Better Homes and Gardens®

500 FIVE INGREDIENT RECIPES

Better Homes and Gardens® Books
Des Moines, Iowa

Better Homes and Gardens® Books
An imprint of Meredith® Books

500 Five-Ingredient Recipes
Editor: Jan Miller
Contributing Editors: Lisa Kingsley, Carrie Mills
Recipe Development: Better Home and Gardens® Test
    Kitchen, Tami Leonard, Jill Lust
Associate Art Director: Mick Schnepf
Illustrator: Ken Carlson
Copy Chief: Terri Fredrickson
Copy and Production Editor: Victoria Forlini
Editorial Operations Manager: Karen Schirm
Managers, Book Production: Pam Kvitne,
    Marjorie J. Schenkelberg
Contributing Copy Editor: Daniel Cubias
Contributing Proofreaders: Maria Duryée,
    Gretchen Kauffman, Susan J. Kling
Indexer: Elizabeth Parson
Electronic Production Coordinator: Paula Forest
Editorial and Design Assistants: Karen McFadden,
    Mary Lee Gavin
Test Kitchen Director: Lynn Blanchard
Test Kitchen Product Supervisor: Marilyn Cornelius

Meredith® Books
Publisher and Editor in Chief: James D. Blume
Design Director: Matt Strelecki
Managing Editor: Gregory H. Kayko
Executive Editor, Food and Crafts: Jennifer Darling

Director, Operations: George A. Susral
Director, Production: Douglas M. Johnston

Vice President and General Manager: Douglas J. Guendel

Better Homes and Gardens® Magazine
Editor in Chief: Karol DeWulf Nickell
Deputy Editor, Food and Entertaining: Nancy Hopkins

Meredith Publishing Group
President, Publishing Group: Stephen M. Lacy
Vice President-Publishing Director: Bob Mate
Meredith Corporation
Chairman and Chief Executive Officer: William T. Kerr

Chairman of the Executive Committee: E. T. Meredith III

All of us at Better Homes and Gardens® Books are
dedicated to providing you with the information and
ideas you need to create delicious foods. We welcome
your comments and suggestions. Write to us at: Better
Homes and Gardens Books, Cookbook Editorial
Department, 1716 Locust St., Des Moines, IA
50309-3023.

If you would like to purchase any of our cooking, crafts,
gardening, home improvement, or home decorating and
design books, check wherever quality books are sold.
Or visit us at: bhgbooks.com

Our seal assures you that every recipe in
500 Five-Ingredient Recipes has been tested in
the Better Homes and Gardens® Test Kitchen.
This means that each recipe is practical and
reliable, and meets our high standards of taste
appeal. We guarantee your satisfaction with this
book for as long as you own it.

CONTENTS

Intro

Easy, family-pleasing weeknight meals with just a handful of ingredients? It sounds too good to be true, but it's the honest-to-goodness truth. There are **no games, tricks, hidden ingredients**, or **steps** in *Better Homes and Gardens 500 Five-Ingredient Recipes*.

With thoughtful combinations and discriminating use of a few high-quality convenience foods, we've turned just five ingredients (or fewer) into **great-taste-guaranteed recipes** that have terrific family appeal. Here are a few notes about **the way we've counted our ingredients:**

WHAT COUNTS:
- Salt and pepper, as one ingredient
- Optional ingredients
- Rice or cooked noodles to be served with a stir-fry or other main dish

WHAT DOESN'T COUNT:
- Water
- Nonstick cooking spray, when it's used to coat a pan
- Serving suggestions of meat, poultry, or fish for recipes in the Sauces & More chapter
- Serving suggestions (such as ice cream) for sauce recipes in the Desserts chapter

The ingredients we call for are common, easy-to-find items you may very well have **sitting on your pantry shelf right now.** You'll be surprised at what you can do.

APPETIZERS

Chapter one

Crunchy Trail Mix

Start to Finish: 5 min.

1½ cups puffed corn cereal, round toasted oat cereal, or crispy corn and rice cereal

1 cup honey-roasted peanuts

½ cup chewy fruit snacks or candy-coated milk chocolate pieces

½ cup raisins

1. Place all ingredients in a self-sealing plastic bag. Seal bag. Shake well to mix.
Makes 7 servings.

Nutrition Facts per serving: 191 cal., 9 g total fat
(2 g sat. fat), 0 mg chol., 108 mg sodium, 28 g carbo.,
1 g fiber, 4 g pro. Daily Values: 4% vit. A, 6% vit. C,
1% calcium, 4% iron

Fruit and Peanut Snack Mix

Start to Finish: 10 min.

1 6-ounce package pretzel, plain, or cheddar cheese-flavored, bite-size, fish-shaped crackers

1 6-ounce package dried cranberries

1 7-ounce package dried apricots, snipped

1 cup peanuts

1. In a medium bowl combine all ingredients. Store in an airtight container.
Makes 12 servings.

Nutrition Facts per serving: 213 cal., 7 g total fat
(1 g sat. fat), 0 mg chol., 206 mg sodium, 35 g carbo.,
3 g fiber, 5 g pro. Daily Values: 1% vit. C, 1% calcium,
11% iron

Sweet Spiced Popcorn

Prep: 10 min. • Bake: 30 min.

8 cups popped popcorn

¾ cup dry roasted peanuts

¼ cup honey

¼ cup butter or margarine

½ teaspoon curry powder or five-spice powder

1. In a large roasting pan combine popcorn and peanuts. In a small saucepan heat and stir honey, butter, and curry powder until butter is melted. Pour over popcorn mixture; toss to coat.

2. Bake popcorn mixture in a 300°F oven for 30 minutes, stirring every 10 minutes. Transfer mixture to a large piece of foil to cool. Store at room temperature in a tightly covered container for up to 1 week.
Makes 8 cups.

Nutrition Facts per ½ cup: 98 cal., 7 g total fat
(2 g sat. fat), 8 mg chol., 32 mg sodium, 9 g carbo.,
1 g fiber, 2 g pro. Daily Values: 2% vit. A, 1% calcium, 2% iron

Almond-Brie Spread

Prep: 5 min. • Stand: 1 hour

2   4½-ounce rounds Brie cheese
2   tablespoons cream sherry or milk
3   tablespoons sliced almonds, toasted
    Crackers

1. Cut the thin, white covering from chilled cheese with a vegetable peeler or small paring knife. Place cheese in a mixing bowl; let stand at room temperature for 1 hour or until softened. Beat with an electric mixer on medium speed for 1 minute. Add sherry; beat until light and smooth. Chop 2 tablespoons of the almonds; stir into cheese mixture.

2. Serve immediately or cover and chill overnight or until serving time. If chilled, let spread stand at room temperature for 30 to 45 minutes before serving. Just before serving, sprinkle with remaining toasted almonds. Serve with crackers.
Makes 20 servings.

Nutrition Facts per serving: 51 cal., 4 g total fat (2 g sat. fat), 13 mg chol., 79 mg sodium, 0 g carbo., 0 g fiber, 3 g pro. Daily Values: 2% vit. A, 3% calcium, 1% iron

Warm Brie

Start to Finish: 15 min.

1   8-ounce round Brie cheese
¼   cup butter or margarine
¼   cup packed brown sugar
¼   cup chopped nuts
1   tablespoon honey

1. Place cheese in a shallow baking dish or pie plate. Bake in a 350°F oven for 10 minutes. Meanwhile, in a small saucepan combine remaining ingredients. Bring sauce to boiling over medium heat, stirring constantly. Pour sauce over cheese. Cut into wedges to serve.
Makes 8 servings.

Nutrition Facts per serving: 206 cal., 16 g total fat (9 g sat. fat), 44 mg chol., 241 mg sodium, 9 g carbo., 0 g fiber, 6 g pro. Daily Values: 8% vit. A, 6% calcium, 2% iron

Toasting Nuts

It may be a small time-saving step, but every little bit counts. You can toast nuts ahead of time and store them in your freezer in a tightly sealed freezer bag. To toast nuts, spread them in a single layer in a shallow baking pan. Bake in a 350°F oven for 5 to 10 minutes or until golden brown, stirring once or twice. Cool completely before storing.

Baked Cheese

Prep: 5 min. • Bake: 20 min.

1   8-ounce package cream cheese
1/3   cup fruit-flavored salsa, such as cherry,
      peach, or raspberry
1/3   cup honey-roasted cashews, finely chopped
      Toasted pita wedges or assorted crackers
      Apple or pear slices

1. Place cream cheese in a pie plate. Spoon
salsa over cheese. Sprinkle with cashews. Bake
in a 350°F oven for 20 minutes or until cheese is
softened and heated through. Serve warm with
pita wedges and apple slices.
Makes 16 servings.

Nutrition Facts per serving: 136 cal., 7 g total fat
(3 g sat. fat), 16 mg chol., 136 mg sodium, 17 g carbo.,
2 g fiber, 3 g pro. Daily Values: 4% vit. A, 3% vit. C,
3% calcium, 4% iron

Fast Fondue

Prep: 10 min. • Bake: 5 min.

1   8-ounce wedge or round Cambozola,
      Camembert, or Brie cheese
      Coarsely ground mixed peppercorns
2   tablespoons chopped walnuts or pecans
      Sliced coarse-grain or crusty bread,
      toasted, or assorted crackers

1. If using a cheese round, peel rind from top of
cheese. Place cheese in a quiche dish or shallow
baking dish. Sprinkle with peppercorns and nuts.
Bake in a 450°F oven for 5 to 8 minutes or until
cheese is softened and just begins to melt. Serve
with toasted bread or crackers.
Makes 8 servings.

Nutrition Facts per serving: 175 cal., 9 g total fat
(5 g sat. fat), 20 mg chol., 411 mg sodium, 15 g carbo.,
1 g fiber, 8 g pro. Daily Values: 13% calcium, 5% iron

Creamy Cheese Spread

Start to Finish: 15 min.

2   cups shredded brick cheese (8 ounces)
1   8-ounce tub cream cheese with chive
        and onion
½   teaspoon bottled hot pepper sauce
        Party rye bread, pumpernickel bread,
        crisp crackers, or bagel chips

1. Bring cheeses to room temperature. In a medium mixing bowl beat the cheeses and hot pepper sauce with an electric mixer on medium speed until the mixture is nearly smooth. Serve with bread, crackers, or bagel chips.
Makes 1½ cups.

Nutrition Facts per tablespoon: 94 cal., 6 g total fat (4 g sat. fat), 18 mg chol., 154 mg sodium, 5 g carbo., 1 g fiber, 3 g pro. Daily Values: 4% vit. A, 10% calcium, 2% iron

Herbed Feta Spread

Start to Finish: 10 min.

1   8-ounce package reduced-fat cream
        cheese (Neufchâtel)
1   4-ounce package crumbled feta cheese
        with garlic and herb
1   tablespoon milk
        Several dashes freshly ground black pepper
        Sweet pepper wedges or other vegetable
        dippers or crackers

1. In a small mixing bowl stir together cheeses, milk, and pepper. Beat with an electric mixer on medium speed until mixture is well combined and of desired spreading consistency. Serve with sweet pepper wedges, other vegetable dippers, or crackers.
Makes 15 to 20 servings.

Nutrition Facts per serving: 119 cal., 8 g total fat (8 g sat. fat), 18 mg chol., 245 mg sodium, 8 g carbo., 0 g fiber, 3 g pro. Daily Values: 6% calcium, 3% iron

Sweet Onion Spread

Prep: 5 min. • Bake: 30 min.

2   medium sweet onions, such as Spanish
    Sweet or Vidalia
2   teaspoons olive oil
2   teaspoons honey
4   large cloves garlic, peeled
    Baguette-style French bread
      slices, toasted

1. Peel and quarter onions. In a large bowl stir together oil and honey. Add onions and garlic, stirring well to coat. Transfer mixture to a lightly greased 2-quart baking dish. Bake in a 350°F oven for 30 to 40 minutes or until onions turn golden brown, stirring occasionally. Remove from oven; let cool.

2. Transfer mixture to a food processor bowl or blender container. Cover and process or blend until smooth. Serve on toasted bread slices.
Makes ½ cup.

Nutrition Facts per 2 tablespoons: 50 cal., 2 g total fat (0 g sat. fat), 0 mg chol., 75 mg sodium, 7 g carbo., 1 g fiber, 1 g pro. Daily Values: 5% vit. C, 1% calcium, 1% iron

Eggplant-Garlic Spread

Prep: 10 min. • Bake: 45 min.

1   medium eggplant
⅓   cup olive oil
2   bulbs garlic, separated into cloves, peeled,
    and thinly sliced
2   tablespoons snipped fresh Italian parsley
    Crackers, toasted pita wedges, or cut-up
      fresh vegetables

1. Halve eggplant lengthwise; brush all over with some of the oil. Grease a shallow baking pan with the remaining oil. Place sliced garlic on the cut side of the eggplant halves. Carefully invert eggplant halves onto the prepared pan, tucking garlic slices under the eggplant. Bake in a 350°F oven for 45 to 60 minutes or until skin begins to wrinkle. Turn off oven; cool eggplant in the oven for 1½ hours.

2. With a large spatula carefully transfer eggplant halves and garlic to a serving platter, cut sides up. Garnish with parsley. Serve with crackers, pita wedges, or vegetables.
Makes 16 servings.

Nutrition Facts per serving: 53 cal., 5 g total fat (1 g sat. fat), 0 mg chol., 2 mg sodium, 3 g carbo., 1 g fiber, 1 g pro. Daily Values: 1% vit. A, 3% vit. C, 1% calcium, 1% iron

Artichoke Dip with Pretzels

Start to Finish: 10 min.

1   14-ounce can artichoke hearts, drained
    and finely chopped
1   8-ounce carton dairy sour cream
½   cup bottled chunky blue cheese
    salad dressing
¼   cup snipped chives or finely chopped
    green onion tops
    Large pretzel rods, small pretzel knots,
    and/or melba toast rounds

1. In a medium bowl stir together artichoke hearts, sour cream, salad dressing, and chives. Transfer to a serving bowl. Serve with pretzels and/or melba toast rounds for dipping.
Makes 40 servings.

Nutrition Facts per serving: 31 cal., 3 g total fat
(1 g sat. fat), 4 mg chol., 56 mg sodium, 1 g carbo.,
0 g fiber, 1 g pro. Daily Values: 1% vit. C, 1% calcium

Fresh Fruit Dip

Start to Finish: 15 min.

1   8-ounce carton vanilla low-fat yogurt
¼   cup unsweetened applesauce
⅛   teaspoon ground cinnamon, nutmeg,
    or ginger
3   cups assorted fresh fruit, such as pineapple
    chunks, strawberries, apple slices,
    and/or peach slices

1. In a small bowl stir together yogurt, applesauce, and cinnamon. To serve, spear fruit with decorative picks and dip into yogurt mixture.
Makes 6 servings.

Nutrition Facts per serving: 27 cal., 0 g total fat
(0 g sat. fat), 1 mg chol., 9 mg sodium, 6 g carbo., 0 g fiber,
1 g pro. Daily Values: 7% vit. C, 2% calcium, 1% iron

Layered Black Bean Dip

Prep: 10 min. • Bake: 20 min.

1   15-ounce can black beans, rinsed
    and drained
¾   cup bottled salsa
2   cups shredded Monterey Jack cheese with
    jalapeño peppers or Monterey Jack
    cheese (8 ounces)
1   medium avocado, halved, seeded, peeled,
    and chopped
    Tortilla chips

1. In a large bowl mash beans with a fork. Stir in salsa and 1 cup of the cheese. Spread bean mixture in bottom of a 9-inch pie plate. Top with avocado and sprinkle with the remaining cheese. Bake, uncovered, in a 350°F oven for 20 minutes or until heated through and cheese is melted. Serve warm with tortilla chips.

Makes 8 to 10 servings.

Nutrition Facts per serving: 291 cal., 18 g total fat
(7 g sat. fat), 25 mg chol., 448 mg sodium, 25 g carbo.,
6 g fiber, 12 g pro. Daily Values: 12% vit. A, 8% vit. C,
27% calcium, 8% iron

Cheesy Pecan Quesadillas

Start to Finish: 15 min.

3   ounces Brie or Muenster cheese, chopped
    (about ¼ cup)
2   8- to 9-inch flour tortillas
2   tablespoons chopped pecans or
    walnuts, toasted
2   tablespoons snipped fresh Italian parsley
    Dairy sour cream

1. Sprinkle cheese over half of each tortilla. Top with nuts and parsley. Fold tortillas in half, pressing gently. In a lightly greased 10-inch skillet or griddle cook quesadillas over medium heat for 2 to 3 minutes or until lightly browned, turning once. Cut quesadillas into wedges. Serve with sour cream.

Makes 4 servings.

Nutrition Facts per serving: 170 cal., 12 g total fat
(6 g sat. fat), 27 mg chol., 202 mg sodium, 9 g carbo.,
0 g fiber, 6 g pro. Daily Values: 4% vit. C, 6% calcium, 5% iron

B.L.T. Bruschetta

Start to Finish: 15 min.

16 ½-inch slices baguette-style French
       bread, toasted
 ½ cup semisoft cheese with garlic and herb
 ½ cup very thinly sliced fresh basil leaves or
       shredded leaf lettuce
 ½ cup chopped tomato
 4 slices bacon, crisp-cooked, drained,
       and crumbled

1. Spread one side of each toast slice with
cheese. Top with remaining ingredients. Serve
bruschetta immediately.
Makes 16 servings.

Nutrition Facts per serving: 75 cal., 4 g total fat
(2 g sat. fat), 8 mg chol., 112 mg sodium, 8 g carbo.,
0 g fiber, 2 g pro. Daily Values: 1% vit. A, 3% vit. C,
1% calcium, 2% iron

Strawberry and Cheese Bites

Start to Finish: 25 min.

1 8-ounce loaf baguette-style French bread
1 8-ounce tub cream cheese
1 tablespoon honey
2 cups strawberries, sliced
¼ cup strawberry jelly

1. Cut bread into ¼-inch slices (24 slices).
Place slices in a single layer on an ungreased
baking sheet. Bake in a 375°F oven about
10 minutes or until lightly brown, turning once.

2. In a small bowl stir together cream cheese
and honey; spread on one side of each bread
slice. Arrange strawberry slices on the cheese.
Heat jelly in a custard cup in a microwave oven
on 100 percent power (high) for 30 seconds or
until melted; stir (or cook and stir in a small
saucepan over low heat until melted). Brush jelly
over strawberries.
Makes 24 servings.

Nutrition Facts per serving: 73 cal., 3 g total fat
(2 g sat. fat), 9 mg chol., 90 mg sodium, 9 g carbo.,
1 g fiber, 2 g pro. Daily Values: 11% vit. C, 2% calcium,
2% iron

Spinach Pizza Bread

Prep: 60 min. • Bake: 30 min.

½ of a 10-ounce package frozen chopped
    spinach
1 16-ounce loaf frozen bread dough, thawed
1 tablespoon olive oil
4 or 5 cloves garlic, minced
½ of a 2-ounce can anchovies, drained and
    cut up (optional)

1. Cook frozen spinach according to package
directions. Drain spinach in a colander. Press
and squeeze to remove excess liquid. Set aside.

2. Roll the bread dough into a 12×9-inch
rectangle. In a medium bowl combine oil, garlic,
and, if desired, anchovies. Stir in drained
spinach. Spread spinach mixture evenly over
dough, leaving a ½-inch border on all sides.

3. Roll up dough, starting from a short side.
Moisten and pinch seams to seal. Place loaf in a
greased 9×5×3- or 8×4×2-inch loaf pan, seam
side down. Cover; let rise in a warm place until
nearly double in size (about 45 minutes).

4. Bake in a 375°F oven for 30 to 40 minutes
or until the bread sounds hollow when you tap it.
(If necessary, cover loosely with foil the last
10 minutes of baking to prevent overbrowning.)
Remove bread from pan. Cool slightly on rack.
Makes 1 loaf (16 servings).

Nutrition Facts per serving: 77 cal., 1 g total fat
(0 g sat. fat), 0 mg chol., 7 mg sodium, 13 g carbo., 0 g fiber,
2 g pro. Daily Values: 11% vit. A, 4% vit. C, 3% calcium,
2% iron

Bread and Cheddar Wedges

Prep: 10 min. • Bake: 15 min.

1 small round loaf of bread (about 8 inches
    in diameter)
1 tablespoon Dijon-style mustard
½ of a 5-ounce jar processed sharp cheddar
    cheese spread (¼ cup)
1 teaspoon grated Parmesan cheese
    Apple slices

1. Cut loaf of bread in half horizontally. Wrap
one half and use another time. Hollow out the
other half, leaving a ½-inch-thick shell. Spread
mustard over inside of bread shell. Spread
cheese spread over mustard. Sprinkle with
Parmesan cheese. Place bread on a baking sheet.

2. Bake in a 400°F oven about 15 minutes or
until cheese begins to bubble. Cut hot bread into
12 wedges; transfer to a serving plate. Serve with
apple slices.
Makes 12 servings.

Nutrition Facts per serving: 89 cal., 2 g total fat
(1 g sat. fat), 4 mg chol., 233 mg sodium, 14 g carbo.,
1 g fiber, 3 g pro. Daily Values: 1% vit. A, 1% vit. C,
6% calcium, 4% iron

Toasted Ravioli

Prep: 25 min. • Bake: 15 min.

1   9-ounce package refrigerated cheese-
    filled ravioli
½   cup Italian-seasoned fine dry bread crumbs
¼   cup milk
1   egg
1½   cups purchased pasta sauce

1. In a large saucepan cook ravioli in boiling water for 3 minutes. Drain well; cool slightly. Place bread crumbs in a shallow dish. In another shallow dish beat together the milk and egg. Dip cooked ravioli in egg mixture; coat with bread crumbs. Place ravioli on a greased baking sheet.

2. Bake in a 425°F oven for 15 minutes or until crisp and golden. Meanwhile, heat sauce in a small saucepan. Serve warm ravioli with sauce. **Makes 10 to 12 servings.**

Nutrition Facts per serving: 141 cal., 3 g total fat
(1 g sat. fat), 32 mg chol., 391 mg sodium, 22 g carbo.,
1 g fiber, 6 g pro. Daily Values: 7% vit. A, 5% vit. C,
6% calcium, 7% iron

Tortellini in Ratatouille Sauce

Start to Finish: 30 min.

    Nonstick cooking spray
2   cups peeled eggplant, cut into bite-size
    cubes
1   medium zucchini, cut into bite-size cubes
1   26-ounce jar marinara sauce
1   cup water
2   9-ounce packages refrigerated cheese-
    filled tortellini

1. Lightly coat a 4-quart Dutch oven with cooking spray. Heat over medium-high heat. Add the eggplant and zucchini. Cook and stir for 5 minutes. Stir in marinara sauce and water. Bring to boiling. Stir in tortellini. Return to boiling; reduce heat. Cook, covered, over medium-low heat for 8 minutes or until tortellini is tender. Serve with decorative picks. **Makes 24 servings.**

Nutrition Facts per serving: 86 cal., 2 g total fat
(1 g sat. fat), 11 mg chol., 210 mg sodium, 13 g carbo.,
2 g fiber, 4 g pro. Daily Values: 3% vit. A, 5% vit. C,
5% calcium, 4% iron

Cheese-Garlic Biscuits

Prep: 10 min. • Bake: 8 min.

2   cups packaged biscuit mix
½   cup shredded cheddar cheese (2 ounces)
⅔   cup milk
¼   cup butter or margarine, melted
½   teaspoon garlic powder

1. In a large bowl combine biscuit mix and cheese; add milk. Stir until just moistened. Drop well-rounded tablespoons of the dough an inch apart onto a greased baking sheet. Bake in a 425°F oven for 8 to 10 minutes or until golden. Combine melted butter and garlic powder; brush over hot biscuits. Serve warm.
Makes 10 to 12 biscuits.

Nutrition Facts per biscuit: 178 cal., 11 g total fat (5 g sat. fat), 20 mg chol., 384 mg sodium, 16 g carbo., 0 g fiber, 4 g pro. Daily Values: 6% vit. A, 9% calcium, 4% iron

Toasted Cheese Pita Chips

Start to Finish: 25 min.

3   pita bread rounds
3   tablespoons butter or margarine, melted
3   tablespoons grated Parmesan or
       Romano cheese

1. Split pita bread rounds in half horizontally. Lightly brush the cut side of each pita bread half with melted butter. Cut each half into 6 wedges. Spread in a single layer on a baking sheet. Sprinkle with grated cheese. Bake in a 350°F oven about 10 minutes or until crisp. Cool. Transfer to an airtight container; store at room temperature for up to 1 week.
Makes 12 servings.

Nutrition Facts per serving: 74 cal., 4 g total fat (2 g sat. fat), 9 mg chol., 135 mg sodium, 8 g carbo., 0 g fiber, 2 g pro. Daily Values: 3% calcium, 2% iron

Parmesan or Romano

You can usually use Parmesan and Romano cheeses interchangeably. Parmesan and Romano cheeses are both pale yellow, hard cheeses that originated in Italy. Both have a sharp, rich flavor; Romano is slightly stronger. Parmesan cheese is made from cow's milk. Romano is often made with a blend of cow's and sheep's or goat's milk.

Italian-Style Chips

Prep: 15 min. • Bake: 8 min.

²⁄₃ cup finely chopped onion

2   tablespoons butter or margarine, melted

1   teaspoon dried Italian seasoning, crushed

4   8-inch flour tortillas
    Salsa (optional)

1. In a small skillet cook the onion in melted butter for 3 to 5 minutes or until tender. Stir in the Italian seasoning. Carefully brush onion mixture evenly over one side of each tortilla. Cut each tortilla into 8 wedges. Spread on an ungreased 15×10×1-inch baking pan. Bake in a 350°F oven for 8 to 10 minutes or until chips are crisp and edges are lightly browned. If desired, serve with salsa.

Makes 8 servings.

Nutrition Facts per serving: 105 cal., 7 g total fat
(2 g sat. fat), 8 mg chol., 127 mg sodium, 9 g carbo.,
0 g fiber, 1 g pro. Daily Values: 1% vit. C, 1% calcium, 4% iron

Focaccia Breadsticks

Prep: 15 min. • Bake: 12 min.

¼   cup oil-packed dried tomatoes

¼   cup grated Romano cheese

2   teaspoons water

1½ teaspoons snipped fresh rosemary or
      ½ teaspoon dried rosemary, crushed

⅛   teaspoon cracked black pepper

1   10-ounce package refrigerated pizza dough

1. Drain dried tomatoes, reserving oil; finely snip tomatoes. In a small bowl combine tomatoes, 2 teaspoons of the reserved oil, the cheese, water, rosemary, and pepper. Set aside.

2. Unroll pizza dough. On a lightly floured surface, roll dough into a 10×8-inch rectangle. Spread tomato mixture crosswise over half of the dough. Fold plain half of dough over filling; press lightly to seal edges. Cut the folded dough lengthwise into ten ½-inch strips. Fold each strip in half and twist two or three times. Place on a lightly greased baking sheet. Bake in a 350°F oven for 12 to 15 minutes or until golden brown. Cool on a wire rack.

Makes 10 breadsticks.

Nutrition Facts per breadstick: 113 cal., 3 g total fat
(1 g sat. fat), 3 mg chol., 263 mg sodium, 18 g carbo.,
1 g fiber, 5 g pro. Daily Values: 1% vit. A, 5% vit. C,
3% calcium, 5% iron

Olive Bread

Prep: 20 min. • Bake: 18 min.

½ cup grated Parmesan cheese
1 2¼-ounce can sliced pitted ripe olives,
    drained
4 to 5 cloves garlic, minced
1 10-ounce package refrigerated pizza dough
    Pizza sauce

1. Set aside 1 tablespoon of the cheese. Stir together olives, garlic, and remaining cheese.

2. On a lightly floured surface, roll the pizza dough into a 14×10-inch rectangle. Sprinkle ⅓ cup of the olive mixture along one short side of the dough in a 2-inch-wide band. Fold dough over filling, allowing about two-thirds of the dough to extend beyond the filling. Add another ⅓ cup of the olive mixture on top of the filled layer, pressing filling lightly. Fold dough back over filling, making about a 3-inch pleat. Repeat filling and folding dough accordion-style once more with remaining filling. Gently pat sides of the loaf to form a 10½×3-inch rectangle; seal ends. Place shaped dough on a lightly greased baking sheet. Brush top of loaf with water and sprinkle with reserved cheese. Bake in a 400°F oven for 18 to 20 minutes or until golden. Serve warm with warm pizza sauce.
Makes 12 servings.

Nutrition Facts per serving: 83 cal., 3 g total fat (1 g sat. fat), 3 mg chol., 285 mg sodium, 11 g carbo., 1 g fiber, 3 g pro. Daily Values: 1% vit. A, 3% vit. C, 7% calcium, 5% iron

Simple Focaccia

Prep: 45 min. • Bake: 15 min.

1 16-ounce package hot roll mix
1 egg
3 tablespoons olive oil
    Coarse salt

1. Lightly grease a 15×10×1-inch baking pan or a 12-inch pizza pan. Set aside.

2. Prepare hot roll mix according to package directions for basic dough, using the egg and substituting 2 tablespoons of the oil for the margarine. Knead dough; allow to rest as directed. If using a baking pan, roll dough into a 15×10-inch rectangle. If using a pizza pan, roll dough into a 12-inch round. Place dough in prepared pan.

3. With your fingertips, press indentations randomly in dough. Brush dough with the remaining 1 tablespoon olive oil; sprinkle lightly with salt. Cover and let rise in a warm place until nearly double in size (about 30 minutes).

4. Bake in a 375°F oven for 15 to 20 minutes or until golden. Cool for 10 minutes on a wire rack. Remove from pan and cool completely.
Makes 12 servings.

Nutrition Facts per serving: 176 cal., 4 g total fat (1 g sat. fat), 18 mg chol., 306 mg sodium, 29 g carbo., 0 g fiber, 6 g pro. Daily Values: 1% vit. A, 6% iron

Soft Pretzels

Prep: 15 min. • Bake: 12 min.

- 1 11-ounce package refrigerated breadsticks (8)
- 1 beaten egg white
- 1 tablespoon water
  Poppy seeds

1. Unroll breadsticks so they lie flat. Gently pull each breadstick into a 16-inch rope. Shape each rope into a pretzel by crossing one end over the other to form a circle, overlapping about 4 inches from each end. Take one end of dough in each hand and twist once where the dough overlaps. Carefully lift each end across to the edge of the circle opposite it. Tuck ends under edges to make pretzel shape. Moisten the ends; press to seal.

2. Place pretzels on a greased baking sheet. Stir together egg white and water; brush over pretzels. Sprinkle with poppy seeds. Bake in a 375°F oven for 12 to 15 minutes or until golden. **Makes 8 pretzels.**

Nutrition Facts per pretzel: 114 cal., 3 g total fat (1 g sat. fat), 0 mg chol., 297 mg sodium, 18 g carbo., 1 g fiber, 4 g pro. Daily Values: 1% calcium, 6% iron

Puff Pastry Cheese Straws

Prep: 18 min. • Bake: 12 min.

- 1 17¼-ounce package frozen puff pastry, thawed
- 1 lightly beaten egg white
  Paprika
  Ground red pepper (optional)
- 1 cup finely shredded sharp cheese, such as aged cheddar, Asiago, or Parmesan (4 ounces)

1. Open 1 sheet of puff pastry on a cutting board. Brush surface lightly with some of the beaten egg white. Sprinkle lightly with paprika and, if desired, red pepper. Sprinkle with half of the cheese. Roll a floured rolling pin over top to gently press the cheese into pastry.

2. Cut puff pastry into long ½-inch strips; gently twist each strip several times. Lay strips 1 inch apart on a baking sheet lined with parchment paper. Repeat with remaining sheet of puff pastry and remaining ingredients. Bake in a 375°F oven for 12 to 14 minutes or until golden. Cool on a wire rack. Serve the same day. **Makes 36 straws.**

Nutrition Facts per straw: 73 cal., 5 g total fat (1 g sat. fat), 3 mg chol., 72 mg sodium, 5 g carbo., 0 g fiber, 1 g pro. Daily Values: 27% calcium

Cheese-Stuffed Pecans

Prep: 20 min. • Chill: 30 min.

1   cup finely shredded Gouda cheese
      (4 ounces)
3   tablespoons dairy sour cream
40 large pecan halves

1. In a medium mixing bowl bring the shredded cheese to room temperature (allow about 30 minutes); add sour cream. Beat with an electric mixer until creamy. Using a scant teaspoon for each, mound cheese mixture onto the flat side of half of the pecans. Top with remaining pecans, flat side down. Cover and chill for 30 minutes.
Makes 10 servings.

Nutrition Facts per serving: 102 cal., 10 g total fat
(3 g sat. fat), 14 mg chol., 94 mg sodium, 1 g carbo.,
1 g fiber, 4 g pro. Daily Values: 2% vit. A, 9% calcium, 1% iron

Toasted Almonds with Rosemary

Start to Finish: 15 min.

8   ounces unblanched almonds or pecan
       halves (about 2 cups)
1½ teaspoons butter or margarine
1   tablespoon finely snipped fresh rosemary
1½ teaspoons brown sugar
¼   to ½ teaspoon salt

1. Spread almonds in a single layer on a baking sheet. Bake in a 350°F oven about 10 minutes or until nuts are lightly toasted and fragrant. Meanwhile, in a medium saucepan melt butter over medium heat until sizzling. Remove from heat. Stir in the rosemary, brown sugar, and salt. Add almonds to butter mixture; toss to coat. Cool slightly before serving.
Makes 16 servings.

Nutrition Facts per serving: 80 cal., 7 g total fat
(1 g sat. fat), 1 mg chol., 37 mg sodium, 3 g carbo.,
1 g fiber, 4 g pro. Daily Values: 4% calcium, 5% iron

Cheesy Potato Wedges

Prep: 10 min. • Bake: 25 min.

1   24-ounce package frozen potato wedges
1   16-ounce jar cheddar cheese pasta sauce
1   2-ounce jar cooked bacon pieces
1   medium tomato, chopped
½   cup sliced green onions

1. Arrange the potato wedges in an even layer on a 15×10×1-inch baking pan. Bake in a 400°F oven for 15 minutes. Remove from oven. Pour sauce over potato wedges; sprinkle with bacon pieces. Bake for 10 minutes more or until potatoes are tender and sauce is heated through. Sprinkle with tomato and onions.
Makes 12 servings.

Nutrition Facts per serving: 146 cal., 8 g total fat
(3 g sat. fat), 18 mg chol., 456 mg sodium, 15 g carbo.,
1 g fiber, 5 g pro. Daily Values: 4% vit. A, 5% vit. C,
5% calcium, 2% iron

Prosciutto-Arugula Roll-Ups

Start to Finish: 30 min.

1   5-ounce container semisoft cheese with
       garlic and herb
2   ounces soft goat cheese (chèvre)
⅓   cup pine nuts or chopped almonds, toasted
4   ounces thinly sliced prosciutto (8 slices)
1½   cups arugula or spinach leaves, stems
       removed (about 2½ ounces)

1. Stir together cheeses and pine nuts. Spread about 2 tablespoons cheese mixture over each prosciutto slice. Top each with arugula. Roll up each slice from a short side. Cut into ½-inch slices. Serve immediately or cover and chill for up to 6 hours.
Makes about 48 slices.

Nutrition Facts per slice: 33 cal., 3 g total fat (1 g sat. fat),
4 mg chol., 55 mg sodium, 0 g carbo., 0 g fiber, 2 g pro.
Daily Values: 1% calcium, 1% iron

Easy Artichoke Roll

Prep: 25 min. • Bake: 30 min.

1   8-ounce package refrigerated crescent
      rolls (8)
½   cup shredded Parmesan cheese (2 ounces)
¼   cup mayonnaise or salad dressing
1   6- to 6½-ounce jar marinated artichoke
      hearts, drained and finely chopped
½   cup chopped sweet pepper

1. On a lightly floured surface, unroll the
crescent roll dough; seal perforations between
rolls. With a lightly floured rolling pin, roll
dough into a 15×8-inch rectangle. In a medium
bowl stir together the cheese and mayonnaise.
Stir in artichoke hearts. Spread mixture on
dough, leaving a ½-inch border on each side.
Sprinkle with sweet pepper. Roll up dough,
beginning at one long edge. Moisten and pinch
edges to seal.

2. Place roll on a lightly greased baking sheet.
Bake in a 350°F oven for 30 minutes or until
golden brown. Let cool slightly before slicing.
Makes 16 servings.

Nutrition Facts per serving: 103 cal., 7 g total fat
(2 g sat. fat), 5 mg chol., 200 mg sodium, 7 g carbo.,
0 g fiber, 2 g pro. Daily Values: 6% vit. A, 17% vit. C,
3% calcium, 3% iron

Zucchini Bites

Start to Finish: 20 min.

1   medium to large zucchini, cut into
      ¼-inch slices
½   of an 8-ounce tub cream cheese with
      salmon (⅓ cup) or ⅓ cup semisoft
      cheese with garlic and herb
1   tablespoon sliced or chopped pitted
      ripe olives
1   tablespoon snipped fresh chives

1. Pat zucchini slices dry with paper towels.
Spread cream cheese over slices. Sprinkle each
with olives and chives. Serve immediately.
Makes 36 slices.

Nutrition Facts per slice: 12 cal., 1 g total fat (1 g sat. fat),
3 mg chol., 27 mg sodium, 1 g carbo., 0 g fiber, 0 g pro.
Daily Values: 1% vit. A, 2% vit. C, 1% calcium

Feta-Stuffed Mushrooms

Prep: 20 min. • Bake: 10 min.

4   portobello mushrooms (5 to 6 ounces each)
1   tablespoon olive oil
1   4-ounce package crumbled feta cheese
      with garlic and herb or crumbled
      feta cheese
¼   cup chopped pitted ripe olives
2   tablespoons snipped oil-pack dried tomatoes

1. Remove and discard mushroom stems. Place mushroom caps, stemmed side up, on a baking sheet. Brush with olive oil (if desired, use the oil from the tomatoes); set aside. In a small bowl stir together remaining ingredients. Divide mixture among mushrooms. Bake in a 425°F oven for 10 minutes or until heated through. To serve, cut each mushroom cap into 4 wedges.
Makes 16 servings.

Nutrition Facts per serving: 40 cal., 3 g total fat
(1 g sat. fat), 6 mg chol., 102 mg sodium, 2 g carbo.,
1 g fiber, 2 g pro. Daily Values: 1% vit. A, 1% vit. C,
5% calcium, 1% iron

Stuffed Mushrooms in Phyllo

Prep: 30 min. • Bake: 11 min.

12   mushrooms (1½ inches in diameter)
4   sheets frozen phyllo dough, thawed
⅓   cup butter, melted
½   of a 5.2-ounce package semisoft cheese
      with garlic and herb (about ⅓ cup)
¼   cup chopped walnuts, toasted

1. Remove stems from mushrooms; set aside for another use. Cook mushroom caps, covered, in a small amount of boiling water for 6 to 8 minutes or until just tender. Drain and invert caps on paper towels.

2. Unfold phyllo dough; keep phyllo covered with plastic wrap, removing sheets as you use them. Brush 1 phyllo sheet with melted butter. Top with a second sheet; brush with melted butter. Layer with remaining phyllo and melted butter. Cut phyllo stack lengthwise into thirds; cut each third crosswise into 4 squares (a total of 12 squares).

3. Place a mushroom on each phyllo square; divide cheese and walnuts evenly among mushrooms. Bring corners of phyllo together over top of mushrooms; pinch to seal. Place on an ungreased baking sheet and brush with remaining melted butter. Bake in a 400°F oven for 11 to 13 minutes or until golden. Serve warm.
Makes 12 servings.

Nutrition Facts per serving: 110 cal., 10 g total fat
(5 g sat. fat), 20 mg chol., 86 mg sodium, 4 g carbo.,
0 g fiber, 2 g pro. Daily Values: 1% calcium, 2% iron

Easy-as-Pie Swiss Appetizer

Prep: 20 min. • Bake: 25 min.

- 4 sheets frozen phyllo dough, thawed
- ¼ cup butter, melted
- 2 cups shredded Swiss cheese (8 ounces)
- 1 20-ounce can apple pie filling
- 2 tablespoons finely chopped pecans or walnuts

1. Unfold phyllo dough; keep phyllo covered with plastic wrap, removing sheets as you use them. Brush 1 phyllo sheet with some of the melted butter. Top with a second sheet; brush with some of the melted butter. Layer with remaining 2 sheets of phyllo and some of the remaining butter.

2. Cut stack of phyllo sheets into 16 rectangles (about 4×3-inch pieces). Brush eight 2½-inch muffin cups with the remaining butter. Place 1 rectangle in each prepared muffin cup. Place another stack crosswise on top of each.

3. Divide 1½ cups of the cheese among the phyllo-lined cups. Spoon apple pie filling over cheese in each cup, mounding slightly. Sprinkle each cup with 1 tablespoon cheese and pecans. Bake in a 350°F oven for 25 to 30 minutes or until golden and cheese melts. Let stand in cups for 5 minutes. Remove from cups; serve warm. **Makes 8 servings.**

Nutrition Facts per serving: 259 cal., 14 g total fat (9 g sat. fat), 42 mg chol., 212 mg sodium, 25 g carbo., 1 g fiber, 9 g pro. Daily Values: 10% vit. A, 1% vit. C, 27% calcium, 3% iron

Olive-Tomato Tarts

Prep: 10 min. • Bake: 12 min.

- ½ of a 17¼-ounce package frozen puff pastry (1 sheet), thawed
- ⅓ cup purchased tapenade or finely chopped pitted ripe olives
- 8 cherry tomatoes, quartered
- ½ of an 8-ounce package crumbled feta cheese

1. Cut puff pastry into sixteen 2½-inch squares. Place each square in a 2½-inch muffin cup. Place about 1 teaspoon of the tapenade on each square. Top with 2 tomato quarters and some of the cheese. Bake in a 425°F oven for 12 to 15 minutes or until pastry is puffed and golden brown. Remove from muffin cups. Serve warm. **Makes 16 tarts.**

Nutrition Facts per tart: 92 cal., 7 g total fat (1 g sat. fat), 6 mg chol., 174 mg sodium, 6 g carbo., 0 g fiber, 2 g pro. Daily Values: 2% vit. C, 4% calcium, 1% iron

Tomato-Pesto Toast

Prep: 15 min. • Broil: 3 min.

2   French-style rolls (about 6 inches long),
       cut into ½-inch slices
¾   cup purchased pesto
2   to 3 plum or Roma tomatoes, cut
       lengthwise into thin slices
⅓   cup crumbled feta cheese
       Coarsely cracked black pepper

1. Arrange bread slices on the rack of an unheated broiler pan. Broil 4 to 5 inches from the heat about 1 minute on each side or until toasted. Spread a scant 1 tablespoon pesto on each slice of toasted bread; top each with a tomato slice. Crumble some of the cheese on top of each tomato slice. Sprinkle with pepper. Watching carefully, broil 4 to 5 inches from the heat for 1 to 2 minutes or until heated through.
Makes 12 to 16 toasts.

Nutrition Facts per toast: 160 cal., 9 g total fat
(2 g sat. fat), 8 mg chol., 289 mg sodium, 15 g carbo.,
1 g fiber, 6 g pro. Daily Values: 2% vit. A, 5% vit. C,
11% calcium, 6% iron

Baked Tomato Melts

Prep: 15 min. • Bake: 15 min.

3   large tomatoes (about 8 ounces each) or
       a variety of smaller tomatoes (about
       1½ pounds)
1   cup shredded Monterey Jack cheese with
       jalapeño peppers or Monterey Jack
       cheese (4 ounces)
1   small sweet pepper, finely chopped
       (about ½ cup)
¼   cup sliced almonds, toasted

1. Cut each tomato into four ½-inch slices. If using smaller tomatoes, halve each one. For each of 4 servings, arrange 3 tomato slices, overlapping slightly, on a foil-lined 15×10×1-inch baking pan. (Or if using smaller tomatoes, arrange in a single layer on a foil-lined 15×10×1-inch baking pan.) Sprinkle with the remaining ingredients. Bake in a 350°F oven about 15 minutes or until cheese is bubbly.
Makes 4 servings.

Nutrition Facts per serving: 203 cal., 14 g total fat
(6 g sat. fat), 25 mg chol., 172 mg sodium, 13 g carbo.,
2 g fiber, 10 g pro. Daily Values: 21% vit. A, 79% vit. C,
20% calcium, 10% iron

Chilled Tomato-Basil Soup

Start to Finish: 20 min.

3 cups peeled, seeded, and coarsely chopped
   tomatoes
1 cup vegetable broth or chicken broth
1 8-ounce can tomato sauce
2 tablespoons snipped fresh basil or
   1 teaspoon dried basil, crushed

1. In a blender container combine tomatoes, broth, and tomato sauce. Cover and blend until smooth. Stir in basil. Cover and chill in the refrigerator until ready to serve.
Makes 4 servings.

Nutrition Facts per serving: 42 cal., 1 g total fat
(0 g sat. fat), 0 mg chol., 520 mg sodium, 9 g carbo.,
2 g fiber, 2 g pro. Daily Values: 34% vit. C, 1% calcium,
4% iron

Cheesy Fruit and Ham Wedges

Prep: 10 min. • Bake: 12 min.

¾ cup mixed dried fruit bits (about ½ of a
   6-ounce package)
½ cup finely chopped cooked ham
½ cup finely chopped walnuts
½ cup shredded fontina cheese (2 ounces)
1 15-ounce package folded refrigerated
   piecrust (2 crusts)

1. For filling, stir together fruit bits, ham, walnuts, and cheese. Unfold piecrusts on a lightly floured surface according to package directions. Transfer 1 crust to a large ungreased baking sheet. Sprinkle filling evenly over crust to within 1 inch of the edge. Brush edge with water; top with the second crust. Flute edge of pastry or press with fork to seal. Cut slits in top pastry to allow steam to escape. Bake in a 425°F oven for 12 to 15 minutes or until golden. Cool slightly on a wire rack. Cut into wedges and serve warm.
Makes 16 servings.

Nutrition Facts per serving: 183 cal., 11 g total fat
(4 g sat. fat), 11 mg chol., 188 mg sodium, 18 g carbo.,
0 g fiber, 3 g pro. Daily Values: 1% vit. A, 3% calcium, 1% iron

Chicken and Rice Spring Rolls

Prep: 25 min. • Chill: 1 hour

8   8-inch round rice papers
16   thin asparagus spears, trimmed
1   cup finely chopped cooked chicken
1   cup cooked long grain rice
¾   cup bottled sweet-and-sour sauce

1. Place some warm water in a shallow dish. Dip each rice paper in warm water and place between damp towels for 5 minutes.

2. Meanwhile, cook asparagus spears in boiling water for 3 minutes. Drain; rinse with cold water. Drain again.

3. In a medium bowl stir together chicken, rice, and ¼ cup of the sweet-and-sour sauce. Place 2 asparagus spears about 1 inch from the bottom edge of one of the rice papers. Place ¼ cup chicken mixture on top of asparagus. Fold up bottom edge of the rice paper over the filling. Fold in the sides; roll up. Repeat with remaining rice papers, asparagus, and chicken mixture.

4. Cover and chill spring rolls for 1 to 2 hours. Cut each spring roll into thirds. Serve with remaining sweet-and-sour sauce.
Makes 24 servings.

Nutrition Facts per serving: 56 cal., 1 g total fat (0 g sat. fat), 5 mg chol., 35 mg sodium, 12 g carbo., 1 g fiber, 3 g pro. Daily Values: 1% vit. A, 2% vit. C, 1% calcium, 3% iron

Tangy Cranberry Meatballs

Prep: 15 min. • Cook: 20 min.

1   16-ounce can jellied cranberry sauce
⅓   cup bottled barbecue or steak sauce
1   tablespoon brown sugar
2   teaspoons Dijon-style mustard
1   18-ounce package original-flavor frozen cooked meatballs (35), one 16-ounce package cocktail wieners, or 1 pound smoked sausage, cut into 1-inch slices

1. In a large saucepan stir together cranberry sauce, barbecue sauce, brown sugar, and mustard. Cook and stir over medium heat until cranberry sauce melts. Stir in meatballs. Reduce heat. Cook, covered, over medium-low heat about 20 minutes or until meatballs are heated through, stirring occasionally. Serve with decorative picks.
Makes 16 to 20 servings.

Nutrition Facts per serving: 149 cal., 8 g total fat (3 g sat. fat), 11 mg chol., 311 mg sodium, 14 g carbo., 1 g fiber, 4 g pro. Daily Values: 1% vit. A, 1% vit. C, 2% calcium, 2% iron

Five-Spice Drummies

**Prep: 5 min • Marinate: 4 hours
Bake: 30 min.**

24   chicken wing drummettes (about 3 pounds)
¼   cup soy sauce
¼   cup orange juice
1   tablespoon honey
2   teaspoons five-spice powder

1. Thaw chicken, if frozen. Place chicken in a self-sealing bag set in a large bowl. In a small bowl stir together remaining ingredients. Pour over chicken in bag. Seal bag and marinate chicken in refrigerator for 4 to 24 hours.

2. Drain chicken, discarding marinade. Arrange chicken in a single layer in a 15×10×1-inch baking pan. Bake, uncovered, in a 400°F oven for 30 to 35 minutes or until chicken is tender and no longer pink and skin starts to brown. **Makes 12 servings.**

Nutrition Facts per serving: 136 cal., 10 g total fat (3 g sat. fat), 47 mg chol., 113 mg sodium, 1 g carbo., 0 g fiber, 11 g pro. Daily Values: 1% vit. A, 2% vit. C, 1% calcium, 3% iron

Buffalo Wings

Prep: 40 min • Broil: 20 min

12   chicken wings (about 2 pounds)
2   tablespoons butter or margarine, melted
2   to 3 tablespoons bottled hot pepper sauce
1   teaspoon paprika
    Bottled blue cheese salad dressing

1. Cut off and discard tips of chicken wings. Cut wings at joints to form 24 pieces. Place the chicken pieces in a shallow nonmetal pan.

2. For sauce, in a small bowl stir together butter, hot pepper sauce, and paprika. Pour mixture over chicken wings, stirring to coat. Cover; let stand at room temperature for 30 minutes.

3. Drain chicken, reserving sauce. Place chicken pieces on the unheated rack of a broiler pan. Brush with some of the reserved sauce. Broil chicken 4 to 5 inches from the heat about 10 minutes or until light brown. Turn chicken pieces; brush again with reserved sauce. Broil for 10 to 15 minutes more or until the chicken is tender and no longer pink. Serve with blue cheese dressing. **Makes 12 servings.**

Nutrition Facts per serving: 262 cal., 24 g total fat (6 g sat. fat), 42 mg chol., 395 mg sodium, 2 g carbo., 0 g fiber, 9 g pro. Daily Values: 7% vit. A, 2% vit. C, 3% calcium, 3% iron

BEVERAGES

Chapter two

Peppy Tomato Sipper

Start to Finish: 10 min.

- 2 cups tomato juice or vegetable juice
- 2 tablespoons lime juice or lemon juice
- 1 teaspoon Worcestershire sauce
- ½ teaspoon prepared horseradish
  Few drops bottled hot pepper sauce

1. In a small pitcher stir together all ingredients. Serve over ice.
Makes 2 servings.

Nutrition Facts per serving: 48 cal., 0 g total fat (0 g sat. fat), 0 mg chol., 911 mg sodium, 12 g carbo., 4 g fiber, 2 g pro. Daily Values: 27% vit. A, 83% vit. C, 3% calcium, 9% iron

Easy Fresh Lemonade

Start to Finish: 15 min.

- 8 cups water
- 2 cups sugar
- 4 cups ice
- 2 7½-ounce containers frozen lemon juice from concentrate, thawed

1. For syrup, in a saucepan bring 2 cups of the water and the sugar to boiling over medium heat. Cook for 5 to 7 minutes or until sugar dissolves. Fill a large bowl with ice. Stir in syrup, lemon juice, and remaining water. Transfer to pitchers.
Makes 14 servings.

Nutrition Facts per serving: 113 cal., 0 g total fat (0 g sat. fat), 0 mg chol., 6 mg sodium, 30 g carbo., 0 g fiber, 0 g pro. Daily Values: 17% vit. C, 1% calcium

Fizzy Kiwi Lemonade

Prep: 20 min. • Chill: 2 hours

- 6 kiwifruit
- 1 cup sugar
- ¾ cup lemon juice
- 1 1-liter bottle carbonated water, chilled

1. Peel kiwifruit. Place the peeled fruit in a blender container; cover and blend until smooth. Strain mixture through a fine sieve placed over a bowl. Discard seeds (some may remain). In a large pitcher combine sugar and lemon juice; stir until sugar is dissolved. Stir in strained kiwi. Cover and chill for 2 to 24 hours.

2. Just before serving, slowly add carbonated water, stirring gently. Serve over ice.
Makes 6 servings.

Nutrition Facts per serving: 196 cal., 1 g total fat (0 g sat. fat), 0 mg chol., 36 mg sodium, 48 g carbo., 0 g fiber, 1 g pro. Daily Values: 167% vit. C, 3% calcium, 3% iron

Apple-Cranberry Punch

Start to Finish: 10 min.

1   32-ounce bottle apple juice or apple cider, chilled
1   32-ounce bottle cranberry juice, chilled
2   cups carbonated water, chilled
     Orange slices (optional)

1. In a punch bowl stir together apple juice and cranberry juice; carefully add the carbonated water. Serve over ice. If desired, add an orange slice to the rim of each glass.
Makes 12 servings.

Nutrition Facts per serving: 86 cal., 0 g total fat
(0 g sat. fat), 0 mg chol., 14 mg sodium, 22 g carbo.,
0 g fiber, 0 g pro. Daily Values: 51% vit. C, 2% iron

Peach Nectar Punch

Start to Finish: 10 min.

4   cups peach nectar, chilled
1   6-ounce can frozen orange juice concentrate, thawed
1   1-liter bottle ginger ale, chilled
2   16-ounce packages frozen unsweetened peach slices

1. In a large punch bowl stir together peach nectar and orange juice concentrate. Slowly stir in ginger ale. Stir in peach slices. Serve over ice.
Makes 18 servings.

Nutrition Facts per serving: 86 cal., 0 g total fat
(0 g sat. fat), 0 mg chol., 8 mg sodium, 22 g carbo.,
1 g fiber, 1 g pro. Daily Values: 21% vit. A, 135% vit. C,
1% calcium, 2% iron

Orange Cream Punch

Start to Finish: 15 min.

1   14-ounce can sweetened condensed milk
1   12-ounce can frozen orange juice concentrate, thawed
     Orange food coloring (optional)
2   1-liter bottles carbonated water or ginger ale, chilled
     Orange sherbet

1. In a punch bowl stir together sweetened condensed milk and orange juice concentrate. If desired, tint with orange food coloring. Slowly add carbonated water. Top with scoops of orange sherbet. Serve immediately.
Makes 16 servings.

Nutrition Facts per serving: 164 cal., 3 g total fat
(2 g sat. fat), 11 mg chol., 75 mg sodium, 33 g carbo.,
0 g fiber, 3 g pro. Daily Values: 3% vit. A, 52% vit. C,
10% calcium, 1% iron

Champagne Fruit Punch

Start to Finish: 20 min.

1   16-ounce package frozen unsweetened
    whole strawberries or sliced peaches,
    thawed

¼   cup sugar

2½ cups orange juice

2   tablespoons lemon juice or lime juice

1   750-milliliter bottle Champagne or
    sparkling wine or 4 cups unsweetened
    pineapple juice, chilled

1. In a blender container or food processor bowl place the thawed fruit and any juice from the fruit. Add the sugar. Cover and blend or process until smooth. Pour fruit mixture through a sieve lined with a double thickness of 100-percent-cotton cheesecloth. Transfer fruit mixture to a 2-quart pitcher. Stir in orange juice and lemon juice. Slowly stir in Champagne.
Makes 12 servings.

Nutrition Facts per serving: 95 cal., 0 g total fat
(0 g sat. fat), 0 mg chol., 2 mg sodium, 14 g carbo.,
1 g fiber, 1 g pro. Daily Values: 1% vit. A, 67% vit. C, 2% iron

Make-Believe Champagne

Start to Finish: 10 min.

1   1-liter bottle carbonated water, chilled

1   1-liter bottle ginger ale, chilled

1   24-ounce bottle unsweetened white grape
    juice, chilled
    Ice cubes

1. In a large pitcher combine the carbonated water, ginger ale, and grape juice. Pour over ice cubes in chilled Champagne or wine glasses.
Makes about 20 servings.

Nutrition Facts per serving: 37 cal., 0 g total fat
(0 g sat. fat), 0 mg chol., 14 mg sodium, 9 g carbo.,
0 g fiber, 0 g pro. Daily Values: 1% iron

Fancy Fruit Float

Start to Finish: 10 min.

2   cups cut-up fruit, such as sliced
    strawberries, halved grapes, sliced
    bananas, orange sections, or chopped
    apple

1   1-liter bottle low-calorie lemon-lime
    carbonated beverage or low-calorie
    ginger ale

2   cups fruit-flavored sherbet

1. Divide the fruit among 4 tall glasses. Fill each glass three-quarters with carbonated beverage and top with a scoop of sherbet.
Makes 4 servings.

Nutrition Facts per serving: 172 cal., 2 g total fat
(1 g sat. fat), 5 mg chol., 83 mg sodium, 39 g carbo.,
2 g fiber, 2 g pro. Daily Values: 2% vit. A, 48% vit. C,
6% calcium, 2% iron

Blueberry Smoothies

Start to Finish: 5 min.

- 2 cups chilled fresh blueberries or frozen blueberries, slightly thawed
- 1 cup chilled pineapple-orange juice, pineapple-orange-strawberry juice, or orange-strawberry-banana juice
- 1 8-ounce carton vanilla low-fat yogurt
- 1 tablespoon sugar
  Fresh or frozen blueberries (optional)

1. In a blender container combine all the ingredients. Cover and blend for 1 to 2 minutes or until almost smooth. Serve immediately in tall glasses. If desired, thread additional blueberries on skewers for garnish.
Makes 3 servings.

Nutrition Facts per serving: 179 cal., 1 g total fat (1 g sat. fat), 4 mg chol., 68 mg sodium, 39 g carbo., 3 g fiber, 5 g pro. Daily Values: 3% vit. A, 66% vit. C, 15% calcium, 1% iron

Berry-Banana Smoothies

Start to Finish: 10 min.

- 1 small banana, peeled, cut up, and frozen
- ¼ cup fresh or frozen assorted berries, such as raspberries, blackberries, and/or strawberries
- 1 cup orange juice
- 3 tablespoons vanilla low-fat yogurt
  Fresh berries (optional)

1. In a blender container combine all ingredients. Cover and blend until smooth. Pour into glasses. If desired, top with additional berries.
Makes 2 servings.

Nutrition Facts per serving: 121 cal., 1 g total fat (0 g sat. fat), 2 mg chol., 18 mg sodium, 28 g carbo., 2 g fiber, 2 g pro. Daily Values: 3% vit. A, 116% vit. C, 6% calcium, 3% iron

Strawberry Smoothies

Start to Finish: 10 min.

- 2 cups fresh strawberries, stemmed and rinsed
- ½ of a 6-ounce can frozen lemonade or limeade concentrate (⅓ cup)
- ⅓ cup sifted powdered sugar
- 2½ to 3 cups ice cubes

1. In a blender container combine the strawberries, lemonade concentrate, and powdered sugar. With the blender running, add ice cubes, 1 at a time, through the opening in the lid until the mixture is slushy.
Makes 4 servings.

Nutrition Facts per serving: 104 cal., 0 g total fat (0 g sat. fat), 0 mg chol., 5 mg sodium, 26 g carbo., 2 g fiber, 1 g pro. Daily Values: 1% vit. A, 76% vit. C, 1% calcium, 3% iron

Apricot-Mint Tea

Prep: 20 min. • Chill: 4 hours

4	cups cold water
10	tea bags
4	12-ounce cans apricot nectar
½	cup fresh mint leaves, slightly crushed
¼	cup sugar

1. In a 4-quart Dutch oven bring the water to boiling; remove from heat. Add tea bags and let steep for 3 to 5 minutes. Discard tea bags. Stir in remaining ingredients. Cover; chill for 4 hours.

2. Pour tea through a strainer into a serving pitcher or punch bowl. Serve over ice.
Makes 10 servings.

Nutrition Facts per serving: 98 cal., 0 g total fat (0 g sat. fat), 0 mg chol., 8 mg sodium, 25 g carbo., 1 g fiber, 1 g pro. Daily Values: 19% vit. A, 5% vit. C, 1% calcium, 8% iron

Ginger-Lemon Tea

Start to Finish: 20 min.

6	cups water
4	teaspoons sugar
1	1-inch piece fresh ginger, thinly sliced
8	lemon peel strips (2½×1 inch each)
8	green tea bags

1. In a large saucepan combine the water, sugar, ginger, and lemon peel. Bring to boiling; reduce heat. Simmer, covered, for 10 minutes. Remove ginger and lemon strips with a slotted spoon; discard.

2. Add tea bags to saucepan. Cover; let steep for 3 to 5 minutes. Remove tea bags; discard. Serve hot.
Makes 6 servings.

Nutrition Facts per serving: 13 cal., 0 g total fat (0 g sat. fat), 0 mg chol., 7 mg sodium, 3 g carbo., 0 g fiber, 0 g pro.

Fizzy Mint-Chocolate Soda

Start to Finish: 10 min.

¼	cup chocolate-flavored syrup
1	pint mint-chocolate chip ice cream
2	cups carbonated water or cream soda, chilled

1. Pour some of the chocolate syrup into the bottoms of 4 tall glasses. Add 1 scoop of ice cream to each glass. Add more chocolate syrup to each glass. Top with another scoop of ice cream. Slowly pour ½ cup carbonated water into each glass.
Makes 4 servings.

Nutrition Facts per serving: 245 cal., 11 g total fat (6 g sat. fat), 26 mg chol., 84 mg sodium, 33 g carbo., 0 g fiber, 4 g pro. Daily Values: 6% vit. A, 10% vit. C, 10% calcium, 3% iron

Raspberry-Coffee Frappé

Start to Finish: 10 min.

- 2 cups strong coffee, chilled
- ¼ cup raspberry-flavored syrup
- ½ cup half-and-half or light cream
- 18 ice cubes (about 2½ cups)
- 6 scoops coffee-flavored ice cream

1. In a blender container place 1 cup of the coffee, the syrup, half-and-half, and ice cubes. Cover; blend until ice is finely crushed. Add remaining coffee. Cover; blend on lowest speed until combined. Pour into glasses. Top each serving with ice cream.
Makes 6 servings.

Nutrition Facts per serving: 243 cal., 14 g total fat (9 g sat. fat), 87 mg chol., 69 mg sodium, 24 g carbo., 0 g fiber, 4 g pro. Daily Values: 8% vit. A, 13% calcium, 1% iron

Mocha au Lait

Start to Finish: 10 min.

- 1½ cups nonfat dry milk powder
- ⅓ cup packed brown sugar
- ½ cup instant coffee crystals
- ⅔ cup miniature semisweet chocolate pieces

1. Combine all ingredients. Store in an airtight container. For each serving, pour ⅔ cup boiling water in a blender container. Add ¼ cup of the mix. Cover tightly; blend until frothy.
Makes 12 servings.

Nutrition Facts per serving: 109 cal., 3 g total fat (1 g sat. fat), 2 mg chol., 55 mg sodium, 15 g carbo., 1 g fiber, 3 g pro. Daily Values: 4% vit. A, 1% vit. C, 12% calcium, 2% iron

Hot Chocolate Mix

Start to Finish: 10 min.

- 1 25.6-ounce package nonfat dry milk powder
- 1 16-ounce jar powdered nondairy creamer
- 1 15- or 16-ounce container presweetened cocoa powder
- 1 13-ounce jar instant malted milk powder
- 1 cup sifted powdered sugar

1. Combine all ingredients. Store in a tightly covered container. For each serving, stir together ½ cup mix and ½ cup boiling water.
Makes 40 servings.

Nutrition Facts per serving: 208 cal., 4 g total fat (4 g sat. fat), 6 mg chol., 202 mg sodium, 33 g carbo., 0 g fiber, 9 g pro. Daily Values: 9% vit. A, 2% vit. C, 29% calcium, 1% iron

Hot Caramel Chocolate

Start to Finish: 15 min.

- ⅓ **cup sugar**
- ⅓ **cup unsweetened cocoa powder**
- ⅓ **cup water**
- 6 **milk chocolate-covered round caramels**
- 6 **cups milk, half-and-half, or light cream**

1. In a large saucepan combine sugar, cocoa powder, and water. Cook and stir over medium heat until sugar is dissolved. Add caramels; stir until melted. Stir in the milk and heat through. **Makes 6 servings.**

Nutrition Facts per serving: 213 cal., 7 g total fat (4 g sat. fat), 19 mg chol., 133 mg sodium, 29 g carbo., 0 g fiber, 10 g pro. Daily Values: 15% vit. A, 3% vit. C, 29% calcium, 5% iron

Nut-Butter Cocoa

Start to Finish: 15 min.

- ½ **cup whipping cream**
- 3½ **cups milk**
- ⅓ **cup chocolate-hazelnut spread**
- 2 **tablespoons creamy peanut butter**
- 3 **bite-size chocolate-covered peanut butter cups, quartered**

1. In a chilled mixing bowl beat whipping cream with an electric mixer on medium to high speed until stiff peaks form (tips stand straight). Cover and chill.

2. In a saucepan combine milk, chocolate-hazelnut spread, and peanut butter. Cook and stir over medium heat until combined and mixture is heated through. Pour mixture into warm mugs. Top each with whipped cream and 2 pieces of peanut butter cups. **Makes 6 servings.**

Nutrition Facts per serving: 310 cal., 21 g total fat (8 g sat. fat), 39 mg chol., 157 mg sodium, 23 g carbo., 1 g fiber, 9 g pro. Daily Values: 17% vit. A, 2% vit. C, 20% calcium, 2% iron

Mocha Java

Start to Finish: 10 min.

- 4 **cups strong coffee**
- ½ **cup semisweet chocolate pieces**
- ¼ **cup sugar**
- 1 **cup half-and-half or light cream**

1. In a small saucepan combine coffee, chocolate pieces, and sugar. Cook and stir over medium heat for 2 to 3 minutes or until chocolate is melted and sugar is dissolved. In another small saucepan heat half-and-half until steaming, stirring occasionally. Divide coffee mixture among 4 mugs. Add warm half-and-half. **Makes 4 servings.**

Nutrition Facts per serving: 232 cal., 13 g total fat (8 g sat. fat), 22 mg chol., 32 mg sodium, 29 g carbo., 1 g fiber, 3 g pro. Daily Values: 5% vit. A, 1% vit. C, 7% calcium, 5% iron

Winter's Day Espresso

Start to Finish: 15 min.

1 cup dairy eggnog
2 cups hot espresso or very strong coffee
1 tablespoon Irish cream-flavored syrup
   Whipped cream
   Ground nutmeg

1. In a saucepan combine eggnog, espresso, and syrup. Heat through. Serve in mugs topped with whipped cream. Sprinkle with nutmeg.
Makes 4 servings.

Nutrition Facts per serving: 117 cal., 7 g total fat (2 g sat. fat), 10 mg chol., 46 mg sodium, 11 g carbo., 0 g fiber, 2 g pro. Daily Values: 2% vit. A, 5% calcium

Chai

Start to Finish: 15 min.

1¼ cups nonfat dry milk powder
 ¼ cup black tea leaves
12 cardamom pods
 4 2-inch pieces stick cinnamon
 2 teaspoons finely shredded lemon peel
 8 cups water

1. In a large saucepan combine all ingredients. Bring to boiling; remove from heat. Cover; let stand for 5 minutes. Strain through a sieve lined with 100-percent-cotton cheesecloth or a clean paper coffee filter.
Makes 8 servings.

Nutrition Facts per serving: 40 cal., 0 g total fat (0 g sat. fat), 2 mg chol., 62 mg sodium, 6 g carbo., 0 g fiber, 4 g pro. Daily Values: 5% vit. A, 2% vit. C, 13% calcium

Hot Scarlet Wine Punch

Start to Finish: 20 min.

1 32-ounce bottle cranberry juice (4 cups)
⅓ cup packed brown sugar
2 inches stick cinnamon
4 whole cloves
1 750-milliliter bottle white Zinfandel

1. In a large saucepan combine cranberry juice, brown sugar, stick cinnamon, and cloves. Bring to boiling; reduce heat. Simmer, uncovered, for 5 minutes. Remove spices. Add white Zinfandel. Heat through.
Makes 14 servings.

Nutrition Facts per serving: 99 cal., 0 g total fat (0 g sat. fat), 0 mg chol., 6 mg sodium, 16 g carbo., 0 g fiber, 0 g pro. Daily Values: 43% vit. C, 1% calcium, 2% iron

Mulled Cider

Start to Finish: 20 min.

8	cups apple cider or apple juice
2	to 4 tablespoons brown sugar
½	teaspoon cardamom seeds
1	teaspoon whole allspice
	Stick cinnamon (optional)

1. In a large saucepan combine cider and brown sugar. For spice bag, place cardamom and allspice on a double-thick, 6-inch square of 100-percent-cotton cheesecloth. Bring corners together and tie with string; add spice bag to cider. Bring cider mixture to boiling; reduce heat. Simmer, covered, for 10 minutes. Discard spice bag. To serve, pour cider into mugs. If desired, garnish each serving with stick cinnamon.
Makes 8 servings.

Nutrition Facts per serving: 135 cal., 0 g total fat (0 g sat. fat), 0 mg chol., 8 mg sodium, 37 g carbo., 0 g fiber, 0 g pro. Daily Values: 4% vit. C, 1% calcium, 8% iron

Cinnamon Sippin' Cider

Start to Finish: 10 min.

3	cups apple cider or apple juice
1	cup cranberry juice
8	inches stick cinnamon, broken

1. In a saucepan combine all ingredients. Bring to boiling; reduce heat. Simmer, uncovered, for 5 minutes. Remove stick cinnamon.
Makes 4 servings.

Nutrition Facts per serving: 107 cal., 0 g total fat (0 g sat. fat), 0 mg chol., 1 mg sodium, 11 g carbo., 0 g fiber, 0 g pro. Daily Values: 40% vit. C, 1% calcium, 4% iron

Hot Strawberry Cider

Start to Finish: 20 min.

8	cups apple cider or apple juice
1	10-ounce package frozen sliced strawberries
4	inches stick cinnamon
1	teaspoon whole cloves
	Fresh strawberry or apple slices or stick cinnamon (optional)

1. In a large saucepan combine all ingredients, except fresh fruit or stick cinnamon. Bring to boiling; reduce heat. Simmer, covered, for 10 minutes. Strain through a sieve lined with 100-percent-cotton cheesecloth. If desired, garnish each serving with a fresh strawberry, apple slice, or stick cinnamon.
Makes 8 servings.

Nutrition Facts per serving: 158 cal., 0 g total fat (0 g sat. fat), 0 mg chol., 9 mg sodium, 43 g carbo., 3 g fiber, 0 g pro. Daily Values: 28% vit. C, 1% calcium, 9% iron

SALADS

Chapter three

Ham and Rye Salad

Prep: 10 min. • Bake: 10 min.

6   slices rye bread, cut into cubes (4 cups)

3   tablespoons butter, melted

1   10-ounce package torn mixed salad greens
     with carrots

1   8-ounce boneless cooked ham slice, cubed

²⁄₃ cup bottled honey-mustard salad dressing

1. Place bread cubes in a large bowl. Add melted butter; toss to coat. Arrange bread cubes in an even layer in a shallow baking pan. Bake in a 350°F oven for 10 to 15 minutes or until toasted, turning once. Set aside to cool.

2. In a large salad bowl toss together bread cubes and remaining ingredients.
Makes 4 to 6 main-dish servings.

Nutrition Facts per serving: 503 cal., 36 g total fat (10 g sat. fat), 65 mg chol., 1,602 mg sodium, 29 g carbo., 4 g fiber, 18 g pro. Daily Values: 12% vit. A, 6% vit. C, 8% calcium, 16% iron

Ham, Melon, and Spinach Salad

Start to Finish: 30 min.

½   of a small cantaloupe

7   cups torn fresh spinach

1   cup cubed cooked lean ham

½   cup pecan halves, toasted

⅓   cup bottled poppy seed salad dressing

1. Use a melon baller to scoop cantaloupe flesh into balls. In a large bowl toss together cantaloupe, spinach, ham, and pecans. Pour dressing over salad. Toss to coat.
Makes 4 main-dish servings.

Nutrition Facts per serving: 286 cal., 20 g total fat (3 g sat. fat), 19 mg chol., 507 mg sodium, 19 g carbo., 4 g fiber, 12 g pro. Daily Values: 119% vit. C, 10% calcium, 24% iron

B.L.T. Salad

Start to Finish: 20 min.

5   cups torn greens or spinach

2   cups grape or cherry tomatoes, halved

½   pound bacon, cooked and crumbled (about
     10 slices)

2   hard-cooked eggs, peeled and chopped

⅓   cup bottled poppy seed salad dressing

1. Place greens in a large bowl. Top with tomatoes, bacon, and eggs. Drizzle with dressing. Toss gently to coat.
Makes 4 main-dish or 8 side-dish servings.

Nutrition Facts per main-dish serving: 251 cal., 20 g total fat (5 g sat. fat), 123 mg chol., 461 mg sodium, 8 g carbo., 2 g fiber, 10 g pro. Daily Values: 50% vit. A, 57% vit. C, 6% calcium, 10% iron

Bacon in a Hurry

For recipes that don't require drippings from just-cooked bacon, save a little time and mess by using precooked bacon that's available in your supermarket. It only needs a brief crisping in the oven or on top of the stove.

Pasta-Salami Salad

Prep: 20 min. • Chill: 4 to 24 hours

12 ounces rotini, cavatelli, or bow tie pasta
1 16-ounce package frozen pepper and onion stir-fry vegetables
4 ounces salami or cooked smoked sausage links
1 cup bottled Italian salad dressing
1 2¼-ounce can sliced pitted ripe olives (½ cup)

1. Cook pasta according to package directions. Place frozen vegetables in a colander; pour pasta and cooking water over vegetables. Drain well.

2. Cut salami into bite-size pieces. In a large bowl toss together pasta mixture, salami, dressing, and olives. Cover and chill for 4 to 24 hours. If necessary, stir in additional Italian dressing before serving.
Makes 6 main-dish servings.

Nutrition Facts per serving: 498 cal., 27 g total fat (5 g sat. fat), 18 mg chol., 765 mg sodium, 52 g carbo., 3 g fiber, 13 g pro. Daily Values: 10% vit. A, 45% vit. C, 2% calcium, 15% iron

Chicken Antipasto Salad

Start to Finish: 10 min.

8 ounces thinly sliced cooked chicken or turkey breast
1 15-ounce can three-bean salad, drained
1 6-ounce jar marinated artichoke hearts
½ cup pitted ripe olives, drained
8 cherry tomatoes

1. Roll each chicken slice; divide among 4 plates. Spoon three-bean salad on each plate. Drain artichoke hearts, reserving marinade (about ¼ cup); arrange artichoke hearts, olives, and tomatoes on each plate. To serve, drizzle reserved artichoke marinade over salads.
Makes 4 main-dish servings.

Nutrition Facts per serving: 258 cal., 10 g total fat (1 g sat. fat), 51 mg chol., 654 mg sodium, 26 g carbo., 7 g fiber, 21 g pro. Daily Values: 11% vit. A, 32% vit. C, 16% iron

Chicken and Greens with Pears

Start to Finish: 15 min.

- 6 cups packaged torn mixed greens or mesclun
- 10 to 12 ounces roasted or grilled chicken breast, sliced
- ¾ cup bottled reduced-calorie or regular blue cheese salad dressing
- 2 pears, cored and sliced
  Freshly ground black pepper (optional)

1. In a large bowl combine the greens, chicken, and dressing; toss gently to coat. Divide among 4 large salad bowls or dinner plates. Arrange pear slices on top of salads. Sprinkle with pepper, if desired.
Makes 4 main-dish servings.

Nutrition Facts per serving: 225 cal., 6 g total fat (2 g sat. fat), 61 mg chol., 639 mg sodium, 16 g carbo., 3 g fiber, 26 g pro. Daily Values: 16% vit. A, 14% vit. C, 9% calcium, 9% iron

Chicken Taco Salad

Prep: 10 min. • Cook: 10 min.

- 1 9-ounce package frozen cooked Southwestern-seasoned chicken breast strips
- 1 15- to 16-ounce can pinto beans, rinsed and drained
- 1 cup frozen whole kernel corn
- ¾ cup salsa
  Tortilla chips

1. In a medium saucepan stir together chicken, beans, corn, and salsa. Bring to boiling; reduce heat. Simmer, covered, for 10 minutes or until heated through, stirring occasionally. Serve with tortilla chips.
Makes 4 main-dish servings.

Nutrition Facts per serving: 320 cal., 9 g total fat (2 g sat. fat), 30 mg chol., 1,066 mg sodium, 42 g carbo., 8 g fiber, 23 g pro. Daily Values: 5% vit. A, 9% vit. C, 9% calcium, 13% iron

Pasta-Chicken Caesar Salad

Start to Finish: 20 min.

- 6 ounces dried radiatore or large bow tie pasta (about 2¼ cups)
- 1 10-ounce package Caesar salad kit (includes lettuce, dressing, croutons, and cheese)
- 1 cup cherry tomatoes, halved
- 1 9-ounce package refrigerated cooked chicken breast strips

1. Cook pasta according to package directions; drain well. Rinse with cold water; drain again. In a very large bowl combine cooked pasta, contents of salad package, and tomatoes; toss to combine. Divide among 4 serving bowls. Arrange chicken strips on top.
Makes 4 main-dish servings.

Nutrition Facts per serving: 377 cal., 14 g total fat (3 g sat. fat), 49 mg chol., 868 mg sodium, 40 g carbo., 3 g fiber, 22 g pro. Daily Values: 32% vit. A, 33% vit. C, 5% calcium, 15% iron

Quick and Crunchy Turkey Salad

Start to Finish: 10 min.

1   16-ounce package shredded cabbage with
      carrot (coleslaw mix)
6   ounces cooked turkey breast, cubed
      (1¼ cups)
1   3-ounce package ramen noodles
⅔   cup bottled orange vinaigrette salad
      dressing
1   11- or 15-ounce can mandarin orange
      sections, drained

1. In a large bowl combine coleslaw mix and
turkey. Remove seasoning packet from noodles;
reserve for another use. Crumble noodles; add to
cabbage mixture. Pour dressing over salad; toss
to coat. Gently stir in the orange sections.
Makes 4 main-dish servings.

Nutrition Facts per serving: 527 cal., 23 g total fat
(1 g sat. fat), 15 mg chol., 1,552 mg sodium, 67 g carbo.,
3 g fiber, 17 g pro. Daily Values: 11% vit. A, 110% vit. C,
7% calcium, 9% iron

Salmon Caesar Salad

Start to Finish: 15 min.

1   10-ounce package Caesar salad kit
      (includes lettuce, dressing, croutons,
      and cheese)
1   small sweet pepper, cut into thin strips
1   small cucumber, quartered lengthwise
      and sliced
6   ounces smoked, poached, or canned
      salmon, skinned, boned, and broken
      into chunks (1 cup)
½   of a lemon, cut into 3 wedges

1. In a large bowl, combine lettuce and
dressing from packaged salad, pepper strips,
and cucumber; toss gently to coat. Add salmon
and the croutons and cheese from packaged
salad; toss gently to combine. Divide among
3 dinner plates. Before serving, squeeze juice
from a lemon wedge over each salad.
Makes 3 main-dish servings.

Nutrition Facts per serving: 251 cal., 18 g total fat
(3 g sat. fat), 23 mg chol., 826 mg sodium, 11 g carbo.,
3 g fiber, 14 g pro. Daily Values: 39% vit. A, 113% vit. C,
8% calcium, 10% iron

Tortellini-Pesto Salad

Prep: 20 min. • Chill: 2 hours

2   cups frozen or refrigerated cheese-filled
     tortellini (about 7 ounces)
4   ounces mozzarella cheese, cubed
1   cup coarsely chopped, seeded tomato
½   cup purchased pesto
¼   cup pine nuts or slivered almonds, toasted

1. Cook tortellini according to package
directions; drain. Rinse with cold water; drain
well. In a large bowl combine tortellini, cheese,
and tomato. Pour pesto over tortellini mixture;
toss lightly to coat. Cover and chill for 2 to
4 hours. Stir in pine nuts just before serving.
Makes 4 main-dish servings.

Nutrition Facts per serving: 360 cal., 15 g total fat
(4 g sat. fat), 51 mg chol., 453 mg sodium, 37 g carbo.,
1 g fiber, 21 g pro. Daily Values: 12% vit. A, 26% vit. C,
16% calcium, 9% iron

Tangy Melon Salad

Start to Finish: 25 min.

3   cups seeded, cubed watermelon, chilled
3   cups seeded, cubed cantaloupe, chilled
1½   to 3 teaspoons sugar
⅓   cup balsamic vinegar
1½   teaspoons fresh ground black pepper
      (optional)

1. Divide watermelon and cantaloupe among
6 dishes. Stir sugar into vinegar until dissolved.
Drizzle some of the vinegar mixture over each
serving. Sprinkle with pepper, if desired.
Makes 6 side-dish servings.

Nutrition Facts per serving: 65 cal., 1 g total fat
(0 g sat. fat), 0 mg chol., 9 mg sodium, 15 g carbo.,
1 g fiber, 1 g pro. Daily Values: 57% vit. A, 68% vit. C,
1% calcium, 2% iron

Orange Dream Fruit Salad

Start to Finish: 15 min.

1   cup chopped, peeled, seeded mango
      or papaya
1   11-ounce can mandarin orange sections,
      drained
1   cup seedless red and/or green grapes,
      halved
½   cup orange-flavored yogurt
¼   teaspoon poppy seeds

1. In a medium bowl combine mango, orange sections, and grapes. In a small bowl stir together yogurt and poppy seeds. Gently stir yogurt mixture into fruit until combined.
Makes 4 to 6 side-dish servings.

Nutrition Facts per serving: 136 cal., 1 g total fat
(0 g sat. fat), 2 mg chol., 26 mg sodium, 32 g carbo.,
2 g fiber, 2 g pro. Daily Values: 46% vit. A, 52% vit. C,
7% calcium, 3% iron

Strawberry-Spinach Salad

Start to Finish: 20 min.

4   cups torn spinach or 2 cups torn spinach
      and 2 cups torn salad greens
1   cup watercress
1   cup sliced fresh strawberries
½   of a small red onion, thinly sliced
½   cup bottled oil-and-vinegar salad dressing
      or poppy seed salad dressing

1. In a large bowl combine spinach, watercress, strawberries, and onion. Pour dressing over salad; toss to coat.
Makes 4 side-dish servings.

Nutrition Facts per serving: 168 cal., 16 g total fat
(2 g sat. fat), 0 mg chol., 468 mg sodium, 8 g carbo.,
2 g fiber, 2 g pro. Daily Values: 41% vit. A, 68% vit. C,
11% iron

Black Cherry-Cranberry Supreme

Prep: 15 min. • Chill: 4³/₄ hours

2 3-ounce packages black cherry-flavored
    gelatin
2 cups boiling water
1 16-ounce can jellied cranberry sauce
1 8-ounce carton dairy sour cream or light
    dairy sour cream
1 cup chopped walnuts or pecans,
    toasted (optional)

1. In a large mixing bowl, dissolve gelatin in the boiling water. Using a wire whisk or rotary beater, lightly beat in cranberry sauce until smooth. Add sour cream; beat until combined. Chill about 45 minutes or until partially set (the consistency of unbeaten egg whites). If desired, fold in nuts.

2. Pour mixture into a 5- or 6-cup mold or an 8×8×2-inch baking dish. Cover and chill for at least 4 hours or until set. Unmold or cut into squares.
Makes 8 to 10 side-dish servings.

Nutrition Facts per serving: 231 cal., 6 g total fat (4 g sat. fat), 13 mg chol., 99 mg sodium, 42 g carbo., 1 g fiber, 3 g pro. Daily Values: 4% vit. A, 3% calcium

Creamy Apple Salad

Start to Finish: 15 min.

3 cups chopped apples (about 3 medium)
1 8-ounce can pineapple tidbits, drained
¹/₂ cup coarsely chopped walnuts
1 small stalk celery, finely chopped
1 4-ounce container frozen whipped dessert
    topping, thawed

1. In a large bowl combine apples, pineapple, walnuts, and celery. Fold whipped dessert topping into apple mixture just until combined.
Makes 8 to 10 side-dish servings.

Nutrition Facts per serving: 173 cal., 13 g total fat (6 g sat. fat), 31 mg chol., 13 mg sodium, 14 g carbo., 2 g fiber, 2 g pro. Daily Values: 7% vit. A, 9% vit. C, 3% calcium, 2% iron

Lemon Sunshine Salad

Prep: 30 min. • Chill: 2 hours

½   cup acini di pepe (tiny, bead-shaped
     pasta)

1   4-serving-size package instant lemon
     pudding mix

1   29-ounce can peach slices in light syrup

2   11-ounce cans mandarin orange sections,
     drained

1   8-ounce container frozen whipped dessert
     topping, thawed

1. Cook pasta according to package directions.
Drain. Stir in pudding mix. Drain peaches,
reserving ½ cup syrup; stir reserved syrup into
pasta mixture. Cut peach slices into bite-size
pieces. Fold peaches and orange sections into
pasta mixture. Cover; chill for 2 hours. Just
before serving, fold in whipped dessert topping.
Makes 15 side-dish servings.

Nutrition Facts per serving: 150 cal., 3 g total fat
(3 g sat. fat), 0 mg chol., 86 mg sodium, 30 g carbo.,
1 g fiber, 1 g pro. Daily Values: 11% vit. A, 16% vit. C,
1% calcium, 4% iron

Marinated Bean Salad

Prep: 20 min. • Chill: 4 to 24 hours

8   ounces fresh green beans, trimmed and cut
     into bite-size pieces, or one 9-ounce
     package frozen cut green beans

2   15- to 19-ounce cans navy, red kidney,
     and/or cannellini beans, rinsed and
     drained

½   cup thinly sliced red onion

½   cup bottled balsamic vinaigrette
     salad dressing

3   tablespoons molasses

1. In a medium saucepan cook fresh green beans
in boiling water for 7 to 10 minutes or until just
tender; drain. (If using frozen green beans, cook
according to package directions; drain.) Rinse
with cold water and drain again.

2. In a large bowl stir together green beans,
canned beans, and onion. Stir together dressing
and molasses. Pour over bean mixture; toss to
coat. Cover and chill for 4 to 24 hours. Serve
with a slotted spoon.
Makes 8 side-dish servings.

Nutrition Facts per serving: 196 cal., 5 g total fat
(1 g sat. fat), 0 mg chol., 656 mg sodium, 31 g carbo.,
6 g fiber, 9 g pro. Daily Values: 3% vit. A, 7% vit. C,
8% calcium, 14% iron

Asian Pea Pod Salad

Start to Finish: 20 min.

6   cups torn romaine
2   cups fresh pea pods, trimmed and
      halved crosswise
⅓   cup bottled Italian salad dressing
1   tablespoon hoisin sauce
1   tablespoon sesame seeds, toasted

1. In a large bowl toss together romaine and pea pods. Stir together dressing and hoisin sauce. Pour over romaine mixture; toss to coat. Sprinkle with sesame seeds.
Makes 6 side-dish servings.

Nutrition Facts per serving: 98 cal., 7 g total fat (1 g sat. fat), 0 mg chol., 153 mg sodium, 6 g carbo., 2 g fiber, 2 g pro. Daily Values: 31% vit. A, 25% vit. C, 4% calcium, 6% iron

Pea and Peanut Salad

Start to Finish: 10 min.

1   10-ounce package frozen peas, thawed
      and drained
1   cup Spanish or honey-roasted peanuts
¼   cup dairy sour cream
2   tablespoons mayonnaise or salad dressing
½   teaspoon sugar

1. In a medium bowl combine peas and peanuts. Stir together sour cream, mayonnaise, and sugar until combined. Stir into pea mixture until coated.
Makes 4 to 6 side-dish servings.

Nutrition Facts per serving: 346 cal., 26 g total fat (5 g sat. fat), 9 mg chol., 131 mg sodium, 17 g carbo., 6 g fiber, 15 g pro. Daily Values: 12% vit. A, 12% vit. C, 5% calcium, 8% iron

Fresh Corn and Tomato Salad

Prep: 40 min. • Stand: 20 min.

6   ears fresh corn, husked
½   of an 8-ounce bottle light Italian salad
    dressing
3   tablespoons snipped fresh rosemary
4   medium Roma tomatoes, cut into
    ½-inch slices
3   cups fresh baby spinach leaves or
    torn spinach

1. Brush each ear of corn with some of the dressing; sprinkle with rosemary. Place brushed ears in a shallow baking pan. Bake in a 425°F oven for 30 minutes, turning once.

2. Cut each ear of corn crosswise into thirds. Set a 1-gallon self-sealing plastic bag in a large shallow bowl; place corn and tomatoes in bag. Pour remaining dressing over vegetables. Seal bag; let stand 20 minutes before serving (or chill for at least 4 hours and up to 24 hours, turning bag once or twice).

3. To serve, arrange spinach leaves on 6 chilled plates. Remove corn and tomatoes from bag with a slotted spoon; reserve dressing. Arrange corn and tomatoes on top of spinach. Pass reserved dressing.
Makes 6 side-dish servings.

Nutrition Facts per serving: 138 cal., 3 g total fat
(0 g sat. fat), 1 mg chol., 414 mg sodium, 28 g carbo.,
5 g fiber, 4 g pro. Daily Values: 27% vit. A, 29% vit. C,
2% calcium, 11% iron

Fruity Wild Rice Salad

Prep: 50 min. • Chill: 4 to 24 hours

⅔   cup uncooked wild rice
½   cup dried cranberries
⅓   cup sliced green onions
½   cup bottled raspberry vinaigrette salad
    dressing or other vinaigrette salad
    dressing
½   cup coarsely chopped pecans, toasted

1. Rinse wild rice in a strainer under cold running water; drain. Cook according to package directions until tender; drain, if necessary. In a medium bowl stir together rice, cranberries, green onions, and salad dressing. Cover and chill for 4 to 24 hours. Stir in pecans before serving.
Makes 6 side-dish servings.

Nutrition Facts per serving: 186 cal., 7 g total fat
(1 g sat. fat), 0 mg chol., 275 mg sodium, 30 g carbo.,
3 g fiber, 4 g pro. Daily Values: 1% vit. A, 2% vit. C,
1% calcium, 4% iron

Cranberry Coleslaw

Start to Finish: 15 min.

- ¼ cup mayonnaise or salad dressing
- 1 to 2 tablespoons honey
- 1 tablespoon vinegar
- ¼ cup chopped fresh cranberries or snipped dried cranberries
- 5 cups shredded cabbage (1 small head)

1. For dressing, in a small bowl stir together mayonnaise, honey, and vinegar. Stir in cranberries. Place shredded cabbage in a large serving bowl. Pour dressing over cabbage; toss to coat. Serve at once or, if desired, cover and chill for 45 minutes.
Makes 6 side-dish servings.

Nutrition Facts per serving: 94 cal., 7 g total fat
(1 g sat. fat), 5 mg chol., 63 mg sodium, 7 g carbo.,
2 g fiber, 1 g pro. Daily Values: 2% vit. A, 32% vit. C,
3% calcium, 2% iron

Ginger-Sesame Slaw

Start to Finish: 25 min.

- 4 cups thinly bias-sliced bok choy
- 2 cups carrot ribbons
- 1 daikon radish (8 ounces), shredded, or 1 cup sliced radishes
- 1 tablespoon finely chopped pickled ginger or 2 teaspoons grated fresh ginger
- ¼ to ½ cup bottled oriental sesame salad dressing

1. In a large bowl stir together bok choy, carrot, radish, and ginger. Add enough dressing to moisten. Serve at once or, if desired, cover and chill for up to 1 hour.
Makes 6 side-dish servings.

Nutrition Facts per serving: 71 cal., 4 g total fat
(1 g sat. fat), 0 mg chol., 106 mg sodium, 9 g carbo.,
2 g fiber, 2 g pro. Daily Values: 234% vit. A, 52% vit. C,
8% calcium, 4% iron

Napa Cabbage Slaw

Start to Finish: 30 min.

- 3 cups finely shredded napa cabbage
- 1 cup finely shredded bok choy
- 2 to 3 tablespoons very thin red sweet pepper strips
- ¼ cup seasoned rice vinegar or white vinegar
- 1 tablespoon toasted sesame oil

1. In a large bowl combine cabbage, bok choy, and pepper strips. Stir together vinegar and oil; pour over salad mixture. Toss to coat.
Makes 6 side-dish servings.

Nutrition Facts per serving: 29 cal., 2 g total fat
(0 g sat. fat), 0 mg chol., 5 mg sodium, 2 g carbo.,
1 g fiber, 1 g pro. Daily Values: 7% vit. A, 27% vit. C,
3% calcium, 1% iron

Fresh Mozzarella Salad

Start to Finish: 10 min.

4   medium tomatoes or 6 Roma tomatoes

4   ounces fresh mozzarella

2   tablespoons bottled balsamic vinaigrette
     salad dressing

½ cup loosely packed fresh basil leaves,
     thinly sliced

    Salt and fresh cracked black pepper

1. Cut tomatoes into ½-inch slices. Cut mozzarella into ¼-inch slices. Arrange tomato and cheese slices on a platter. Drizzle with vinaigrette. Sprinkle basil on top. Sprinkle with salt and pepper.
Makes 8 side-dish servings.

Nutrition Facts per serving: 64 cal., 4 g total fat
(2 g sat. fat), 11 mg chol., 174 mg sodium, 4 g carbo.,
1 g fiber, 3 g pro. Daily Values: 12% vit. A, 20% vit. C,
8% calcium, 2% iron

Mediterranean-Style Pasta Salad

Prep: 25 min. • Chill: 4 hours

1½ cups dried mostaccioli pasta

1   cup halved cherry or grape tomatoes

⅓ cup sliced pitted kalamata or other
     ripe olives

1   4-ounce package crumbled feta cheese

½ cup bottled balsamic vinaigrette
     salad dressing

1. Cook pasta according to package directions; drain. Rinse with cold water; drain well. In a large bowl combine the cooked pasta with remaining ingredients; toss to coat. Cover and chill for 4 to 8 hours. Stir gently before serving.
Makes 4 to 5 side-dish servings.

Nutrition Facts per serving: 335 cal., 17 g total fat
(5 g sat. fat), 25 mg chol., 792 mg sodium, 36 g carbo.,
2 g fiber, 9 g pro. Daily Values: 8% vit. A, 14% vit. C,
15% calcium, 8% iron

Strawberry Vinaigrette

Start to Finish: 5 min.

1 cup cut-up fresh or frozen strawberries
2 tablespoons red wine vinegar
½ teaspoon sugar
⅛ teaspoon cracked black pepper

1. In a blender container combine all ingredients. Cover and blend until smooth. If desired, store in the refrigerator for up to 24 hours.
Makes 1 cup.

Nutrition Facts per tablespoon: 3 cal., 0 g total fat (0 g sat. fat), 0 mg chol., 0 mg sodium, 1 g carbo., 0 g fiber, 0 g pro. Daily Values: 9% vit. C

Lime Vinaigrette

Start to Finish: 10 min.

¼ cup salad oil
¼ teaspoon finely shredded lime peel
2 tablespoons lime juice
¼ teaspoon grated fresh ginger or dash
     ground ginger

1. In a screw-top jar combine all ingredients. Cover; shake well. Use at once or store in the refrigerator for up to 3 days. Shake before using.
Makes ⅓ cup.

Nutrition Facts per tablespoon: 98 cal., 11 g total fat (2 g sat. fat), 0 mg chol., 0 mg sodium, 1 g carbo., 0 g fiber, 0 g pro. Daily Values: 4% vit. C, 1% calcium, 1% iron

Lemon-Nut Vinaigrette

Start to Finish: 10 min.

¼ cup walnut oil, salad oil, or olive oil
1 teaspoon finely shredded lemon peel or
     lime peel
¼ cup lemon juice or lime juice
2 tablespoons ground walnuts, almonds, or
     pecans
1 tablespoon honey

1. In a small bowl stir together all ingredients. Use at once or cover and store in the refrigerator for up to 3 days. Stir before using.
Makes ⅔ cup.

Nutrition Facts per tablespoon: 66 cal., 6 g total fat (1 g sat. fat), 0 mg chol., 0 mg sodium, 2 g carbo., 0 g fiber, 0 g pro. Daily Values: 5% vit. C

Berry-Melon Vinaigrette

Start to Finish: 15 min.

- 1 cup seeded watermelon chunks
- 1 cup hulled, halved strawberries
- 2 tablespoons white balsamic vinegar
- 1 tablespoon sugar
- 1 teaspoon finely shredded orange peel

1. In a blender container or food processor bowl combine all ingredients. Cover and blend or process until smooth. Use at once or cover and store in the refrigerator for up to 3 days. Shake well before using.
Makes about 2 cups.

Nutrition Facts per 2 tablespoons: 11 cal., 0 g total fat
(0 g sat. fat), 0 mg chol., 1 mg sodium, 3 g carbo., 0 g fiber,
0 g pro. Daily Values: 11% vit. C

Spicy Citrus Dressing

Start to Finish: 10 min.

- $\frac{1}{4}$ cup lemon juice or lime juice
- 2 tablespoons honey
- 1 tablespoon salad oil
- $\frac{1}{4}$ teaspoon ground cinnamon, allspice,
      or cardamom
- $\frac{1}{8}$ teaspoon paprika

1. In a screw-top jar combine all ingredients. Cover; shake well. Use at once or store in the refrigerator for up to 3 days. Shake before serving.
Makes about $\frac{1}{3}$ cup.

Nutrition Facts per tablespoon: 53 cal., 3 g total fat
(0 g sat. fat), 0 mg chol., 1 mg sodium, 8 g carbo., 0 g fiber,
0 g pro. Daily Values: 1% vit. A, 10% vit. C, 1% iron

Apricot Nectar Dressing

Start to Finish: 5 min.

- $\frac{1}{2}$ cup plain low-fat yogurt
- 1 tablespoon brown sugar
- $\frac{1}{8}$ teaspoon ground cinnamon
      Dash nutmeg
- $\frac{1}{4}$ to $\frac{1}{2}$ cup apricot nectar

1. In a small bowl stir together yogurt, brown sugar, cinnamon, and nutmeg. Add apricot nectar to make the dressing of drizzling consistency. Stir until smooth. Use at once or cover and store in the refrigerator for 3 to 5 days.
Makes $\frac{3}{4}$ to 1 cup.

Nutrition Facts per tablespoon: 12 cal., 0 g total fat
(0 g sat. fat), 1 mg chol., 8 mg sodium, 2 g carbo., 0 g fiber,
1 g pro. Daily Values: 2% vit. A, 2% calcium

Poppy Seed Dressing

Start to Finish: 5 min.

1/3	cup orange juice
3	tablespoons salad oil
1	tablespoon Dijon-style mustard
1	teaspoon poppy seeds
2	to 3 dashes bottled hot pepper sauce

1. In a small bowl whisk together all ingredients. Use at once or cover and store in the refrigerator for up to 3 days. Stir dressing before using.
Makes 1/2 cup.

Nutrition Facts per tablespoon: 54 cal., 5 g total fat (1 g sat. fat), 0 mg chol., 11 mg sodium, 1 g carbo., 0 g fiber, 0 g pro. Daily Values: 9% vit. C, 1% calcium, 1% iron

Chutney Salad Dressing

Start to Finish: 10 min.

1/4	cup mango chutney
1	cup mayonnaise or salad dressing
1/2	cup dairy sour cream

1. Cut up any large pieces in chutney. In a small bowl stir together all ingredients. Use at once or cover and store in the refrigerator for up to 1 week.
Makes 1 3/4 cups.

Nutrition Facts per tablespoon: 71 cal., 7 g total fat (1 g sat. fat), 6 mg chol., 49 mg sodium, 2 g carbo., 0 g fiber, 0 g pro. Daily Values: 3% vit. A, 2% vit. C, 1% calcium

Thousand Island Dressing

Start to Finish: 20 min.

1 1/2	cups mayonnaise or salad dressing
1/4	cup chili sauce
1	hard-cooked egg, chopped
1	tablespoon finely chopped onion
1	tablespoon pickle relish

1. In a small bowl stir together all ingredients. Use at once or cover and store in the refrigerator for up to 3 days.
Makes 2 cups.

Nutrition Facts per tablespoon: 80 cal., 8 g total fat (1 g sat. fat), 10 mg chol., 87 mg sodium, 1 g carbo., 0 g fiber, 0 g pro. Daily Values: 1% vit. C

Creamy Garlic Dressing

Start to Finish: 5 min.

½ cup plain low-fat yogurt

⅓ cup low-fat Italian salad dressing

1 tablespoon grated Parmesan cheese

1 small garlic clove, minced

1. In a small bowl stir together all ingredients. Use at once or cover and store in the refrigerator for up to 3 days.
Makes 1 cup.

Nutrition Facts per tablespoon: 12 cal., 1 g total fat (0 g sat. fat), 1 mg chol., 50 mg sodium, 1 g carbo., 0 g fiber, 1 g pro. Daily Values: 2% calcium

Creamy Salad Dressing

Start to Finish: 5 min.

¼ cup plain low-fat yogurt

2 tablespoons light mayonnaise dressing or salad dressing

2 tablespoons fat-free milk

1 tablespoon snipped fresh parsley or chives

¼ teaspoon dried basil, oregano, or thyme, crushed (optional)

1. In a small bowl stir together all ingredients. Use at once or cover and store in the refrigerator for up to 3 days.
Makes ½ cup.

Nutrition Facts per tablespoon: 19 cal., 1 g total fat (0 g sat. fat), 2 mg chol., 48 mg sodium, 1 g carbo., 0 g fiber, 1 g pro. Daily Values: 1% vit. A, 1% vit. C, 2% calcium

Herb-Buttermilk Dressing

Start to Finish: 5 min.

⅔ cup light mayonnaise dressing or salad dressing

⅓ cup buttermilk

1 teaspoon snipped fresh tarragon or ¼ teaspoon dried tarragon, crushed

1 to 2 teaspoons milk (optional)

1. In a small bowl stir together mayonnaise dressing, buttermilk, and tarragon. If necessary, stir in enough milk to make of desired consistency. Use at once or cover and store in the refrigerator for up to 3 days.
Makes about 1 cup.

Nutrition Facts per tablespoon: 35 cal., 3 g total fat (1 g sat. fat), 3 mg chol., 65 mg sodium, 2 g carbo., 0 g fiber, 0 g pro. Daily Values: 1% calcium

Using Fresh or Dried Herbs

If you don't have the fresh herbs called for in a recipe, you can substitute dried. Use one-third less of the dried herb than fresh. For instance, if a recipe calls for 1 tablespoon of fresh herb, use 1 teaspoon of dried. If you don't have a particular herb on hand, try these substitutions:

Sage: use savory, marjoram, or rosemary

Basil: use oregano or thyme

Thyme: use basil, marjoram, oregano, or savory

Cilantro: use parsley

Mint: use basil, marjoram, or rosemary

Honey-Mustard Dressing

Start to Finish: 5 min.

- ⅓ **cup salad oil**
- 2 **tablespoons lemon juice**
- 2 **tablespoons honey**
- 2 **tablespoons coarse-grain brown mustard or Dijon-style mustard**
- 1 **clove garlic, minced**

1. In a small bowl stir together all ingredients. Use dressing at once or cover and store in the refrigerator for up to 3 days. Stir before using. **Makes ¾ cup.**

Nutrition Facts per tablespoon: 67 cal., 6 g total fat (1 g sat. fat), 0 mg chol., 34 mg sodium, 3 g carbo., 0 g fiber, 0 g pro. Daily Values: 3% vit. C, 1% calcium, 1% iron

Herbed Crouton Sticks

Prep: 15 min. • Bake: 25 min.

- 1 **8-ounce baguette-style French bread**
- ½ **cup butter or margarine**
- 1 **tablespoon snipped fresh basil or ½ teaspoon dried basil, crushed**
- ⅛ **teaspoon garlic powder**

1. Cut baguette in half horizontally. Cut bread into 3½×1-inch strips; set aside. In a 12-inch skillet melt butter. Stir in basil and garlic powder. Add half the bread sticks, stirring until coated with butter mixture. Arrange sticks in a single layer in a shallow baking pan. Repeat with remaining sticks.

2. Bake, uncovered, in a 300°F oven for 25 to 30 minutes or until sticks are dry and crisp, turning once. Cool completely. Store, tightly covered, at room temperature for up to 3 days or in the freezer for up to 3 months. **Makes about 24 sticks.**

Nutrition Facts per stick: 62 cal., 4 g total fat (3 g sat. fat), 11 mg chol., 99 mg sodium, 5 g carbo., 0 g fiber, 1 g pro. Daily Values: 3% vit. A, 1% calcium, 1% iron

Garlic Croutons

Start to Finish: 15 min.

- 2 **cups 1- to 1½-inch French or Italian bread cubes (about 2 ounces)**
- 2 **large cloves garlic, minced**
- 1 **teaspoon dried seasoning, crushed (such as Italian herbs, Greek seasoning, herbes de Provence, bouquet garni seasoning, or desired spice blend)**
- 1 **tablespoon cooking oil**
- 1 **tablespoon butter or margarine**

1. Place bread cubes in a bowl. In a large skillet cook and stir garlic and desired seasoning in hot oil and butter over medium-low heat for 30 seconds. Drizzle over bread cubes, tossing to coat well.

2. Pour cubes into skillet. Cook over medium-low heat for 6 to 8 minutes or until cubes are lightly brown and crisp, stirring occasionally. Remove from pan. Drain on paper towels. Store tightly covered for up to 1 week. **Makes 16 servings.**

Nutrition Facts per serving: 24 cal., 2 g total fat (0 g sat. fat), 2 mg chol., 30 mg sodium, 2 g carbo., 0 g fiber, 0 g pro. Daily Values: 1% vit. A, 1% iron

MAIN DISHES

Chapter four

Barbecue Meat Loaf

Prep: 15 min. • Bake: 45 min.

1	beaten egg
¼	cup fine dry bread crumbs
½	cup bottled barbecue sauce
1	pound lean ground beef
2	4-inch pieces string cheese (about 2 ounces)

1. In a medium bowl combine egg, bread crumbs, and ¼ cup of the barbecue sauce; add beef and mix well.

2. In a 2-quart rectangular baking dish pat about two-thirds of the meat mixture into a 7×3-inch rectangle. Place the cheese lengthwise in the center of the rectangle. Pat remaining meat mixture on top, sealing it around the cheese. Bake, uncovered, in a 350°F oven for 40 to 45 minutes or until center of the loaf registers 160°F on an instant-read thermometer. Spoon remaining barbecue sauce over loaf; bake for 5 minutes more.
Makes 4 servings.

Nutrition Facts per serving: 394 cal., 25 g total fat (10 g sat. fat), 144 mg chol., 735 mg sodium, 13 g carbo., 0 g fiber, 26 g pro. Daily Values: 6% vit. A, 12% calcium, 14% iron

Instant-Read Thermometers
Instant-read thermometers are used to check the internal temperature of food toward the end of cooking time. They should not be left in food as it cooks in the oven or microwave. To use a digital instant-read thermometer, insert the thermometer tip into the food at least ¼ inch for 10 seconds. For a dial instant-read thermometer, insert the tip into the food to a depth of 2 to 3 inches.

Taco Pizza

Prep: 15 min. • Bake: 20 min.

8	ounces lean ground beef and/or bulk pork sausage
1	medium green sweet pepper, chopped (¾ cup)
1	11½-ounce package refrigerated corn bread twists
½	cup purchased salsa
3	cups shredded taco cheese (12 ounces)

1. In a skillet cook beef and pepper over medium heat until meat is brown; drain. Set aside.

2. Unroll corn bread dough (do not separate into strips). Press dough into the bottom and up the edges of a greased 12-inch pizza pan. Spread salsa on top of dough. Sprinkle with meat mixture and cheese. Bake in a 400°F oven about 20 minutes or until bottom of crust is golden brown. Cut into wedges.
Makes 6 slices.

Nutrition Facts per slice: 465 cal., 30 g total fat (15 g sat. fat), 73 mg chol., 870 mg sodium, 27 g carbo., 1 g fiber, 22 g pro. Daily Values: 16% vit. A, 26% vit. C, 31% calcium, 13% iron

Italian Pizza Burgers

Prep: 15 min. • Broil: 11 min.

- 4   3¾-ounce purchased uncooked hamburger patties
- 4   ¾-inch slices sourdough bread
- 1   cup purchased mushroom pasta sauce
- 1   cup shredded provolone or mozzarella cheese (4 ounces)
- 2   tablespoons thinly sliced fresh basil

1. Place patties on the unheated rack of a broiler pan. Broil 3 to 4 inches from heat for 10 to 12 minutes or until done (160°F), turning once. Add the bread slices to broiler pan the last 2 to 3 minutes of broiling; turn once to toast evenly.

2. Meanwhile, in a medium saucepan cook pasta sauce over medium heat, stirring occasionally, until heated through. Place 1 patty on each bread slice. Spoon pasta sauce over patties; sprinkle with cheese. Broil for 1 to 2 minutes more or until cheese is melted. Top with basil.
Makes 4 servings.

Nutrition Facts per serving: 504 cal., 30 g total fat
(13 g sat. fat), 96 mg chol., 815 mg sodium, 27 g carbo.,
2 g fiber, 30 g pro. Daily Values: 18% vit. A, 13% vit. C,
26% calcium, 18% iron

Bacon Cheeseburgers

Prep: 15 min. • Broil: 11 min.

- 1¼   pounds lean ground beef
- 8   thin slices co-jack or cheddar cheese (4 ounces)
- 4   slices bacon, crisp-cooked and crumbled
- 4   hamburger buns, split and toasted
- ¼   cup dairy sour cream French onion dip

1. Shape ground beef into eight ¼-inch patties. Place 1 cheese slice on each of 4 patties; sprinkle with crumbled bacon. Top with remaining patties; seal edges well.

2. Place patties on the unheated rack of a broiler pan. Broil 3 to 4 inches from the heat for 10 to 12 minutes or until done (160°F), turning once. Place remaining 4 cheese slices on top of patties. Broil for 1 minute more.

3. Meanwhile, spread cut sides of buns with onion dip. Serve burgers on buns.
Makes 4 servings.

Nutrition Facts per serving: 635 cal., 41 g total fat
(19 g sat. fat), 133 mg chol., 691 mg sodium, 25 g carbo.,
1 g fiber, 37 g pro. Daily Values: 4% vit. A, 23% calcium,
20% iron

Meatball Oven Dinner

Prep: 5 min. • Bake: 45 min.

16   1-ounce frozen cooked Italian-style
       meatballs, thawed
 2   cups purchased three-cheese pasta sauce
 8   frozen cheddar-garlic biscuits or one
       10-ounce package refrigerated
       flaky buttermilk biscuits (10)

1. Cut meatballs in half and place in the bottom of a 2-quart rectangular baking dish. Pour pasta sauce over meatballs. Bake, covered, in a 375°F oven for 20 to 25 minutes or until sauce is bubbly. Top meatball mixture with biscuits. Bake, uncovered, about 25 minutes more for frozen biscuits (about 20 minutes more for refrigerated biscuits) or until biscuits are golden brown.
Makes 8 servings.

Nutrition Facts per serving: 402 cal., 24 g total fat (12 g sat. fat), 49 mg chol., 1,424 mg sodium, 29 g carbo., 4 g fiber, 18 g pro. Daily Values: 9% vit. A, 5% vit. C, 15% calcium, 16% iron

Saucy Meatball Sandwich

Start to Finish: 20 min.

1¼   pounds frozen cooked Italian-style
        meatballs (18)
 1   26- to 28-ounce jar pasta sauce
 ½   cup coarsely chopped onion (1 medium)
 6   hoagie buns, split and toasted
 1   cup shredded Italian-style cheese blend
       (4 ounces)

1. In a large saucepan combine the frozen meatballs, pasta sauce, and onion. Bring to boiling; reduce heat. Simmer, covered, for 10 minutes or until meatballs are heated through, stirring occasionally. Spoon hot meatball mixture into split buns. Spoon any remaining sauce over meatballs. Sprinkle with cheese.
Makes 6 servings.

Nutrition Facts per serving: 802 cal., 36 g total fat (14 g sat. fat), 74 mg chol., 2,293 mg sodium, 88 g carbo., 9 g fiber, 32 g pro. Daily Values: 8% vit. A, 9% vit. C, 27% calcium, 36% iron

Upside-Down Pizza Casserole

Prep: 20 min. • Bake: 15 min.

1½ pounds lean ground beef
 1 15-ounce can Italian-style tomato sauce
1½ cups shredded mozzarella cheese
       (6 ounces)
 1 10-ounce package refrigerated biscuits (10)

1. In a large skillet cook beef until brown; drain off fat. Stir in tomato sauce; heat through. Transfer mixture to a 2-quart rectangular baking dish. Sprinkle with cheese. Flatten each biscuit with your hands; arrange the biscuits on top of cheese. Bake in a 400°F oven about 15 minutes or until biscuits are golden.
Makes 5 servings.

Nutrition Facts per serving: 642 cal., 40 g total fat (16 g sat. fat), 116 mg chol., 1,102 mg sodium, 30 g carbo., 2 g fiber, 34 g pro. Daily Values: 34% vit. A, 12% vit. C, 64% calcium, 46% iron

Cacciatore-Style Penne

Start to Finish: 30 min.

 1 pound dried penne
 8 ounces ground beef or bulk Italian sausage
 1 medium green sweet pepper, chopped
 1 6-ounce can sliced mushrooms, drained
 1 14-ounce jar pasta sauce

1. Cook pasta according to package directions; drain well. Keep warm. Meanwhile, in a large skillet cook ground beef and pepper until meat is brown and pepper is tender. Drain fat. Stir in mushrooms and pasta sauce; heat through. Toss with hot pasta in large serving bowl.
Makes 6 servings.

Nutrition Facts per serving: 420 cal., 10 g total fat (3 g sat. fat), 27 mg chol., 580 mg sodium, 63 g carbo., 4 g fiber, 18 g pro. Daily Values: 7% vit. A, 30% vit. C, 4% calcium, 20% iron

Thai Beef Stir-Fry

Prep: 10 min. • Cook: 5 min.

4   ounces rice noodles
1   16-ounce package frozen pepper and onion
        stir-fry vegetables
2   tablespoons cooking oil
12 ounces beef stir-fry strips
½   cup bottled Thai peanut stir-fry sauce

1. Prepare noodles according to package directions. Drain and set aside. In a large skillet cook vegetables in 1 tablespoon hot oil over medium-high heat for 2 to 3 minutes or until just tender. Drain; transfer vegetables to a bowl. In the skillet cook and stir beef strips in remaining oil for 2 to 3 minutes or until desired doneness. Return vegetables to skillet; add sauce. Stir to combine; heat through. Serve over noodles.
Makes 4 servings.

Nutrition Facts per serving: 404 cal., 16 g total fat (4 g sat. fat), 50 mg chol., 597 mg sodium, 39 g carbo., 3 g fiber, 23 g pro. Daily Values: 42% vit. A, 28% vit. C, 3% calcium, 15% iron

Stir-Fry Time-Saver

Stir-fries are quick and convenient one-dish meals. You can get dinner on the table even more quickly when you use meats and poultry that are precut by your supermarket's butcher. If you must cut your own beef strips for the recipe above, the task is easier if you partially freeze the meat first. Place it in the freezer for 30 minutes before cooking time, then cut thin strips.

Saucy Strip Steak

Prep: 10 min. • Cook: 3 min. • Grill: 11 min.

⅔   cup orange marmalade
2   tablespoons butter or margarine
1   teaspoon snipped fresh rosemary or
        ¼ teaspoon dried rosemary, crushed
4   8-ounce boneless beef top loin steaks, cut
        about 1 inch thick
    Salt and black pepper

1. In a small saucepan combine marmalade, butter, and rosemary. Cook and stir over low heat until butter is melted. Set aside.

2. Sprinkle both sides of steaks with salt and pepper. Grill steaks on the rack of an uncovered grill directly over medium coals to desired doneness, turning once and brushing with marmalade mixture during the last 5 minutes. (Allow 11 to 15 minutes for medium rare and 14 to 18 minutes for medium.) Transfer steaks to a serving platter. Spoon any remaining marmalade mixture over steaks.
Makes 4 servings.

Nutrition Facts per serving: 464 cal., 14 g total fat (7 g sat. fat), 123 mg chol., 357 mg sodium, 35 g carbo., 0 g fiber, 49 g pro. Daily Values: 5% vit. A, 4% vit. C, 6% calcium, 27% iron

Steak and Mushrooms

Start to Finish: 20 min.

4   beef tenderloin steaks, cut 1 inch thick
       (about 1 pound)
1   tablespoon olive oil
8   ounces crimini, shiitake, baby portobello,
       and/or button mushrooms, sliced
       (3 cups)
¼   cup seasoned beef broth
¼   cup whipping cream

1. In a large skillet cook steaks in hot oil over medium heat to desired doneness, turning once. (Allow 7 to 9 minutes for medium rare or 10 to 13 minutes for medium.) Transfer steaks to a serving platter; keep warm.

2. In the same skillet cook and stir mushrooms for 4 to 5 minutes or until tender. Stir in broth and cream. Cook and stir over medium heat about 2 minutes or until slightly thickened. Spoon mushroom mixture over steaks.
Makes 4 servings.

Nutrition Facts per serving: 271 cal., 18 g total fat
(7 g sat. fat), 90 mg chol., 116 mg sodium, 2 g carbo.,
0 g fiber, 26 g pro. Daily Values: 5% vit. A, 2% calcium,
19% iron

Beef Tenderloin with Blue Cheese

Prep: 10 min. • Cook: 10 min.

4   beef tenderloin steaks, cut 1 inch thick
       (about 1 pound)
½   teaspoon garlic salt
⅓   cup dairy sour cream
3   tablespoons crumbled blue cheese
3   tablespoons chopped walnuts, toasted

1. Sprinkle both sides of steaks with garlic salt. Lightly coat a large skillet with nonstick cooking spray. Heat skillet over medium-high heat. Add steaks. Reduce heat to medium and cook to desired doneness, turning once. (Allow 10 to 11 minutes for medium rare or 12 to 13 minutes for medium.) Transfer steaks to a serving platter.

2. Meanwhile, in a small bowl stir together sour cream and blue cheese. Spoon sour cream mixture on top of steaks. Sprinkle with walnuts.
Makes 4 servings.

Nutrition Facts per serving: 264 cal., 17 g total fat
(6 g sat. fat), 81 mg chol., 255 mg sodium, 2 g carbo.,
0 g fiber, 26 g pro. Daily Values: 3% vit. A, 6% calcium,
18% iron

Steak with Creamy Onion Sauce

Prep: 10 min. • Broil: 22 min.

1   medium sweet onion, such as Maui or Walla
    Walla, thinly sliced
4   6-ounce rib eye beef steaks, cut about
    1 inch thick
1   tablespoon Mediterranean seasoning blend
    or lemon-pepper seasoning
1   8-ounce container dairy sour cream
2   tablespoons capers, drained

1. Place onion slices on the rack of an unheated broiler pan. Broil 3 to 4 inches from heat for 5 minutes; turn onions. Meanwhile, sprinkle steaks with 1½ teaspoons of the seasoning blend. Place steaks on the broiler pan rack with onion. Broil steaks and onions for 5 minutes more or until onions are brown. Remove onions to a cutting board. Broil steaks to desired doneness (allow 12 to 14 minutes more for medium rare or 15 to 18 minutes more for medium), turning once.

2. Meanwhile, coarsely chop onion. In a small saucepan combine sour cream, cooked onion, capers, and remaining seasoning blend. Cook over medium-low heat until heated through (do not boil). Transfer steaks to serving plates. Spoon sauce over steaks.
Makes 4 servings.

Nutrition Facts per serving: 398 cal., 22 g total fat (11 g sat. fat), 106 mg chol., 472 mg sodium, 4 g carbo., 0 g fiber, 39 g pro. Daily Values: 9% vit. A, 3% vit. C, 8% calcium, 17% iron

Grilled B.L.T. Steak

Start to Finish: 30 min.

2   12-ounce boneless beef top loin steaks,
    cut 1¼ inches thick
2   slices bacon
½   cup bottled balsamic vinaigrette salad
    dressing
8   slices tomato
2   cups mixed baby greens

1. Trim fat from steaks. Grill steaks on the rack of an uncovered grill over medium coals until desired doneness, turning once halfway through grilling. (Allow 14 to 18 minutes for medium rare or 18 to 22 minutes for medium.)

2. Meanwhile, in a large skillet cook bacon over medium heat until crisp. Remove bacon and drain on paper towels. Crumble bacon and set aside. Drain fat, reserving 1 tablespoon drippings in skillet. Add vinaigrette. Cook and stir over high heat about 1 minute, scraping up browned bits. Remove from heat.

3. To serve, halve steaks. Place a piece of steak on each of 4 dinner plates. Top each with tomato slices, cooked bacon, mixed greens, and some of dressing from the skillet.
Makes 4 servings.

Nutrition Facts per serving: 556 cal., 42 g total fat (14 g sat. fat), 122 mg chol., 636 mg sodium, 5 g carbo., 1 g fiber, 38 g pro. Daily Values: 6% vit. A, 12% vit. C, 2% calcium, 17% iron

Zesty Grilled Sirloin

Prep: 35 min. • Marinate: 24 hours
Grill: 20 min.

1½   **ounces dried red chiles (7 or 8), such as guajillo, ancho, or pasilla**

1   **tablespoon ground cumin**

½   **cup olive oil**

1   **2¾- to 3-pound beef top sirloin steak, cut 1½ inches thick**

1. Wearing plastic gloves, use scissors to remove the stalk end from chiles. Split chiles; remove and discard seeds. In a dry skillet toast chiles over medium heat for 3 to 4 minutes or until fragrant, turning once or twice.

2. Transfer chiles to a small bowl. Cover with at least 1 cup of hot water; soak for 30 minutes. Drain, reserving 1 cup soaking water. Place the drained chiles in a blender container or food processor bowl.

3. In the same skillet, toast cumin over medium heat for 1 to 2 minutes or until it becomes fragrant, stirring often. Place cumin and oil in the blender or food processor with chiles. Blend or process until nearly smooth, adding enough of the soaking water to make a medium-thick paste. Set aside.

4. Trim fat from steak. Place steak in a plastic bag set in a shallow dish. Spread chile paste on both sides of steak. Close bag. Marinate in the refrigerator for 24 hours, turning occasionally.

5. Drain steak, reserving marinade. Place steak on the rack of an uncovered grill directly over medium coals. Grill to desired doneness, turning once and brushing occasionally with reserved marinade during first half of grilling. Allow 20 to 24 minutes for medium rare and 24 to 28 minutes for medium. Discard remaining marinade. Thinly slice steak across the grain.
Makes 12 servings.

Nutrition Facts per serving: 185 cal., 9 g total fat (2 g sat. fat), 63 mg chol., 56 mg sodium, 3 g carbo., 1 g fiber, 23 g pro. Daily Values: 19% vit A., 2% vit C., 1% calcium, 16% iron

Sirloin with Mustard and Chives

Prep: 10 min. • Grill: 9 min.

4   **boneless beef sirloin or rib eye steaks, cut ¾ inch thick (about 1½ pounds)**

2   **teaspoons garlic-pepper seasoning**

½   **cup dairy sour cream**

2   **tablespoons Dijon-style mustard**

1   **tablespoon snipped fresh chives**

1. Sprinkle both sides of steaks with 1½ teaspoons of the seasoning. Grill steaks on the rack of an uncovered grill directly over medium coals to desired doneness, turning once. (Allow 9 to 11 minutes for medium rare and 11 to 13 minutes for medium.) Transfer steaks to a serving platter.

2. In a small bowl combine sour cream, mustard, chives, and remaining seasoning. Spoon over steaks.
Makes 4 servings.

Nutrition Facts per serving: 277 cal., 12 g total fat (5 g sat. fat), 114 mg chol., 619 mg sodium, 2 g carbo., 0 g fiber, 37 g pro. Daily Values: 5% vit. A, 1% vit. C, 5% calcium, 25% iron

Steak with Tarragon Butter

Start to Finish: 30 min.

¼ cup butter, softened
1 clove garlic, minced
1 teaspoon lemon juice
½ teaspoon dried tarragon, crushed
2 1-pound beef porterhouse, T-bone, or
    sirloin steaks, cut 1½ inches thick

1. In a bowl stir together butter, garlic, lemon juice, and tarragon. Chill butter mixture while preparing steaks.

2. Without cutting into meat, cut the fat edges at 1-inch intervals. Place steaks on the unheated rack of a broiler pan. Broil steaks 3 to 4 inches from the heat to desired doneness, turning once. (Allow 18 to 21 minutes for medium rare or 22 to 27 minutes for medium.) Cut steaks into serving-size pieces. Serve with tarragon butter.
Makes 6 servings.

Nutrition Facts per serving: 207 cal., 14 g total fat
(7 g sat. fat), 64 mg chol., 128 mg sodium, 0 g carbo.,
0 g fiber, 20 g pro. Daily Values: 6% vit. A, 1% vit. C,
2% calcium, 8% iron

Prosciutto-Wrapped Tenderloin

Start to Finish: 20 min.

1 ounce sliced prosciutto, chopped
1 small carrot, shredded
1 green onion, sliced
4 beef tenderloin steaks, cut 1 inch thick
4 thin slices prosciutto

1. For stuffing, combine chopped prosciutto, carrot, and green onion. Cut a slit horizontally in each steak to form a pocket. Fill pockets with stuffing. Cut sliced prosciutto into 1-inch strips. Wrap prosciutto around each steak. Secure with toothpicks.

2. Place steaks on the unheated rack of a broiler pan. Broil 3 to 4 inches from the heat to desired doneness, turning once. (Allow 12 to 14 minutes for medium rare or 15 to 18 minutes for medium.)
Makes 4 servings.

Nutrition Facts per serving: 296 cal., 13 g total fat
(5 g sat. fat), 115 mg chol., 516 mg sodium, 1 g carbo.,
0 g fiber, 40 g pro. Daily Values: 51% vit. A, 2% vit. C,
2% calcium, 28% iron

Spinach-Stuffed Flank Steak

Prep: 20 min. • Broil: 10 min.

¼ cup dried tomatoes (not oil-packed)
1 1-pound beef flank steak or top round
    steak, trimmed of separable fat
1 10-ounce package frozen chopped spinach,
    thawed and well drained
2 tablespoons grated Parmesan cheese
2 tablespoons snipped fresh basil

1. In a small bowl soak dried tomatoes in
enough hot water to cover for 10 minutes.
Drain. Snip into small pieces.

2. Meanwhile, make shallow diagonal cuts at
1-inch intervals in a diamond pattern on both
sides of steak. Place steak between 2 pieces of
plastic wrap. Pound into 12×8-inch rectangle.
Discard plastic wrap.

3. Spread spinach over steak. Sprinkle with
tomatoes, cheese, and basil. Starting from a
short side, roll up steak. Secure with toothpicks
at 1-inch intervals, starting ½ inch from one end.
Cut between toothpicks into eight 1-inch slices.

4. Place slices, cut sides down, on the
unheated rack of a broiler pan. Broil 3 to
4 inches from the heat to desired doneness,
turning once. (Allow 10 to 12 minutes for
medium rare or 12 to 16 minutes for medium.)
Remove toothpicks.
Makes 4 servings.

Nutrition Facts per serving: 281 cal., 9 g total fat
(4 g sat. fat), 45 mg chol., 521 mg sodium, 18 g carbo.,
12 g fiber, 37 g pro. Daily Values: 576% vit. A, 97% vit. C,
45% calcium, 54% iron

Basil-Beef Sirloin

Prep: 15 min. • Roast: 50 min.

1 3- to 3½-pound boneless beef sirloin
    roast, cut 1¾ inches thick
¼ teaspoon each salt and black pepper
2 cups lightly packed fresh basil leaves,
    snipped
8 cloves garlic, minced (2 tablespoons)
2 teaspoons olive oil

1. Make five or six 5-inch-long slits along the
top of the roast, cutting almost through it.
Sprinkle with salt and pepper. In a medium bowl
combine basil and garlic; stuff mixture into the
slits in meat. Tie meat with heavy-duty string to
hold slits closed. Drizzle with oil.

2. Place meat on a rack in a shallow roasting
pan. Insert an oven-safe meat thermometer.
Roast, uncovered, in a 425°F oven for
15 minutes. Reduce oven temperature to
350°F; roast for 35 to 45 minutes more or
until desired doneness (160°F for medium).
Let meat stand, covered, for 10 minutes
(temperature of meat will rise slightly).
Makes 10 to 12 servings.

Nutrition Facts per serving: 255 cal., 13 g total fat
(5 g sat. fat), 91 mg chol., 121 mg sodium, 1 g carbo.,
0 g fiber, 31 g pro. Daily Values: 23% iron

German-Style Beef Roast

Prep: 30 min. • Roast: 2½ hours

1   3-pound boneless beef round rump roast
1   12-ounce can beer
1   cup catsup
1   tablespoon brown sugar
¼   teaspoon black pepper

1. Trim any excess fat from the roast. Place in a 4-quart Dutch oven. In a bowl stir together beer and catsup. Pour over roast. Bake, covered, in a 325°F oven for 2½ hours or until tender. Remove roast from Dutch oven. Cover meat; let stand while finishing sauce.

2. Meanwhile, stir brown sugar and pepper into the sauce. Bring sauce to boiling; reduce heat. Simmer, uncovered, for 10 minutes or until slightly thickened. Slice roast. Skim fat from sauce; serve sauce with meat.
Makes 8 to 10 servings.

Nutrition Facts per serving: 278 cal., 7 g total fat
(2 g sat. fat), 89 mg chol., 470 mg sodium, 11 g carbo.,
1 g fiber, 39 g pro. Daily Values: 6% vit. A, 8% vit. C,
2% calcium, 10% iron

Easy Elegant Beef Roast

Prep: 15 min. • Roast: 1¾ hours

1   4- to 6-pound beef rib roast
    Salt and black pepper
2   tablespoons olive oil
1   tablespoon dried minced onion
2   teaspoons bottled minced garlic

1. Cut 1-inch pockets on fat side of the roast at 3-inch intervals. Sprinkle roast with salt and pepper. In a small bowl combine the remaining ingredients; rub onto roast and into pockets.

2. Place roast, fat side up, in a roasting pan. Insert an oven-safe meat thermometer into the thickest portion of meat without touching fat or bone. Roast in a 350°F oven for 1¾ to 2¼ hours for medium rare (135°F) or 2¼ to 2¾ hours for medium (150°F). Transfer to serving platter; cover with foil. Let stand for at least 15 minutes before carving (temperature will rise 5° during standing).
Makes 10 to 12 servings.

Nutrition Facts per serving: 296 cal., 18 g total fat
(7 g sat. fat), 91 mg chol., 83 mg sodium, 1 g carbo.,
0 g fiber, 31 g pro. Daily Values: 1% vit. C, 1% calcium,
19% iron

Stroganoff-Sauced Beef Roast

Prep: 15 min. • Cook: 15 min.

1 16-ounce package cooked beef pot roast
   with gravy
2 cups shiitake, crimini, or button
   mushrooms
½ cup dairy sour cream French onion dip
2 cups hot cooked noodles

1. Transfer beef with gravy to a large skillet (leave meat whole). Remove stems from shiitake mushrooms; halve or quarter mushrooms. Add mushrooms to skillet. Cook, covered, over medium-low heat for 15 minutes or until heated through, stirring mushrooms once and turning roast once. Break meat into bite-size pieces. Stir onion dip into meat mixture; heat through (do not boil). Stir in noodles.
Makes 3 to 4 servings.

Nutrition Facts per serving: 542 cal., 7 g total fat (11 g sat. fat), 99 mg chol., 787 mg sodium, 46 g carbo., 4 g fiber, 8 g pro. Daily Values: 2% calcium, 20% iron

Speedy Beef Stew

Prep: 15 min. • Cook: 10 min.

1 17-ounce package refrigerated cooked
   beef roast au jus
2 10¾-ounce cans condensed beefy
   mushroom soup
1 16-ounce package frozen mixed vegetables
4 teaspoons snipped fresh basil or
      1½ teaspoons dried basil, crushed
1½ cups milk

1. Cut beef into bite-size pieces, if necessary. In a 4-quart Dutch oven combine beef and au jus, soup, vegetables, and dried basil, if using. Bring to boiling; reduce heat. Simmer, covered, for 10 minutes. Stir in milk and fresh basil, if using. Heat through. Ladle into soup bowls.
Makes 4 servings.

Nutrition Facts per serving: 386 cal., 15 g total fat (7 g sat. fat), 80 mg chol., 1,688 mg sodium, 33 g carbo., 5 g fiber, 33 g pro. Daily Values: 132% vit. A, 10% vit. C, 15% calcium, 23% iron

Oven-Barbecued Beef Sandwiches

Prep: 10 min. • Bake: 2 hours

1   10¾-ounce can condensed cream of
      chicken or mushroom soup
1¼ cups bottled barbecue sauce
1   4- to 6-pound beef roast, such as
      boneless chuck
1   1-ounce envelope dry onion soup mix
      Onion buns or kaiser rolls, toasted

1. In a roasting pan pour soup and barbecue sauce over roast. Sprinkle dry soup mix over roast. Bake, covered, in a 350°F oven about 2 hours or until tender enough to slice. (For shredded meat, cook about 3 hours or until very tender.)

2. Drain off fat and remove any bones from roast. Slice or shred the meat and serve on buns. Spoon sauce over meat.
Makes 6 to 8 servings.

Nutrition Facts per serving: 887 cal., 53 g total fat (20 g sat. fat), 179 mg chol., 1,446 mg sodium, 42 g carbo., 2 g fiber, 56 g pro. Daily Values: 14% vit. A, 6% vit. C, 10% calcium, 45% iron

Deli Roast Beef Sandwich

Start to Finish: 10 min.

8   ounces thinly sliced deli roast beef
4   slices pumpernickel, rye, or whole
      wheat bread
½   cup deli coleslaw
      Herb-pepper seasoning

1. Arrange the roast beef on 2 slices of bread. Spread coleslaw over beef; sprinkle with herb-pepper seasoning. Top with the remaining slices of bread. Cut each sandwich in half.
Makes 2 servings.

Nutrition Facts per serving: 369 cal., 8 g total fat (2 g sat. fat), 80 mg chol., 507 mg sodium, 34 g carbo., 5 g fiber, 39 g pro. Daily Values: 4% vit. A, 16% vit. C, 6% calcium, 23% iron

Greek-Style Pitas

Prep: 15 min. • Chill: 1 hour

1   cup deli creamy cucumber and onion salad
½   cup chopped tomato
1   teaspoon snipped fresh dill
4   wheat or white pita bread rounds, halved
      crosswise
12 ounces thinly sliced cooked deli roast beef

1. In a bowl combine salad, tomato, and dill;
cover and chill for 1 hour. Line pita halves
with roast beef. Spoon salad mixture into each
pita half.
Makes 4 servings.

Nutrition Facts per serving: 380 cal., 10 g total fat
(3 g sat. fat), 82 mg chol., 427 mg sodium, 39 g carbo.,
1 g fiber, 34 g pro. Daily Values: 2% vit. A, 12% vit. C,
3% calcium, 21% iron

Middle Eastern Pitas

Start to Finish: 10 min.

1   7- or 8-ounce container roasted garlic-
      flavored hummus
4   pita bread rounds, halved crosswise
12 ounces thinly sliced deli roast beef
½   cup plain yogurt
½   cup chopped cucumber

1. Spread hummus in the pita halves. Add roast
beef to pitas. In a small bowl stir together yogurt
and cucumber; spoon over roast beef in pitas.
Makes 4 servings.

Nutrition Facts per serving: 463 cal., 18 g total fat
(6 g sat. fat), 70 mg chol., 735 mg sodium, 44 g carbo.,
3 g fiber, 34 g pro. Daily Values: 1% vit. A, 2% vit. C,
12% calcium, 26% iron

Reuben Loaf

Prep: 60 min. • Bake: 25 min.

1   16-ounce package hot roll mix
1   cup bottled Thousand Island salad dressing
1   pound sliced cooked corned beef
8   ounces Swiss cheese, shredded
1   14- to 16-ounce jar or can sauerkraut,
     rinsed and drained

1. Prepare the hot roll mix according to package directions. Let rest 5 minutes. Meanwhile, line a very large baking sheet with foil; grease foil. Set aside.

2. Divide dough in half; roll each portion into a 12×8-inch rectangle. Spread ¼ cup dressing over each dough portion. Layer half of the corned beef, cheese, and sauerkraut evenly on each dough portion to within 1 inch of the edges. Starting from a long side, roll each portion into a loaf. Brush edges with water; press to seal.

3. Place loaves, seam side down, on prepared baking sheet. Lightly cover and let rise in a warm place for 30 minutes. Make 4 diagonal slits, ¼ inch deep, in the top of each loaf. Bake in a 375°F oven for 25 to 30 minutes or until golden brown. Serve with remaining dressing.
Makes 10 servings.

Nutrition Facts per serving: 492 cal., 27 g total fat (8 g sat. fat), 91 mg chol., 1,305 mg sodium, 41 g carbo., 1 g fiber, 22 g pro. Daily Values: 6% vit. A, 10% vit. C, 23% calcium, 16% iron

Cheesy Reuben Potatoes

Start to Finish: 25 min.

1   8-ounce can sauerkraut, rinsed and
     drained (about 1 cup)
1   cup bottled Thousand Island salad dressing
4   medium baking potatoes (6 to 8 ounces
     each)
4   ounces sliced process Swiss cheese, halved
     diagonally
1   6-ounce package corned beef, cut into
     bite-size pieces (about 1 cup)

1. Combine sauerkraut and dressing; set aside. Scrub potatoes and pierce with a fork. Arrange about 1 inch apart on a large microwave-safe plate. Microwave on 100 percent power (high) for 12 to 18 minutes or until tender, turning the potatoes after 6 minutes. Remove from oven. Cover with foil; let stand for 6 minutes. Cut each potato open.

2. Top potatoes with half of the cheese, the sauerkraut mixture, and corned beef. Top with the remaining cheese. Microwave for 3 to 4 minutes more or until cheese melts, turning the dish a half-turn once.
Makes 4 servings.

Nutrition Facts per serving: 566 cal., 36 g total fat (11 g sat. fat), 80 mg chol., 1,262 mg sodium, 39 g carbo., 4 g fiber, 25 g pro. Daily Values: 9% vit. A, 55% vit. C, 31% calcium, 21% iron

Vegetable and Pastrami Panini

Start to Finish: 15 min.

4   thin slices provolone cheese (2 ounces)
8   ½-inch slices sourdough or Vienna bread
1   cup roasted or grilled vegetables from the
      deli or deli-marinated vegetables,
      coarsely chopped
4   thin slices pastrami (3 ounces)
1   tablespoon olive oil

1. Place a cheese slice on 4 of the bread slices. Spread vegetables evenly over cheese. Top with pastrami and remaining bread slices. Brush outsides of sandwiches with oil.

2. Heat a large nonstick skillet or griddle over medium heat. Cook sandwiches 4 to 6 minutes or until bread is golden brown and cheese is melted, turning once. Halve sandwiches.
Makes 4 servings.

Nutrition Facts per serving: 254 cal., 9 g total fat
(3 g sat. fat), 30 mg chol., 658 mg sodium, 30 g carbo.,
1 g fiber, 13 g pro. Daily Values: 38% vit. C, 13% calcium,
13% iron

Mu Shu-Style Pork Roll-Ups

Prep: 12 min. • Cook: 5 min.

4   10-inch flour tortillas
12 ounces lean boneless pork, cut into strips
1   teaspoon toasted sesame oil
2   cups frozen stir-fry vegetables
¼   cup plum or hoisin sauce

1. Wrap tortillas tightly in foil. Heat in a 350°F oven for 10 minutes to soften. (Or wrap tortillas in white, microwave-safe paper towels; microwave on high for 15 to 30 seconds or until tortillas are softened.)

2. In a large skillet cook and stir the pork strips in hot oil over medium-high heat for 2 to 3 minutes or until no pink remains. Add the vegetables. Cook and stir for 3 to 4 minutes or until vegetables are crisp-tender.

3. Spread each tortilla with plum sauce and place ¼ of meat mixture just below the center of each tortilla. Fold the bottom edge of each tortilla up and over the filling. Fold in the sides until they meet; roll up over the filling.
Makes 4 servings.

Nutrition Facts per serving: 302 cal., 8 g total fat
(2 g sat. fat), 53 mg chol., 311 mg sodium, 34 g carbo.,
2 g fiber, 22 g pro. Daily Values: 20% vit. A, 15% vit. C,
7% calcium, 14% iron

Thyme Pork Chops

Prep: 15 min. • Roast: 45 min.

6 center-cut pork loin rib chops, cut
    1½ inches thick
    Salt and black pepper
2 tablespoons olive oil
1 tablespoon snipped fresh thyme or
    ½ teaspoon dried thyme, crushed

1. Trim fat from chops. Season chops lightly with salt and pepper. In a bowl stir together oil and thyme; brush over all sides of chops. Place chops on a rack in a shallow roasting pan. Roast, uncovered, in a 350°F oven for 45 to 50 minutes or until juices run clear (160°F). **Makes 6 servings.**

Nutrition Facts per serving: 391 cal., 19 g total fat (6 g sat. fat), 129 mg chol., 108 mg sodium, 0 g carbo., 0 g fiber, 51 g pro. Daily Values: 1% vit. A, 2% vit. C, 1% calcium, 11% iron

Pork Chops Dijon

Start to Finish: 30 min.

3 tablespoons Dijon-style mustard
2 tablespoons low-calorie Italian salad
    dressing
¼ teaspoon black pepper
4 pork loin chops, cut ½ inch thick
    (1¼ pounds)
    Nonstick cooking spray
1 medium onion, halved and sliced

1. In a small bowl combine mustard, dressing, and pepper; set aside. Trim excess fat from chops. Coat a 10-inch skillet with cooking spray. Heat skillet over medium-high heat. Add chops; brown on both sides. Remove from skillet.

2. Add onion to skillet. Cook and stir over medium heat for 3 minutes. Push onion aside; return chops to skillet. Spread mustard mixture over chops. Cook, covered, over medium-low heat for 15 minutes or until meat juices run clear (160°F). Serve onion over chops. **Makes 4 servings.**

Nutrition Facts per serving: 153 cal., 5 g total fat (2 g sat. fat), 58 mg chol., 218 mg sodium, 4 g carbo., 1 g fiber, 21 g pro. Daily Values: 3% vit. C, 4% calcium, 6% iron

Pork Chops with Chili-Apricot Glaze

Prep: 15 min. • Broil: 16 min.

¼   cup apricot jam or preserves
¼   cup chili sauce
1   tablespoon sweet-hot mustard or
     brown mustard
1   tablespoon water
4   boneless pork top loin chops, cut 1 inch
     thick (about 1½ pounds)

1. For glaze, cut up any large pieces in jam. In a small saucepan combine jam, chili sauce, mustard, and water. Cook and stir over medium-low heat until heated through.

2. Meanwhile, trim excess fat from chops. Place chops on the unheated rack of a broiler pan. Broil 4 to 5 inches from heat for 8 minutes. Turn chops; brush generously with glaze. Broil 8 to 12 minutes more or until juices run clear (160°F). Spoon any remaining glaze over chops before serving.
Makes 4 servings.

Nutrition Facts per serving: 244 cal., 9 g total fat (3 g sat. fat), 64 mg chol., 303 mg sodium, 18 g carbo., 0 g fiber, 21 g pro. Daily Values: 2% vit. A, 3% vit. C, 1% calcium, 7% iron

Bigger and Better Saucy Pork Chops

Prep: 10 min. • Bake: 2 hours
Broil: 10 min.

6   center-cut pork loin rib chops, cut
     1½ inches thick (about 3 pounds)
⅓   cup packed brown sugar
¼   cup hot water
½   cup bottled chili sauce
⅓   cup catsup
1   teaspoon dry mustard

1. Trim fat from chops. Arrange chops in a single layer on a rack in a roasting pan. Pour hot water into bottom of pan up to the level of the rack. Cover pan with foil. Bake in a 350°F oven for 2 hours or until chops are tender.

2. For the sauce, stir together brown sugar and the ¼ cup hot water. Stir in remaining ingredients. Spoon sauce generously over chops. Place chops on the unheated rack of a broiler pan. Broil 5 to 6 inches from the heat for 10 to 12 minutes or until sauce begins to glaze chops, turning once. Heat any remaining sauce and pass with chops.
Makes 6 servings.

Nutrition Facts per serving: 421 cal., 12 g total fat (4 g sat. fat), 135 mg chol., 529 mg sodium, 20 g carbo., 1 g fiber, 55 g pro. Daily Values: 6% vit. A, 10% vit. C, 6% calcium, 11% iron

Easy Pork Chops Supreme

Prep: 10 min. • Bake: 1 hour

1   **cup catsup**
1/3 **cup honey**
1   **teaspoon bottled hot pepper sauce**
6   **pork loin chops, cut 3/4 inch thick**
        (1 1/2 to 1 3/4 pounds)
6   **lemon slices**

1. Stir together catsup, honey, and hot pepper sauce. Arrange chops in a 12×7 1/2×2-inch baking dish. Pour sauce over chops. Top each chop with a slice of lemon. Bake, uncovered, in a 350°F oven about 1 hour or until meat is tender and juices run clear (160°F).
Makes 6 servings.

Nutrition Facts per serving: 230 cal., 5 g total fat (2 g sat. fat), 48 mg chol., 512 mg sodium, 26 g carbo., 1 g fiber, 20 g pro. Daily Values: 8% vit. A, 13% vit. C, 1% calcium, 6% iron

Beer-Glazed Pork Chops

Prep: 15 min. • Marinate: 6 to 24 hours
Grill: 30 min.

4   **boneless pork top loin chops, cut 1 1/4 inches**
        thick (about 1 3/4 pounds)
1   **12-ounce bottle stout (dark beer)**
1/4 **cup honey mustard**
3   **cloves garlic, minced**
1   **teaspoon caraway seeds**

1. Trim fat from chops. Place chops in a self-sealing plastic bag set in a shallow dish. For marinade, stir together the remaining ingredients; pour over chops. Close bag. Marinate in the refrigerator for 6 to 24 hours, turning the bag occasionally.

2. Remove chops; pour marinade into a small saucepan. Bring to boiling; reduce heat. Simmer, uncovered, about 15 minutes or until marinade is reduced by half. In a covered grill arrange heated coals around a drip pan. Test for medium heat above the pan. Place chops on grill rack over drip pan. Cover and grill for 30 to 35 minutes or until the juices run clear (160°F), brushing chops frequently with marinade during the last 10 minutes of grilling. Discard any remaining marinade.
Makes 4 servings.

Nutrition Facts per serving: 327 cal., 11 g total fat (4 g sat. fat), 108 mg chol., 90 mg sodium, 5 g carbo., 0 g fiber, 44 g pro. Daily Values: 1% vit. C, 1% calcium, 7% iron

Country Chops and Peppers

Start to Finish: 20 min.

4   pork loin chops, cut ¾ inch thick (about
     1½ pounds)
     Seasoned salt and black pepper
     Nonstick cooking spray
1   medium sweet pepper, cut into strips
1   tablespoon butter or margarine
⅓   cup white wine Worcestershire sauce or
     2 tablespoons Worcestershire sauce and
     ¼ cup water

1. Sprinkle chops lightly on both sides with seasoned salt and pepper; press gently onto meat. Coat a large cold skillet with cooking spray. Heat skillet. Cook chops in hot skillet over medium high heat for 5 minutes. Turn and top with sweet pepper strips. Cook, covered, for 5 to 7 minutes more or until meat juices run clear (160°F) and vegetables are crisp-tender. Remove chops and vegetables; keep warm.

2. In the same skillet melt butter, scraping up crusty bits. Add Worcestershire sauce. Cook and stir over medium heat until mixture thickens slightly. Remove from heat. Place chops on dinner plates; top with vegetables. Pour sauce over vegetables.
Makes 4 servings.

Nutrition Facts per serving: 282 cal., 11 g total fat
(5 g sat. fat), 101 mg chol., 282 mg sodium, 6 g carbo.,
1 g fiber, 38 g pro. Daily Values: 6% vit. A, 38% vit. C,
6% calcium, 9% iron

Peppery Pork Chops

Start to Finish: 30 min.

2   teaspoons paprika
1   teaspoon garlic salt
½   teaspoon black pepper
4   pork loin chops, cut ¾ inch thick
     Dairy sour cream

1. In a small bowl stir together paprika, garlic salt, and pepper. Rub each chop with paprika mixture. Place chops on the unheated rack of a broiler pan. Broil 4 to 5 inches from the heat for 8 minutes. Turn chops and broil for 7 to 9 minutes more or until juices run clear (160°F). Serve with sour cream.
Makes 4 servings.

Nutrition Facts per serving: 246 cal., 12 g total fat
(5 g sat. fat), 87 mg chol., 310 mg sodium, 2 g carbo.,
0 g fiber, 31 g pro. Daily Values: 17% vit. A, 2% vit. C,
5% calcium, 7% iron

Maple-Pecan Pork Chops

Start to Finish: 15 min.

4   boneless pork loin chops, cut ¾ inch thick
      (about 1 pound)
      Salt and black pepper
4   tablespoons butter or margarine, softened
2   tablespoons maple-flavored syrup
⅓   cup chopped pecans, toasted

1. Sprinkle both sides of chops with salt and pepper. In a 12-inch skillet cook chops in 1 tablespoon of the butter over medium-high heat for 9 to 13 minutes or until juices run clear (160°F), turning once. Transfer chops to a serving platter. Meanwhile, in a small bowl combine the remaining butter and the syrup. Spread butter mixture evenly over chops. Let stand for 1 minute or until melted. Sprinkle with pecans.
Makes 4 servings.

Nutrition Facts per serving: 333 cal., 23 g total fat (10 g sat. fat), 98 mg chol., 310 mg sodium, 8 g carbo., 1 g fiber, 23 g pro. Daily Values: 9% vit. A, 1% vit. C, 3% calcium, 7% iron

Pork Tenderloin with Sweet Potatoes

Prep: 10 min. • Cook: 15 min.

1   ¾-pound pork tenderloin
1   large onion, cut into wedges
1   tablespoon cooking oil
2   10-ounce or one 16-ounce package(s)
      frozen candied sweet potatoes, thawed
1   tablespoon snipped fresh thyme or
      ½ teaspoon dried thyme, crushed

1. Cut tenderloin into ½-inch slices. In a large skillet cook slices and onion in hot oil for 6 minutes or until pork is tender and juices run clear, turning slices once. Remove slices from the skillet; set aside.

2. Add sweet potatoes with sauce and dried thyme, if using, to onions in skillet. Bring to boiling; reduce heat. Cook, covered, over medium heat for 10 minutes or until potatoes are tender. Return pork to skillet. Heat through. Stir in fresh thyme, if using.
Makes 4 servings.

Nutrition Facts per serving: 386 cal., 13 g total fat (2 g sat. fat), 55 mg chol., 484 mg sodium, 44 g carbo., 4 g fiber, 20 g pro. Daily Values: 342% vit. A, 25% vit. C, 3% calcium, 10% iron

Pork with Sweet Cherry Sauce

Start to Finish: 20 min.

1 1-pound pork tenderloin
   Nonstick cooking spray
³⁄₄ cup cranberry juice or apple juice
2 teaspoons spicy brown mustard
1 teaspoon cornstarch
1 cup sweet cherries (such as Rainier or
      Bing), halved and pitted, or 1 cup
      frozen unsweetened pitted dark sweet
      cherries, thawed

1. Trim fat from pork; cut pork crosswise into
1-inch slices. Place each slice between 2 pieces
of plastic wrap. With the heel of your hand,
press each slice into a ¹⁄₂-inch medallion.
Discard plastic wrap.

2. Coat an unheated large nonstick skillet with
cooking spray. Heat skillet over medium-high
heat. Add pork; cook for 6 minutes or until meat
is slightly pink in center and juices run clear,
turning once. Transfer to a serving platter;
cover and keep warm.

3. Combine cranberry juice, mustard, and
cornstarch; add to skillet. Cook and stir until
thickened and bubbly. Cook and stir for
2 minutes more. Stir cherries into cranberry
mixture in skillet. Spoon over meat.
Makes 4 servings.

Nutrition Facts per serving: 197 cal., 5 g total fat
(2 g sat. fat), 81 mg chol., 127 mg sodium, 12 g carbo.,
0 g fiber, 26 g pro. Daily Values: 31% vit. C, 1% calcium,
10% iron

Pork Medallions with Apples

Start to Finish: 15 min.

1 1-pound pork tenderloin
2 cloves garlic, minced
2 tablespoons olive oil or butter
1 20-ounce can sliced apples, drained
2 teaspoons fresh snipped thyme or
      ¹⁄₂ teaspoon dried thyme, crushed

1. Cut tenderloin crosswise into ¹⁄₂-inch slices. In
a 12-inch skillet cook garlic in oil over medium-
high heat for 15 seconds. Carefully place the pork
slices into the hot oil. Cook for 2 minutes on each
side or until browned and no longer pink in center.
Add drained apples and thyme. Cook, covered, for
1 minute or until apples are heated through.
Makes 4 servings.

Nutrition Facts per serving: 292 cal., 11 g total fat
(2 g sat. fat), 73 mg chol., 61 mg sodium, 24 g carbo.,
2 g fiber, 24 g pro. Daily Values: 2% vit. A, 4% vit. C,
2% calcium, 10% iron

Pork Loin with Vegetables

Prep: 14 min. • Roast: 35 min.

2½ cups peeled baby carrots
12   ounces tiny new potatoes, quartered
 1   12- to 16-ounce pork tenderloin
⅔   cup apricot preserves
¼   cup white wine vinegar or white vinegar

1. In a medium saucepan cook carrots and potatoes in a small amount of boiling water for 4 minutes; drain. Meanwhile, place tenderloin in a 13×9×2-inch baking pan. Arrange carrots and potatoes around pork. Roast, uncovered, in 425°F oven for 20 minutes.

2. In a small bowl stir together the preserves and vinegar; brush some of the mixture over meat. Drizzle remaining preserves mixture over vegetables; toss to coat. Roast, uncovered, for 15 minutes more or until vegetables and meat are tender and meat juices run clear (160°F). Stir vegetable mixture.

3. Cover; let meat and vegetables stand for 10 minutes. Slice meat and place on a serving platter. Transfer vegetables to the serving platter with a slotted spoon. Drizzle pan juices over meat and vegetables.
Makes 4 servings.

Nutrition Facts per serving: 365 cal., 2 g total fat
(1 g sat. fat), 50 mg chol., 84 mg sodium, 62 g carbo.,
5 g fiber, 23 g pro. Daily Values: 431% vit. A, 36% vit. C,
5% calcium, 14% iron

Peachy Pork Tenderloin

**Prep: 10 min. • Marinate: 4 hours
Grill: 30 min.**

 1   ¾-pound pork tenderloin
⅓   cup peach nectar
 3   tablespoons light teriyaki sauce
 2   tablespoons snipped fresh rosemary or
     2 teaspoons dried rosemary, crushed
 1   tablespoon olive oil

1. Trim fat from the tenderloin. Place tenderloin in a plastic bag set in a shallow dish. For marinade, in a small bowl combine remaining ingredients. Pour over meat; seal bag. Marinate in the refrigerator for 4 to 24 hours, turning occasionally. Drain meat, discard marinade.

2. In a grill with a cover arrange heated coals around a drip pan. Test for medium heat above the pan. Place meat on the grill rack over drip pan. Cover and grill for 30 to 40 minutes or until meat is slightly pink in center and juices run clear (160°F). Remove meat from grill. Cover with foil; let stand for 10 minutes before slicing.
Makes 4 servings.

Nutrition Facts per serving: 162 cal., 7 g total fat
(2 g sat. fat), 60 mg chol., 285 mg sodium, 6 g carbo.,
0 g fiber, 19 g pro. Daily Values: 2% vit. C, 1% calcium,
8% iron

Pineapple-Glazed Pork

Prep: 10 min. • Grill: 30 min.

¹⁄₂ of a 6-ounce can frozen pineapple juice
concentrate (¹⁄₃ cup)

1 tablespoon Dijon-style mustard

1 teaspoon snipped fresh rosemary or
¹⁄₄ teaspoon dried rosemary, crushed

1 clove garlic, minced

2 12-ounce pork tenderloins

1. For sauce, in a small saucepan heat juice concentrate, mustard, rosemary, and garlic over medium heat about 5 minutes or until slightly thickened, stirring once.

2. In a covered grill arrange heated coals around a drip pan. Test for medium heat above pan. Place pork on grill over drip pan. Brush with sauce. Cover and grill for 30 to 45 minutes or until juices run clear (160°F), brushing again with sauce during the last 10 minutes of grilling. Remove pork from grill. Cover with foil; let stand for 10 minutes before slicing.
Makes 6 servings.

Nutrition Facts per serving: 154 cal., 4 g total fat
(1 g sat. fat), 81 mg chol., 121 mg sodium, 2 g carbo.,
0 g fiber, 25 g pro. Daily Values: 13% vit. C, 9% iron

Pork with Cider and Cream

Start to Finish: 25 min.

1 ³⁄₄-pound pork tenderloin

2 tablespoons butter or margarine

¹⁄₂ cup whipping cream

1 2¹⁄₂-ounce can whole mushrooms, drained

2 tablespoons calvados, apple jack, brandy,
or apple juice

1. Cut pork tenderloin into 1-inch slices. Place each slice between 2 sheets of plastic wrap. Pound lightly to ¹⁄₂-inch thickness.

2. In a large skillet cook pork in butter over medium-high heat for 4 minutes. Turn and cook 4 to 6 minutes more or until juices run clear. Transfer meat to a serving platter; keep warm.

3. Stir remaining ingredients into drippings in skillet. Bring to boiling; reduce heat. Simmer for 3 to 5 minutes or until slightly thickened. Pour sauce over pork.
Makes 4 servings.

Nutrition Facts per serving: 279 cal., 20 g total fat
(12 g sat. fat), 112 mg chol., 183 mg sodium, 2 g carbo.,
0 g fiber, 19 g pro. Daily Values: 13% vit. A, 1% vit. C,
3% calcium, 7% iron

Soy and Sesame Pork

**Prep: 5 min. • Marinate: 24 hours
Roast: 45 min.**

1   **1-pound pork tenderloin**
¼   **cup light soy sauce**
1   **tablespoon catsup**
¼   **teaspoon garlic powder**
2   **to 3 tablespoons toasted sesame seeds**

1. Place tenderloin in a plastic bag set in a shallow dish. In a small bowl combine soy sauce, catsup, and garlic powder; pour over pork. Turn pork to coat all sides. Seal bag. Marinate in the refrigerator for 24 hours, turning occasionally.

2. Drain pork, discard marinade. Place pork on a rack in a shallow roasting pan. Insert an oven-safe meat thermometer. Roast, uncovered, in a 325°F oven for 45 to 60 minutes or until thermometer registers 160°F. Sprinkle sesame seeds on a piece of foil. Carefully roll pork in sesame seeds. Cut into thin slices.
Makes 4 servings.

Nutrition Facts per serving: 162 cal., 5 g total fat
(1 g sat. fat), 73 mg chol., 357 mg sodium, 2 g carbo.,
1 g fiber, 25 g pro. Daily Values: 1% vit. A, 2% vit. C,
2% calcium, 10% iron

Barbecued Ribs and Sauerkraut

Prep: 15 min. • Cook: 25 min.

1   **14½-ounce can sauerkraut, rinsed and drained**
2   **cups loose-pack diced hash brown potatoes with onion and peppers**
1   **30.4-ounce package cooked pork ribs in barbecue sauce**
¼   **cup chicken broth**

1. In a large nonstick skillet combine sauerkraut and potatoes. Cut ribs into 2-rib portions; arrange on top of sauerkraut mixture. Combine any barbecue sauce from package and chicken broth; drizzle over mixture in the skillet. Cook, covered, over medium heat about 25 minutes or until heated through.
Makes 4 servings.

Nutrition Facts per serving: 582 cal., 32 g total fat
(12 g sat. fat), 84 mg chol., 2,004 mg sodium, 45 g carbo.,
6 g fiber, 30 g pro. Daily Values: 26% vit. A, 40% vit. C,
10% calcium, 26% iron

Cranberry-Glazed Pork Ribs

Prep: 10 min. • Grill: 45 min.

1   8-ounce can whole cranberry sauce (1 cup)
3   inches stick cinnamon
1   tablespoon Dijon-style mustard
1   teaspoon finely shredded orange peel
1½   pounds boneless country-style pork ribs

1. For sauce, cook and stir cranberry sauce, stick cinnamon, mustard, and orange peel over medium heat for 5 minutes or until bubbly. Set aside.

2. Arrange heated coals around a drip pan in a covered grill. Test for medium heat above pan. Place ribs on grill over drip pan. Brush with sauce. Cover and grill for 45 to 60 minutes or until ribs are tender and juices run clear, brushing ribs occasionally with sauce. Heat any remaining sauce. Remove and discard stick cinnamon. Pass remaining sauce with ribs.
Makes 6 servings.

Nutrition Facts per serving: 255 cal., 14 g total fat
(5 g sat. fat), 65 mg chol., 124 mg sodium, 15 g carbo.,
0 g fiber, 16 g pro. Daily Values: 3% vit. C, 1% calcium,
5% iron

Smoked Chops and Potatoes

Start to Finish: 20 min.

3   medium potatoes, sliced (about 1 pound)
1   cup loose-pack frozen broccoli,
       cauliflower, and carrots
4   smoked pork chops, cut ½ to ¾ inch thick
1   12-ounce jar brown gravy

1. In a large skillet cook potatoes and frozen vegetables, covered, in a small amount of boiling water for 6 to 8 minutes or until tender. Drain in colander.

2. In the same skillet arrange chops. Place potatoes and vegetables over chops. Spoon gravy over all. Cook, covered, over medium-low heat for 7 to 8 minutes or until heated through.
Makes 4 servings.

Nutrition Facts per serving: 349 cal., 19 g total fat
(7 g sat. fat), 60 mg chol., 1,452 mg sodium, 24 g carbo.,
3 g fiber, 23 g pro. Daily Values: 10% vit. A, 34% vit. C,
2% calcium, 11% iron

Smoked Pork Chop Skillet

Start to Finish: 25 min.

- 4   cooked smoked pork chops, cut ¾ inch thick (1¾ pounds)
- 1   16-ounce package frozen French-style green beans
- ¼   cup water
- 1½   teaspoons snipped fresh sage or ½ teaspoon dried leaf sage, crushed
- ½   cup balsamic vinegar

1. Cook chops in a large nonstick skillet over medium heat for 3 to 5 minutes on each side or until lightly brown. Remove from skillet; keep warm. Add green beans, water, and sage to skillet; return chops to skillet. Cook, covered, over medium heat for 5 minutes.

2. Meanwhile, in a small saucepan boil vinegar gently about 5 minutes or until reduced to ¼ cup. Brush chops with vinegar; drizzle remaining vinegar over green bean mixture.
Makes 4 servings.

Nutrition Facts per serving: 257 cal., 14 g total fat (5 g sat. fat), 47 mg chol., 749 mg sodium, 18 g carbo., 3 g fiber, 17 g pro. Daily Values: 10% vit. A, 20% vit. C, 5% calcium, 8% iron

Brown Sugar-Glazed Ham

Prep: 10 min. • Bake: 1 hour 35 min.

- 1   5- to 6-pound cooked bone-in ham (rump half or shank portion)
- 1½   cups packed brown sugar
- 1½   cups red wine vinegar
- 4   sprigs fresh mint

1. If desired, score ham by making diagonal cuts 1 inch apart in fat in a diamond pattern. Place on a rack in a shallow roasting pan. Insert an oven-safe meat thermometer so it does not touch bone. Bake in a 325°F oven until thermometer registers 125°F. For rump, allow 1¼ to 1½ hours; for shank, allow 1¾ to 2 hours.

2. Meanwhile, for glaze, in a medium saucepan stir together remaining ingredients. Bring to boiling; reduce heat. Boil gently, uncovered, about 30 minutes or until reduced to 1 cup. Remove from heat. Remove and discard mint. Brush ham with some of the glaze.

3. Bake ham for 20 to 30 minutes more or until thermometer registers 135°F, brushing occasionally with additional glaze. Let stand for 15 minutes before carving. (The meat temperature will rise 5°F during standing.) Bring any remaining glaze to boiling; serve with ham.
Makes 16 to 20 servings.

Nutrition Facts per serving: 232 cal., 8 g total fat (3 g sat. fat), 51 mg chol., 1,305 mg sodium, 22 g carbo., 0 g fiber, 20 g pro. Daily Values: 33% vit. C, 2% calcium, 12% iron

Fruited Baked Ham

Prep: 10 min. • Roast: 1½ hours

1   3- to 4-pound cooked boneless ham
½   cup apricot preserves
1   cup cherry preserves
¼   cup orange juice

1. Place ham in a shallow roasting pan. If desired, score ham by making diagonal cuts 1 inch apart in fat in a diamond pattern. Insert an oven-safe meat thermometer. Roast, uncovered, in a 325°F oven for 1½ to 2¼ hours or until thermometer registers 135°F. Let stand for 15 minutes before carving. (The meat temperature will rise 5°F during standing.)

2. Meanwhile, for sauce, snip the large pieces of apricot in the preserves. In a saucepan combine apricot and cherry preserves and orange juice. Heat through. Serve over ham.
Makes 12 to 16 servings.

Nutrition Facts per serving: 292 cal., 6 g total fat (2 g sat. fat), 62 mg chol., 1,518 mg sodium, 28 g carbo., 0 g fiber, 29 g pro. Daily Values: 10% vit. C, 2% calcium, 7% iron

Ham Steaks with Spicy Apricot Glaze

Prep: 10 min. • Broil: 8 min.

3   tablespoons apricot jam or preserves
2   tablespoons coarse-grain mustard
1   teaspoon cider vinegar
⅛   teaspoon ground red pepper
1   pound fully cooked boneless ham, cut into
        four ½-inch slices

1. For the glaze, in a small bowl stir together jam, mustard, vinegar, and pepper. Place ham on the unheated rack of a broiler pan. Broil ham 5 inches from the heat for 8 to 10 minutes or until brown, turning once and brushing occasionally with glaze.
Makes 4 servings.

Nutrition Facts per serving: 190 cal., 6 g total fat (2 g sat. fat), 51 mg chol., 1,273 mg sodium, 12 g carbo., 0 g fiber, 21 g pro. Daily Values: 34% vit. C, 1% calcium, 11% iron

Ham Slice with Basil-Cherry Sauce

Prep: 10 min. • Cook: 8 min.

1   1- to 1¼-pound cooked center-cut ham
    slice, cut ½ inch thick
2   tablespoons butter or margarine
1   15- to 17-ounce can pitted dark sweet
    cherries
2   teaspoons cornstarch
2   teaspoons fresh snipped basil or
    ½ teaspoon dried basil, crushed

1. In a 12-inch skillet cook the ham in
1 tablespoon of the butter over medium heat
for 8 to 10 minutes or until ham is heated
through, turning once. Transfer to a serving
platter; keep warm.

2. Meanwhile, drain canned cherries, reserving
juice; set cherries aside. In a small saucepan
stir reserved cherry juice into cornstarch. Cook
and stir until thickened and bubbly; cook and
stir for 2 minutes more. Stir in cherries, basil,
and remaining butter until melted and heated
through. Serve sauce over ham.
Makes 4 servings.

Nutrition Facts per serving: 338 cal., 18 g total fat
(8 g sat. fat), 74 mg chol., 1,285 mg sodium, 20 g carbo.,
2 g fiber, 23 g pro. Daily Values: 8% vit. A, 7% vit. C,
2% calcium, 7% iron

Old-Fashioned Beans and Ham

Prep: 35 min. • Stand: 1 hour
Cook: 1¼ hours

1   pound pinto beans
12 cups water
1   meaty smoked pork hock (1 to 1½ pounds)
1   large onion, chopped (1 cup)

1. Rinse beans. In a 4-quart Dutch oven combine
beans and 8 cups of the water. Bring to boiling;
reduce heat. Simmer, covered, for 2 minutes.
Remove from heat. Cover and let stand for 1 hour.
(Or omit simmering and soak beans in cold water
overnight in a covered pan.)

2. Drain and rinse beans. In the same pan
combine the beans, the remaining 4 cups of
water, pork hock, and onion. Bring to boiling;
reduce heat. Simmer, covered, for 1¼ to
1¾ hours or until beans are tender and
beginning to split. Remove from heat.

3. Remove pork hock; cool slightly. Trim meat
from pork hock; chop meat. Return meat to
bean mixture; heat through.
Makes 6 servings.

Nutrition Facts per serving: 288 cal., 2 g total fat
(1 g sat. fat), 9 mg chol., 192 mg sodium, 50 g carbo.,
19 g fiber, 19 g pro. Daily Values: 9% vit. C, 9% calcium,
21% iron

Ham and Beans with Escarole

Prep: 10 min. • Cook: 8 min.

- 2 **15-ounce cans Great Northern beans**
- 1 **tablespoon olive oil**
- 6 **cloves garlic, minced**
- 2 **cups cooked smoked ham, cut into bite-size strips**
- 3 **cups chopped escarole or spinach**

1. Drain beans, reserving liquid. In a large nonstick skillet heat oil over medium heat. Add garlic; cook and stir for 1 minute. Add beans and ham to the skillet. Cook about 5 minutes or until heated through, stirring occasionally. Stir in escarole; cook, covered, for 2 to 5 minutes more or until greens are wilted. If desired, thin mixture with some of the reserved liquid from beans.
Makes 4 servings.

Nutrition Facts per serving: 324 cal., 8 g total fat
(2 g sat. fat), 39 mg chol., 1,443 mg sodium, 33 g carbo.,
11 g fiber, 29 g pro. Daily Values: 15% vit. A, 6% vit. C,
20% calcium, 23% iron

Ham and Broccoli-Topped Spuds

Prep: 10 min. • Bake: 40 min.

- 4 **medium baking potatoes (6 to 8 ounces each)**
- 2 **10-ounce packages frozen cut broccoli in cheese sauce**
- 2 **cups chopped cooked ham**
- ½ **teaspoon caraway seeds**

1. Scrub potatoes; pat dry. Prick potatoes with a fork. Bake potatoes in a 425°F oven for 40 to 60 minutes or until tender. Roll each potato gently under your hand. Cut each potato open.

2. Meanwhile, cook broccoli in pouches according to package directions. Place contents of pouches in a medium saucepan. Add ham and caraway; heat through. Top each potato with broccoli mixture.
Makes 4 servings.

Nutrition Facts per serving: 338 cal., 10 g total fat
(3 g sat. fat), 44 mg chol., 1,713 mg sodium, 38 g carbo.,
6 g fiber, 24 g pro. Daily Values: 25% vit. A, 130% vit. C,
10% calcium, 18% iron

Ham and Asparagus Pasta

Start to Finish: 20 min.

4   cups farfalle (bow ties), rotini
     (corkscrews), or other medium pasta
1   10-ounce package frozen cut asparagus
     or broccoli
8   ounces cooked ham slices, cut into thin
     strips
1   8-ounce container soft-style cream cheese
     with chives and onion
1/3 cup milk

1. Cook pasta according to package directions,
adding asparagus the last 5 minutes and ham
the last minute of cooking time. Drain; return to
pan. In a 2-cup measure stir cream cheese into
milk; add to the pasta mixture in the pan. Stir
gently over medium heat until heated through.
Makes 4 servings.

Nutrition Facts per serving: 505 cal., 24 g total fat
(12 g sat. fat), 140 mg chol., 905 mg sodium, 45 g carbo.,
1 g fiber, 25 g pro. Daily Values: 19% vit. A, 43% vit. C,
7% calcium, 23% iron

Ham and Cheese Calzones

Prep: 15 min. • Bake: 15 min.

1   10-ounce package refrigerated pizza dough
1/4 cup coarse-grain mustard
6   ounces sliced Swiss or provolone cheese
8   ounces cubed cooked ham (1 1/2 cups)
1/2 teaspoon caraway seeds

1. Line a baking sheet with foil; lightly grease
foil. Unroll pizza dough. On a lightly floured
surface roll or pat dough into a 15×10-inch
rectangle. Cut dough in half crosswise and
lengthwise to make 4 rectangles. Spread
mustard over rectangles. Divide half of the
cheese among rectangles, placing cheese on
half of each and cutting or tearing to fit as
necessary. Top with ham and sprinkle with
caraway seeds. Top with remaining cheese.
Brush edges with water. Fold dough over filling
to opposite edge, stretching slightly if
necessary. Seal edges with a fork.

2. Place calzones on the prepared baking sheet.
Prick tops to allow steam to escape. Bake in a
400°F oven about 15 minutes or until golden
brown. Let stand for 5 minutes before serving.
Makes 4 servings.

Nutrition Facts per serving: 421 cal., 21 g total fat
(10 g sat. fat), 72 mg chol., 1,390 mg sodium, 28 g carbo.,
1 g fiber, 30 g pro. Daily Values: 7% vit. A, 44% calcium,
16% iron

Canadian Bacon Pizza

Prep: 15 min. • Bake: 15 min.

1   16-ounce package Italian bread shell
     (Boboli)
1   6-ounce jar marinated artichoke hearts
1   5.2-ounce container semisoft cheese with
     garlic and herb
1   3.5-ounce package pizza-style Canadian-
     style bacon (1½ inches in diameter)
1   medium sweet pepper, cut into bite-size
     strips

1. Place bread shell on a large baking sheet.
Drain artichoke hearts, reserving 1 tablespoon
of the marinade. Coarsely chop artichokes; set
aside. In a small bowl combine cheese and
reserved marinade. Spread half of the cheese
mixture over bread shell; top with Canadian
bacon, pepper, and artichoke hearts. Spoon
remaining cheese mixture by teaspoons over
toppings. Bake in a 350°F oven for 15 minutes
or until heated through.
Makes 4 to 6 servings.

Nutrition Facts per serving: 529 cal., 24 g total fat
(9 g sat. fat), 54 mg chol., 1,136 mg sodium, 58 g carbo.,
2 g fiber, 23 g pro. Daily Values: 2% vit. A, 158% vit. C,
16% calcium, 16% iron

Denver Potato Casserole

Prep: 20 min. • Bake: 1 hour 5 min.

4   medium Yukon gold potatoes, thinly sliced
     (1⅓ pounds)
8   ounces cubed cooked ham
1   medium sweet pepper, chopped (¾ cup)
1   small sweet yellow onion, chopped (⅓ cup)
1   cup shredded co-jack cheese (4 ounces)

1. In a greased 2-quart square baking dish
layer half of the potatoes, half of the ham, half
of the pepper, half of the onion, and half of the
cheese. Repeat with the remaining ham,
pepper, and onion. Top with the remaining
potatoes. Bake, covered, in a 350°F oven for
45 minutes. Uncover and bake 15 minutes more
or until potatoes are tender. Sprinkle with
remaining cheese. Bake, uncovered, 5 minutes
more or until cheese is melted.
Makes 4 servings.

Nutrition Facts per serving: 315 cal., 12 g total fat
(6 g sat. fat), 56 mg chol., 1,010 mg sodium, 27 g carbo.,
3 g fiber, 24 g pro. Daily Values: 6% vit. A, 71% vit. C,
21% calcium, 12% iron

Sausage-Grits Casserole

Prep: 20 min. • Bake: 35 min.

1 cup quick-cooking grits
1 pound bulk pork sausage
½ cup chopped onion
2 beaten eggs
1 8-ounce package shredded cheddar cheese
    (2 cups)

1. Prepare grits according to package directions. Meanwhile, in a large skillet cook sausage and onion until meat is brown and onion is tender, stirring to break up the sausage. Drain.

2. In a large bowl combine grits, sausage mixture, eggs, and 1½ cups of the cheese. Spread in a greased 3-quart rectangular baking dish; sprinkle with remaining cheese. Bake, uncovered, in a 350°F oven about 35 minutes or until set.
Makes 8 to 12 servings.

Nutrition Facts per serving: 404 cal., 21 g total fat (13 g sat. fat), 115 mg chol., 476 mg sodium, 17 g carbo., 0 g fiber, 17 g pro. Daily Values: 9% vit. A, 2% vit. C, 22% calcium, 8% iron

Sausage-Sauced Polenta

Start to Finish: 20 minutes

2 16-ounce tubes wild mushroom-flavored
    polenta or other flavored polenta
1 pound bulk pork sausage or Italian sausage
1 26- to 27¾-ounce jar chunky garden-style
    pasta sauce
¼ cup finely shredded or grated Parmesan
    cheese
    Snipped fresh parsley or cilantro

1. Cut each tube of polenta into 9 slices; set aside. In a 12-inch skillet cook sausage until brown. Drain off fat. Stir in sauce; heat to boiling. Place polenta slices on top of sauce. Simmer, covered, for 5 minutes or until heated through. Sprinkle with cheese and parsley.
Makes 6 servings.

Nutrition Facts per serving: 490 cal., 26 g total fat (10 g sat. fat), 47 mg chol., 1,194 mg sodium, 41 g carbo., 5 g fiber, 15 g pro. Daily Values: 14% vit. A, 12% vit. C, 9% calcium, 14% iron

Italian Sausage Spiral

Prep: 25 min. • Bake: 35 min.

- 1 pound bulk Italian sausage
- 1 1-pound loaf frozen bread dough, thawed
- 1 27½-ounce jar tomato, garlic, and basil pasta sauce
- 1 8-ounce package shredded Italian-style cheese blend (2 cups)
- 5 cups baby spinach (about 5 ounces)

1. In a large skillet cook sausage until no pink remains. Drain fat; set sausage aside.

2. On a lightly floured surface, roll bread dough to an 18×12-inch rectangle. Spread 1 cup of the sauce on the dough to within ¼ inch of the edge. Layer sausage, 1¼ cups of the cheese, and spinach on top of the sausage. Starting from a short side, roll up the dough; brush edges with water and pinch to seal. Place seam side down on a greased baking sheet. Cover; let rest for 15 minutes.

3. Uncover and bake in a 375°F oven for 25 minutes. Cover loosely with foil and bake 10 minutes more. Meanwhile, in a small saucepan heat remaining pasta sauce. To serve, cut spiral into 8 slices; top with remaining sauce and cheese.
Makes 8 servings.

Nutrition Facts per serving: 481 cal., 22 g total fat
(10 g sat. fat), 61 mg chol., 886 mg sodium, 42 g carbo.,
4 g fiber, 21 g pro. Daily Values: 41% vit. A, 37% vit. C,
25% calcium, 15% iron

Hot and Saucy Tortellini

Start to Finish: 25 min.

- 7 to 8 ounces dried cheese-filled tortellini (about 1¾ cups)
- 8 ounces bulk Italian sausage
- 1 13- to 14-ounce jar red pasta sauce
- 1 16-ounce bottle salsa
- 2 tablespoons snipped fresh cilantro

1. Cook tortellini according to package directions; drain well. Keep pasta warm. Meanwhile, in a large skillet cook sausage until no longer pink; drain. Stir in pasta sauce and salsa. Bring to boiling; reduce heat. Simmer, covered, for 5 minutes. Stir pasta and half of the cilantro into sauce mixture; heat through. Transfer to a serving bowl or platter. Sprinkle with remaining cilantro.
Makes 4 servings.

Nutrition Facts per serving: 450 cal., 20 g total fat
(5 g sat. fat), 38 mg chol., 1,848 mg sodium, 42 g carbo.,
3 g fiber, 21 g pro. Daily Values: 22% vit. A, 35% vit. C,
23% calcium, 15% iron

One-Pot Pesto Pasta

Prep: 15 min. • Cook: 25 min.

1   pound bulk sweet Italian sausage or
     ground beef
3   cups reduced-sodium chicken broth
8   ounces spaghetti, broken
3   tablespoons purchased basil pesto
¼   cup finely shredded Parmesan cheese

1. In a large saucepan cook sausage until no longer pink, stirring occasionally. Drain fat. Stir in broth; bring to boiling. Gradually add spaghetti. Reduce heat. Simmer, covered, for 25 minutes or until spaghetti is tender and most of the liquid is absorbed, stirring occasionally. Remove from heat. Stir in pesto. Transfer to serving dish. Sprinkle with cheese.
Makes 4 servings.

Nutrition Facts per serving: 659 cal., 35 g total fat (12 g sat. fat), 84 mg chol., 1,253 mg sodium, 46 g carbo., 1 g fiber, 29 g pro. Daily Values: 1% vit. A, 2% vit. C, 9% calcium, 17% iron

A Spoonful of Pesto

Pesto is the perfect condiment for adding flavor in a hurry. Try these simple ideas to finish off that partial container:
•Spread a spoonful on top of grilled fish or poultry.
•Slather some on the toasted bun of a grilled hamburger or chicken sandwich.
•Spoon some pesto under the skin of a whole chicken before roasting.

Bow Ties with Sausage and Sweet Peppers

Start to Finish: 25 min.

8   ounces dried bow tie pasta
¾   pound fresh spicy Italian sausage links
2   medium sweet peppers, cut into bite-
     size pieces
½   cup vegetable broth or beef broth
¼   teaspoon coarsely ground black pepper

1. Cook pasta according to package directions. Meanwhile, cut sausage into bite-size pieces. In a large skillet cook sausage and sweet peppers over medium-high heat until sausage is brown. Drain off fat.

2. Add broth and black pepper to skillet. Bring to boiling; reduce heat. Simmer, uncovered, for 5 minutes. Remove from heat. Drain pasta. Toss pasta with sausage mixture.
Makes 4 servings.

Nutrition Facts per serving: 479 cal., 22 g total fat (8 g sat. fat), 111 mg chol., 713 mg sodium, 45 g carbo., 3 g fiber, 21 g pro. Daily Values: 65% vit. A, 160% vit. C, 4% calcium, 18% iron

Smoked Sausage Pasta Bake

Prep: 25 min. • Bake: 15 min.

12 ounces cavatelli or rotini pasta
 1 26- to 28-ounce jar purchased spicy
     tomato pasta sauce
 6 ounces cooked smoked sausage, halved
     lengthwise and sliced
¾ cup bottled roasted red sweet peppers,
     drained and coarsely chopped
 1 cup shredded provolone or mozzarella
     cheese (4 ounces)

1. Cook pasta according to package directions;
drain well. Return pasta to pan. Stir sauce,
sausage, and roasted peppers into pasta,
tossing gently to coat. Spoon pasta mixture into
four greased 14- to 16-ounce casseroles.
Sprinkle with cheese. Bake in a 375°F oven for
15 to 20 minutes or until cheese is melted and
pasta mixture is heated through.
Makes 4 servings.

Nutrition Facts per serving: 654 cal., 25 g total fat
(12 g sat. fat), 38 mg chol., 995 mg sodium, 77 g carbo.,
6 g fiber, 26 g pro. Daily Values: 5% vit. A, 144% vit. C,
30% calcium, 20% iron

Quick Sausage-Noodle Soup

Start to Finish: 20 min.

1 14½-ounce can diced tomatoes with green
    pepper and onion, undrained
4 cups water
8 ounces cooked smoked sausage, halved
    lengthwise and thinly sliced
1 medium sweet pepper, cut into bite-size
    strips (1 cup)
2 3-ounce packages chicken-flavored
    ramen noodles

1. In a large saucepan combine the undrained
tomatoes, water, sausage, sweet pepper, and
seasoning packets from the noodles (set noodles
aside). Bring to boiling. Break noodles into
quarters; add to saucepan. Return to boiling; boil
noodles for 2 to 3 minutes or until tender.
Makes 4 servings.

Nutrition Facts per serving: 462 cal., 27 g total fat
(6 g sat. fat), 39 mg chol., 2,001 mg sodium, 36 g carbo.,
2 g fiber, 19 g pro. Daily Values: 3% vit. A, 52% vit. C,
5% calcium, 8% iron

Honey-Mustard Lamb Chops

Prep: 10 min. • Broil: 10 min.

4   lamb chops, cut 1 inch thick (about
    1 pound)
2   small zucchini, halved lengthwise
1   tablespoon Dijon-style mustard
1   tablespoon honey
1½ teaspoons snipped fresh rosemary or
    ½ teaspoon dried rosemary, crushed

1. Trim fat from chops. Arrange chops and zucchini, cut sides up, on the unheated rack of a broiler pan. In a small bowl stir together the remaining ingredients. Spread some of the mustard mixture on top of the chops.

2. Broil chops and zucchini 3 to 4 inches from the heat for 5 minutes. Turn chops and zucchini; spread more of the mustard mixture on the chops. Broil for 5 to 10 minutes more to desired doneness (160°F for medium) and until zucchini is tender, spreading the remaining mustard mixture on zucchini the last 3 minutes of broiling.
Makes 2 servings.

Nutrition Facts per serving: 182 cal., 6 g total fat (2 g sat. fat), 60 mg chol., 99 mg sodium, 12 g carbo., 1 g fiber, 21 g pro. Daily Values: 6% vit. A, 11% vit. C, 4% calcium, 13% iron

Orange-Mustard Lamb Chops

Start to Finish: 15 min.

8   lamb chops, cut 1 inch thick (about
    2 pounds)
3   tablespoons orange marmalade
4   teaspoons Dijon-style mustard

1. Trim fat from chops. Place chops on the unheated rack of a broiler pan. Broil 3 to 4 inches from the heat to desired doneness, turning once. Allow 10 to 15 minutes for medium (160°F).

2. Meanwhile, in a small saucepan stir together marmalade and mustard. Cook and stir over medium heat until heated through. To serve, spoon over chops.
Makes 4 servings.

Nutrition Facts per serving: 172 cal., 6 g total fat (23 g sat. fat), 60 mg chol., 90 mg sodium, 10 g carbo., 1 g fiber, 20 g pro. Daily Values: 2% vit. C, 2% calcium, 10% iron

Balsamic-Glazed Lamb and Greens

Start to Finish: 25 min.

1   cup balsamic vinegar
8   lamb loin or rib chops, cut 1 inch thick
      (about 2 pounds)
3   cups sugar snap peas, strings and tips
      removed
6   cups torn mixed salad greens
¼   cup hazelnuts or coarsely chopped walnuts,
      toasted

1. For glaze, in a small saucepan bring vinegar just to boiling. Boil gently, uncovered, about 10 minutes or until vinegar is reduced to ⅓ cup. Set aside.

2. Meanwhile, trim fat from chops. Broil chops on the unheated rack of a broiler pan 3 to 4 inches from the heat to desired doneness, turning once. Allow 10 to 15 minutes for medium (160°F).

3. In a small saucepan cook peas, covered, in a small amount of boiling salted water for 2 to 4 minutes or until crisp-tender. Drain. Divide greens among 4 dinner plates. Top each with 2 chops and some of the peas. Drizzle with glaze; sprinkle with nuts.
Makes 4 servings.

Nutrition Facts per serving: 293 cal., 10 g total fat (2 g sat. fat), 60 mg chol., 68 mg sodium, 24 g carbo., 3 g fiber, 23 g pro. Daily Values: 7% vit. A, 44% vit. C, 6% calcium, 21% iron

Lemon and Herb-Roasted Chicken

Prep: 15 min. • Roast: 1¾ hours

1   medium lemon
1   tablespoon olive oil
1   5- to 6-pound whole roasting chicken
2   cloves garlic, finely chopped
2½   teaspoons herbes de Provence or
        Greek seasoning

1. Halve the lemon; squeeze 2 tablespoons lemon juice from the lemon. Reserve lemon halves. Stir together oil and lemon juice; brush over chicken. In a small bowl combine garlic and herbes de Provence; rub onto chicken. Place the squeezed lemon halves in body cavity of the chicken.

2. If desired, skewer neck skin to back; tie legs to tail and twist wing tips under back. Place chicken, breast side up, on a rack in a shallow pan. If desired, insert an oven-safe meat thermometer into the center of an inside thigh muscle. Do not allow thermometer bulb to touch bone.

3. Roast, uncovered, in a 325°F oven for 1¾ to 2½ hours or until drumsticks move easily in their sockets, chicken is no longer pink, and meat thermometer registers 180°F. Let stand, covered, for 15 minutes before carving.
Makes 8 to 12 servings.

Nutrition Facts per serving: 447 cal., 33 g total fat (9 g sat. fat), 148 mg chol., 111 mg sodium, 1 g carbo., 0 g fiber, 35 g pro. Daily Values: 5% vit. A, 7% vit. C, 3% calcium, 11% iron

Roast Chicken with Fruit and Pesto

Prep: 20 min. • Roast: 1³/₄ hours

1   cup apricot or peach preserves

¹/₂   cup snipped dried apricots or peaches

¹/₄   teaspoon ground ginger

²/₃   cup purchased basil pesto

1   5- to 6-pound whole roasting chicken

1. In a medium bowl stir together preserves, apricots, and ginger. Remove ¹/₃ cup of mixture; place in a small bowl. Stir in pesto; set aside. Set aside remaining preserve mixture for sauce.

2. Rinse inside of chicken; pat dry. Slip your fingers between the skin and breast meat of the bird. Spoon some of the pesto mixture under the skin and spread over the breast meat. Spread some of the pesto mixture into the neck cavity. Pull neck skin to back; fasten with a small skewer. Spread some of the pesto mixture into the body cavity. Rub remaining pesto mixture over outside of chicken. Tie the drumsticks to the tail. Twist the wing tips under the chicken.

3. Place chicken, breast side up, on a rack in a shallow roasting pan. Insert an oven-safe meat thermometer into the center of 1 of the thigh muscles. The bulb should not touch bone. Roast, uncovered, in a 325°F oven for 1³/₄ to 2¹/₂ hours or until drumsticks move easily in their sockets, chicken is no longer pink, and meat thermometer registers 180°F. When the bird is two-thirds done, cut the band of skin or string between the drumsticks so the thighs cook evenly. Transfer chicken to a platter; let stand 15 minutes before carving.

4. Meanwhile, in a small saucepan heat reserved preserve mixture over low heat until preserves have melted and mixture is heated through. Serve sauce with sliced chicken.
Makes 8 to 10 servings.

Nutrition Facts per serving: 873 cal., 57 g total fat (12 g sat. fat), 208 mg chol., 323 mg sodium, 36 g carbo., 1 g fiber, 52 g pro. Daily Values: 18% vit. A, 12% vit. C, 4% calcium, 18% iron

Oven-Barbecued Chicken

Prep: 10 min. • Bake: 45 min.

2   pounds meaty chicken pieces (breasts, thighs, and drumsticks)

¹/₃   cup orange marmalade

¹/₃   cup bottled barbecue sauce

2   tablespoons Worcestershire sauce

2   tablespoons lemon juice

1. Skin chicken, if desired. Arrange chicken pieces in a foil-lined 13×9×2-inch baking pan; set aside. In a small bowl combine remaining ingredients; pour over chicken.

2. Bake, uncovered, in a 375°F oven for 45 to 55 minutes or until chicken is tender and no longer pink (170°F for breasts; 180°F for thighs and drumsticks), spooning sauce over chicken occasionally.
Makes 4 to 6 servings.

Nutrition Facts per serving: 345 cal., 13 g total fat (2 g sat. fat), 104 mg chol., 357 mg sodium, 22 g carbo., 2 g fiber, 34 g pro. Daily Values: 4% vit. A, 13% vit. C, 4% calcium, 11% iron

Hot Barbecued Chicken

**Prep: 10 min. • Marinate: 2 hours
Grill: 50 min.**

2½ to 3 pounds meaty chicken pieces (breasts,
          thighs, and drumsticks)
  1 2½-ounce bottle hot sauce (¼ cup)
  3 tablespoons catsup
  3 tablespoons Worcestershire sauce

1. Place chicken pieces in a self-sealing plastic
bag set in a bowl. For marinade, combine
remaining ingredients. Pour marinade over
chicken pieces; close bag. Marinate in the
refrigerator for 2 to 3 hours.

2. Drain chicken, discard marinade. In a covered
grill arrange heated coals around a drip pan. Test
for medium heat above the pan. Place chicken
over pan. Cover and grill chicken for 50 to
60 minutes or until no longer pink (170°F for
breasts; 180°F for thighs and drumsticks).
Makes 6 servings.

Nutrition Facts per serving: 285 cal., 17 g total fat
(5 g sat. fat), 110 mg chol., 201 mg sodium, 2 g carbo.,
0 g fiber, 29 g pro. Daily Values: 5% vit. A, 6% vit. C,
2% calcium, 8% iron

Honey-Mustard Baked Chicken

Prep: 5 min. • Bake: 35 min.

2½ to 3 pounds meaty chicken pieces (breasts,
          thighs, and drumsticks)
  1 tablespoon cooking oil
  ⅓ cup brown mustard
  1 tablespoon soy sauce
  1 to 2 tablespoons honey

1. Skin chicken, if desired. Place the chicken
pieces in a lightly greased shallow baking pan.
Bake in a 425°F oven for 15 minutes. Meanwhile,
in a small bowl stir together remaining
ingredients. Brush mixture generously over
chicken pieces. Bake for 20 to 25 minutes more
or until chicken is tender and no longer pink
(170°F for breasts; 180°F for thighs and
drumsticks), brushing chicken frequently with
mustard mixture.
Makes 6 servings.

Nutrition Facts per serving: 259 cal., 14 g total fat
(3 g sat. fat), 86 mg chol., 409 mg sodium, 4 g carbo.,
0 g fiber, 29 g pro. Daily Values: 3% calcium, 8% iron

French-Onion Baked Chicken

Prep: 20 min. • Bake: 35 min.

2   **pounds chicken thighs or drumsticks**
1/3   **cup creamy ranch salad dressing or French salad dressing**
1/4   **teaspoon bottled hot pepper sauce**
1   **2.8-ounce can French-fried onions, crumbled**
1/2   **cup crushed cornflakes**

1. Skin chicken. In a shallow bowl stir together salad dressing and hot pepper sauce. In another bowl combine onions and cornflakes.

2. In a 3-quart rectangular baking dish with a rack arrange chicken pieces, meaty side up. Brush with salad dressing mixture. Sprinkle with onion mixture, pressing mixture onto chicken.

3. Bake, uncovered, in a 425°F oven for 35 to 40 minutes or until chicken is tender and no longer pink (180°F), covering loosely the last 10 minutes, if necessary, to prevent overbrowning.
Makes 4 servings.

Nutrition Facts per serving: 408 cal., 24 g total fat (3 g sat. fat), 108 mg chol., 558 mg sodium, 18 g carbo., 0 g fiber, 28 g pro. Daily Values: 2% vit. A, 5% vit. C, 2% calcium, 17% iron

Papaya-Glazed Chicken

Prep: 15 min. • Bake: 35 min.

2 1/2 **to 3 pounds meaty chicken pieces (breasts, thighs, and drumsticks)**
1/2   **teaspoon seasoned salt**
1   **cup chopped, peeled papaya**
1   **tablespoon frozen orange juice concentrate**
1   **tablespoon water**
1/2   **to 1 teaspoon curry powder**

1. Skin chicken, if desired. Place chicken pieces in a 3-quart rectangular baking dish. Sprinkle with seasoned salt. Bake in a 425°F oven for 20 minutes. Meanwhile, in a blender container or food processor bowl combine remaining ingredients. Cover and blend or process until smooth. Remove chicken from oven; brush papaya mixture generously over chicken. Bake for 15 to 20 minutes more or until chicken is no longer pink (170°F for breasts; 180°F for thighs and drumsticks), brushing several times with papaya mixture.
Makes 6 servings.

Nutrition Facts per serving: 228 cal., 11 g total fat (3 g sat. fat), 86 mg chol., 204 mg sodium, 4 g carbo., 0 g fiber, 28 g pro. Daily Values: 2% vit. A, 31% vit. C, 2% calcium, 7% iron

Peach-Glazed Chicken

Prep: 10 min. • Bake: 50 min.

- 2 **pounds meaty chicken pieces (breasts, thighs, and drumsticks)**
- ¼ **cup French salad dressing**
- 2 **tablespoons peach jam, large pieces cut up**
- 1 **tablespoon water**
- 1 **teaspoon dried minced onion or**
  2 tablespoons finely chopped onion

1. Skin chicken, if desired. Place chicken pieces in a 13×9×2-inch baking pan. For glaze, stir together remaining ingredients. Brush glaze lightly over chicken. Bake, uncovered, in a 375°F oven for 45 to 55 minutes or until chicken is tender and no longer pink (170°F for breasts; 180°F for thighs and drumsticks). Brush with remaining glaze; bake 5 minutes more.
Makes 4 servings.

Nutrition Facts per serving: 353 cal., 19 g total fat (5 g sat. fat), 106 mg chol., 306 mg sodium, 10 g carbo., 0 g fiber, 34 g pro. Daily Values: 4% vit. A, 1% calcium, 10% iron

Sweet and Spicy Chicken

Prep: 15 min. • Cook: 45 min.

- 3 **pounds meaty chicken pieces (breasts, thighs, and drumsticks)**
- 3 **cloves garlic, minced**
- 2 **tablespoons cooking oil**
- ¾ **cup bottled sweet-and-sour sauce**
- ¾ **cup bottled hot-style barbecue sauce**

1. Skin chicken, if desired. In a 12-inch skillet cook and stir garlic in 1 tablespoon hot oil over medium heat for 1 minute. Using a slotted spoon, transfer garlic to a medium mixing bowl. Stir sweet-and-sour sauce and barbecue sauce into garlic in bowl; set sauce mixture aside.

2. Add remaining oil to skillet; add chicken pieces. Cook, uncovered, over medium heat for 10 minutes, turning to brown evenly. Add more oil, if necessary. Reduce heat; cover tightly. Cook for 25 minutes. Uncover; pour sauce mixture over chicken. Bring to boiling over medium heat. Cook, uncovered, over medium heat for 10 minutes more or until chicken is tender and no longer pink (170°F for breasts; 180°F for thighs and drumsticks), spooning sauce over chicken occasionally. Transfer chicken to a serving platter. Stir sauce and spoon over chicken.
Makes 6 servings.

Nutrition Facts per serving: 399 cal., 18 g total fat (4 g sat. fat), 104 mg chol., 606 mg sodium, 21 g carbo., 0 g fiber, 33 g pro. Daily Values: 5% vit. C, 2% calcium, 8% iron

Orange-Plum Chicken

Prep: 15 min. • Bake: 45 min.

- ⅓ **cup plum preserves**
- 1 **tablespoon soy sauce**
- 2 **to 2½ pounds meaty chicken pieces (breasts, thighs, and drumsticks)**
- ⅓ **cup orange juice**
- 1 **teaspoon cornstarch**

1. In a small bowl stir together plum preserves and soy sauce. In a 3-quart rectangular baking dish arrange chicken pieces so they don't touch. Brush chicken pieces with plum mixture.

2. Bake, uncovered, in a 375°F oven for 45 to 55 minutes or until chicken is tender and no longer pink (170°F for breasts; 180°F for thighs and drumsticks). Remove chicken from dish, reserving juices; keep warm.

3. Pour reserved juices into a 2-cup glass measure. Skim fat from juices, if necessary. Transfer juices to a small saucepan. Combine orange juice and cornstarch; stir into reserved juices. Cook and stir over medium heat until thickened and bubbly. Cook and stir for 2 minutes more. Serve over chicken.
Makes 4 servings.

Nutrition Facts per serving: 421 cal., 21 g total fat (6 g sat. fat), 132 mg chol., 339 mg sodium, 21 g carbo., 0 g fiber, 35 g pro. Daily Values: 4% vit. A, 25% vit. C, 3% calcium, 9% iron

Chutney Chicken

Start to Finish: 35 min.

- 2 **to 2½ pounds meaty chicken pieces (breasts, thighs, and drumsticks)**
- ½ **of a 9-ounce jar chutney (about ⅓ cup)**
- 1 **tablespoon butter or margarine**
- 1 **tablespoon lemon juice**
- ⅛ **teaspoon black pepper**

1. Place chicken pieces, skin side down, on the unheated rack of a broiler pan. Broil 4 to 5 inches from the heat for 15 to 18 minutes or until chicken is lightly brown.

2. Meanwhile, for sauce, in a small saucepan stir together remaining ingredients. Cook over medium heat until butter melts and mixture bubbles, stirring occasionally.

3. Turn chicken pieces and broil for 10 to 15 minutes more or until chicken is tender and no longer pink (170°F for breasts; 180°F for thighs and drumsticks), brushing chicken with some of the sauce during the last 2 minutes of broiling. Spoon remaining sauce over chicken.
Makes 4 servings.

Nutrition Facts per serving: 334 cal., 16 g total fat (5 g sat. fat), 112 mg chol., 138 mg sodium, 13 g carbo., 0 g fiber, 34 g pro. Daily Values: 15% vit. A, 15% vit. C, 2% calcium, 8% iron

Old-Fashioned Fried Chicken

Prep: 10 min. • Cook: 25 min.

½   **cup all-purpose flour**

½   **teaspoon each salt and black pepper**

1   **5-ounce can evaporated milk**

⅔   **cup water**

2   **cups cooking oil**

2½ **to 3 pounds meaty chicken pieces (breasts, thighs, and drumsticks)**

1. In a shallow dish stir together flour, salt, and pepper. Set aside. In a bowl stir together milk and water; set aside. In a 12-inch skillet over medium heat, heat ½ inch of oil. Dip chicken pieces in milk mixture; roll in flour mixture.

2. Cook chicken, uncovered, in hot oil for 10 minutes or until golden on the bottom. Turn and cook pieces 15 minutes more or until chicken is tender and no longer pink (170°F for breasts; 180°F for thighs and drumsticks). Remove chicken from skillet; drain on paper towels. Serve warm.
Makes 4 to 6 servings.

Nutrition Facts per serving: 495 cal., 32 g total fat (8 g sat. fat), 125 mg chol., 419 mg sodium, 15 g carbo., 0 g fiber, 34 g pro. Daily Values: 4% vit. A, 5% vit. C, 11% calcium, 11% iron

Oven-Fried Coconut Chicken

Prep: 10 min. • Bake: 45 min.

½   **cup flaked coconut**

¼   **cup fine dry seasoned bread crumbs**

2½ **to 3 pounds meaty chicken pieces (breasts, thighs, and drumsticks)**

¼   **cup butter or margarine, melted**

1. In a shallow bowl stir together coconut and bread crumbs; set aside. Brush chicken pieces with melted butter. Roll chicken pieces in coconut mixture to coat all sides. In a 15×10×1- or a 13×9×2-inch baking pan arrange chicken, skin side up, so pieces don't touch. Drizzle any remaining butter over chicken. Bake in a 375°F oven for 45 to 50 minutes or until chicken is tender and no longer pink (170°F for breasts; 180°F for thighs and drumsticks). Do not turn.
Makes 6 servings.

Nutrition Facts per serving: 332 cal., 21 g total fat (10 g sat. fat), 108 mg chol., 284 mg sodium, 6 g carbo., 0 g fiber, 29 g pro. Daily Values: 6% vit. A, 2% calcium, 7% iron

Garlic Clove Chicken

Prep: 20 min. • Bake: 45 min.

  Nonstick cooking spray
2 to 2½ pounds meaty chicken pieces
     (breasts, thighs, and drumsticks),
     skinned
25 cloves garlic (about ½ cup or 2 to 3 bulbs)
¼ cup dry white wine
  Salt
  Ground red pepper

1. Coat a large skillet with cooking spray. Heat skillet over medium heat. Add chicken pieces; cook over medium heat for 10 minutes, turning to brown evenly. Place chicken pieces in an 8-inch square baking dish. Add unpeeled garlic cloves. Pour wine over chicken. Lightly sprinkle with salt and red pepper. Bake, covered, in a 325°F oven for 45 to 50 minutes or until chicken is tender and no longer pink (170°F for breasts; 180°F for thighs and drumsticks).
Makes 4 servings.

Nutrition Facts per serving: 194 cal., 3 g total fat
(1 g sat. fat), 96 mg chol., 232 mg sodium, 6 g carbo.,
0 g fiber, 31 g pro. Daily Values: 1% vit. A, 14% vit. C,
5% calcium, 8% iron

Tuscan Chicken

Start to Finish: 50 min.

2 to 2½ pounds meaty chicken pieces
     (breasts, thighs, and drumsticks)
2 tablespoons olive oil
1¼ teaspoons pesto seasoning
½ cup whole kalamata olives
½ cup dry white wine or chicken broth

1. In a 12-inch skillet cook chicken pieces in hot oil over medium heat for 15 minutes, turning to brown evenly. Reduce heat. Drain excess oil. Sprinkle seasoning evenly over chicken. Add olives. Pour white wine over all. Cover tightly and cook for 25 minutes. Uncover; cook for 5 to 10 minutes more or until chicken is tender and no longer pink (170°F for breasts; 180°F for thighs and drumsticks).
Makes 4 servings.

Nutrition Facts per serving: 334 cal., 18 g total fat
(4 g sat. fat), 104 mg chol., 280 mg sodium, 2 g carbo.,
1 g fiber, 34 g pro. Daily Values: 1% vit. A, 3% calcium,
9% iron

Asian Chicken and Vegetables

Prep: 10 min. • Bake: 40 min.

8　chicken drumsticks and/or thighs, skinned (about 2 pounds)
1　tablespoon cooking oil
1½　teaspoons five-spice powder
⅓　cup purchased plum sauce or sweet-and-sour sauce
1　14-ounce package frozen baby whole potatoes, broccoli, carrots, baby corn, and red pepper mix or one 16-ounce package frozen stir-fry vegetables

1. Arrange chicken pieces in a 13×9×2-inch baking pan. Brush chicken with oil; sprinkle with 1 teaspoon of the five-spice powder. Bake, uncovered, in a 400°F oven for 25 minutes.

2. Meanwhile, in a large bowl combine the remaining five-spice powder and plum sauce. Add frozen vegetables; toss to coat. Move chicken pieces to one side of baking pan. Add vegetable mixture to other side of pan. Bake for 15 to 20 minutes more or until chicken is tender and no longer pink (180°F), stirring vegetables once during baking. Using a slotted spoon, transfer chicken and vegetables to a serving platter.
Makes 4 servings.

Nutrition Facts per serving: 277 cal., 9 g total fat (2 g sat. fat), 98 mg chol., 124 mg sodium, 21 g carbo., 2 g fiber, 30 g pro. Daily Values: 21% vit. A, 19% vit. C, 5% calcium, 11% iron

Blue Ribbon Cranberry Chicken

Prep: 15 min. • Bake: 1½ hours

1　16-ounce can whole cranberry sauce
1　cup Russian salad dressing or French salad dressing
1　envelope (½ of a 2-ounce package) onion soup mix
2½　to 3 pounds meaty chicken pieces (breasts, thighs, and drumsticks)
　Hot cooked rice (optional)

1. In a bowl stir together cranberry sauce, salad dressing, and soup mix. Skin chicken, if desired. Arrange chicken pieces, meaty side down, in a 3-quart rectangular baking dish. Pour cranberry mixture over chicken pieces.

2. Bake, uncovered, in a 325°F oven about 1½ hours or until the chicken is tender and no longer pink (170°F for breasts; 180°F for thighs and drumsticks), stirring glaze and spooning over chicken once or twice. Serve over hot cooked rice.
Makes 4 to 6 servings.

Nutrition Facts per serving: 803 cal., 47 g total fat (9 g sat. fat), 141 mg chol., 919 mg sodium, 53 g carbo., 1 g fiber, 43 g pro. Daily Values: 9% vit. A, 10% vit. C, 4% calcium, 13% iron

Firecracker Fried Chicken

Prep: 10 min. • Marinate: 1 to 24 hours
Cook: 25 min.

8   chicken drumsticks (about 2 pounds)
1   2-ounce bottle hot pepper sauce (¼ cup)
⅓   cup self-rising flour
2   tablespoons yellow cornmeal
      Cooking oil (about 3 cups)

1. If desired, skin drumsticks. Place chicken in a self-sealing plastic bag set in a shallow dish. Pour hot pepper sauce over chicken. Seal bag. Marinate in the refrigerator for 1 to 24 hours, turning bag occasionally.

2. Drain chicken; discard marinade. In another plastic bag combine flour and cornmeal. Add chicken, a few pieces at a time, shaking to coat.

3. In a 12-inch skillet heat ½ inch oil over medium heat until a bread cube dropped into oil sizzles. Carefully add chicken to skillet. Cook, uncovered, over medium heat for 25 to 30 minutes or until chicken is tender and no longer pink (180°F), turning occasionally. Drain on paper towels; transfer to a serving platter. **Makes 4 servings.**

Nutrition Facts per serving: 328 cal., 22 g total fat (4 g sat. fat), 76 mg chol., 406 mg sodium, 10 g carbo., 0 g fiber, 22 g pro. Daily Values: 4% vit. A, 6% vit. C, 105% iron

Honey-Glazed Chicken Drumsticks

Prep: 10 min. • Bake: 45 min.

3   tablespoons honey
3   tablespoons Dijon-style mustard
1   teaspoon lemon juice
1   teaspoon finely shredded orange peel
8   chicken drumsticks (about 2 pounds)

1. For sauce, stir together honey, mustard, lemon juice, and orange peel. Set aside. Place drumsticks on a rack in a roasting pan. Bake in a 375°F oven for 45 to 55 minutes or until tender and no longer pink (180°F), brushing with sauce during last half of baking time. **Makes 4 servings.**

Nutrition Facts per serving: 241 cal., 9 g total fat (2 g sat. fat), 87 mg chol., 370 mg sodium, 14 g carbo., 0 g fiber, 26 g pro. Daily Values: 1% vit. A, 2% vit. C, 1% calcium, 8% iron

Self-Rising Flour

If you don't happen to have self-rising flour on hand, you can make your own. Stir together 1 cup of all-purpose flour, 1 teaspoon baking powder, ½ teaspoon salt, and ¼ teaspoon baking soda. Makes 1 cup of self-rising flour.

Sweet-Hot Chicken

Prep: 10 min. • Bake: 45 min.

8   chicken drumsticks and/or thighs
     (about 2 pounds)
¼   cup finely chopped green onions
¼   cup honey
¼   teaspoon garlic powder
     Dash ground red pepper

1. Arrange chicken pieces in a 15×10×1-inch baking pan. Bake in a 375°F oven for 30 minutes. Meanwhile, stir together remaining ingredients. Brush chicken with honey mixture. Bake for 15 to 20 minutes more or until chicken is tender and no longer pink (180°F).
Makes 4 servings.

Nutrition Facts per serving: 308 cal., 13 g total fat (4 g sat. fat), 123 mg chol., 103 mg sodium, 18 g carbo., 0 g fiber, 29 g pro. Daily Values: 3% vit. A, 7% vit. C, 2% calcium, 9% iron

Garlic-Roasted Chicken

Prep: 10 min. • Bake: 35 min.

4   chicken breast halves (about 2 pounds)
1   tablespoon lemon juice
1   teaspoon olive oil or cooking oil
4   cloves garlic, minced
½   teaspoon seasoned salt

1. Place chicken, skin side up, in a lightly greased roasting pan. In a small bowl combine remaining ingredients. Brush mixture on chicken breast halves. Bake in a 425°F oven for 35 minutes or until chicken is tender and no longer pink (170°F).
Makes 4 servings.

Nutrition Facts per serving: 317 cal., 17 g total fat (5 g sat. fat), 115 mg chol., 282 mg sodium, 1 g carbo., 0 g fiber, 38 g pro. Daily Values: 2% vit. A, 7% vit. C, 2% calcium, 7% iron

Marinated Chicken Breasts

Prep: 20 min. • Marinate: 8 hours
Grill: 50 min.

- 4   to 6 chicken breast halves (1¼ to 2 pounds)
- 1½   cups dry white wine
- ½   cup olive oil
- 1   tablespoon dried Italian seasoning, crushed
- 2   teaspoons minced fresh garlic

1. Skin chicken, if desired. Place chicken in a self-sealing plastic bag set in a shallow baking dish. Stir together remaining ingredients. Pour over chicken. Close bag. Marinate in the refrigerator for 8 hours or overnight.

2. Drain chicken, reserving marinade. In a covered grill arrange preheated coals around a drip pan. Test for medium heat above the pan. Place chicken on a grill rack, bone side up, over the pan. Cover and grill for 50 to 60 minutes or until chicken is tender and no longer pink (170°F), turning once. Brush chicken once with reserved marinade halfway through grilling.
Makes 4 to 6 servings.

Nutrition Facts per serving: 404 cal., 25 g total fat (6 g sat. fat), 115 mg chol., 93 mg sodium, 1 g carbo., 0 g fiber, 38 g pro. Daily Values: 2% vit. A, 3% vit. C, 3% calcium, 9% iron

German-Style Chicken

Prep: 10 min. • Bake: 45 min.

- ¼   cup Dusseldorf mustard or horseradish mustard
- 2   tablespoons dry sherry
- ½   teaspoon sweet Hungarian paprika or ¼ teaspoon hot Hungarian paprika
- 4   skinless, boneless chicken breast halves (about 1¼ pounds)
- ½   cup soft rye bread crumbs

1. Combine mustard, sherry, and paprika. Brush 2 tablespoons of mustard mixture evenly over top of chicken. Place chicken, mustard side up, in a 3-quart rectangular baking dish. Sprinkle with bread crumbs, patting lightly. Bake, uncovered, in a 375°F oven for 45 to 50 minutes or until chicken is tender and no longer pink (170°F). Serve with remaining mustard mixture.
Makes 4 servings.

Nutrition Facts per serving: 232 cal., 9 g total fat (2 g sat. fat), 83 mg chol., 306 mg sodium, 4 g carbo., 0 g fiber, 31 g pro. Daily Values: 4% vit. A, 3% calcium, 10% iron

Why Marinate?

Marinades tenderize and flavor meats, poultry, and fish. They usually consist of an acid (such as vinegar, lemon juice, or wine), seasonings, and cooking or olive oil. Because marinades contain acid, always marinate in a ceramic, glass, or stainless steel container—never aluminum. Better yet, use a big plastic bag to simplify cleanup. Turn the bag occasionally to ensure that the marinade is evenly distributed.

Chicken with Dried Fruit and Honey

Start to Finish: 25 min.

- 8   skinless, boneless chicken thighs (about 1½ pounds)
- ½   teaspoon pumpkin pie spice or ¼ teaspoon ground ginger
- 1   tablespoon butter
- 1   cup mixed dried fruit bits
- ¼   cup honey
- ⅓   cup water

1. Sprinkle one side of chicken thighs with pumpkin pie spice. In a 12-inch skillet cook thighs in hot butter about 2 minutes on each side or until brown. Stir in remaining ingredients. Bring to boiling; reduce heat. Simmer, covered, for 10 to 15 minutes or until chicken is tender and no longer pink (180°F). **Makes 4 servings.**

Nutrition Facts per serving. 301 cal., 9 g total fat (4 g sat. fat), 149 mg chol., 171 mg sodium, 41 g carbo., 0 g fiber, 35 g pro. Daily Values: 4% vit. A, 8% vit. C, 3% calcium, 11% iron

Balsamic Chicken over Greens

Prep: 15 min. • Marinate: 1 hour
Broil: 12 min.

- 4   skinless, boneless chicken breast halves (about 1¼ pounds)
- 1   cup bottled balsamic vinaigrette salad dressing
- 3   cloves garlic, minced
- ¼   teaspoon crushed red pepper
- 8   cups torn mixed salad greens

1. Place chicken in a self-sealing plastic bag set in a shallow dish. For marinade, stir together ½ cup of the vinaigrette, the garlic, and red pepper. Pour marinade over chicken; close bag. Marinate in the refrigerator for 1 to 4 hours, turning occasionally.

2. Drain chicken, reserving marinade. Place chicken on the unheated rack of a broiler pan. Broil 4 to 5 inches from heat for 12 to 15 minutes or until chicken is tender and no longer pink (170°F), turning once and brushing once with marinade halfway through broiling. Discard any remaining marinade.

3. Arrange greens on serving plates. Cut chicken into strips. Place chicken on top of greens. Drizzle with remaining vinaigrette. **Makes 4 servings.**

Nutrition Facts per serving: 284 cal., 13 g total fat (2 g sat. fat), 82 mg chol., 525 mg sodium, 7 g carbo., 1 g fiber, 34 g pro. Daily Values: 21% vit. A, 14% vit. C, 6% calcium, 8% iron

Chicken with Cranberry Sauce

Start to Finish: 20 min.

- 4 skinless, boneless chicken breast halves (about 1¼ pounds)
- 1 tablespoon butter or margarine
- ½ of a 16-ounce can whole cranberry sauce (1 cup)
- 2 tablespoons honey
- ½ teaspoon ground ginger

1. In a large skillet cook chicken in hot butter over medium heat for 12 to 14 minutes or until chicken is tender and no longer pink (170°F), turning once. Remove chicken from skillet, reserving drippings in skillet. Cover; keep warm.

2. For sauce, stir remaining ingredients into reserved drippings in skillet; heat through. To serve, spoon sauce over chicken.
Makes 4 servings.

Nutrition Facts per serving: 274 cal., 5 g total fat (2 g sat. fat), 74 mg chol., 110 mg sodium, 31 g carbo., 1 g fiber, 27 g pro. Daily Values: 3% vit. A, 4% vit. C, 2% calcium, 5% iron

Pepper and Peach Fajita Chicken

Start to Finish: 30 min.

- 4 skinless, boneless chicken breast halves (about 1¼ pounds)
- 1½ teaspoons fajita seasoning
- 2 tablespoons olive oil or butter
- 1½ cups sweet pepper strips
- 1 medium fresh peach or nectarine, cut into thin slices, or 1 cup frozen peach slices, thawed

1. Sprinkle both sides of chicken with seasoning. In a large skillet cook chicken in 1 tablespoon of the oil over medium heat for 12 to 14 minutes or until chicken is tender and no longer pink (170°F), turning once. Transfer chicken to a serving platter; keep warm.

2. Add remaining oil to skillet. Add pepper strips. Cook and stir for 3 minutes or until pepper strips are crisp-tender. Gently stir in peach slices. Cook for 1 to 2 minutes more or until heated through. Spoon pepper strips and peach mixture over chicken.
Makes 4 servings.

Nutrition Facts per serving: 243 cal., 9 g total fat (1 g sat. fat), 82 mg chol., 150 mg sodium, 7 g carbo., 2 g fiber, 33 g pro. Daily Values: 64% vit. A, 155% vit. C, 2% calcium, 7% iron

Molasses and Orange-Glazed Chicken

Prep: 5 min. • Broil: 12 min.

- 2 **tablespoons frozen orange juice concentrate, thawed**
- 2 **tablespoons molasses**
- ¼ **teaspoon onion powder**
- 4 **skinless, boneless chicken breast halves (about 1¼ pounds)**
  Salt and black pepper

1. For glaze, in a small bowl stir together orange juice concentrate, molasses, and onion powder. Season chicken with salt and pepper; place on the unheated rack of a broiler pan. Broil 4 to 5 inches from the heat for 6 minutes. Brush with some of the glaze. Turn chicken; brush with remaining glaze. Broil for 6 to 9 minutes more or until chicken is tender and no longer pink (170°F).
Makes 4 servings.

Nutrition Facts per serving: 202 cal., 23 g total fat (1 g sat. fat), 82 mg chol., 116 mg sodium, 10 g carbo., 0 g fiber, 33 g pro. Daily Values: 1% vit. A, 23% vit. C, 4% calcium, 8% iron

Tangy Lemon Chicken

Prep: 10 min. • Marinate: 2 hours
Grill: 12 min.

- 4 **skinless, boneless chicken breast halves (about 1¼ pounds)**
- ½ **cup bottled creamy Italian salad dressing**
- 1 **tablespoon finely shredded lemon peel**
- ¼ **cup lemon juice**
  Dash black pepper

1. Place chicken in a self-sealing plastic bag set in a bowl. For marinade, in a small bowl stir together remaining ingredients. Pour over chicken. Seal bag. Marinate in the refrigerator for 2 to 4 hours, turning bag occasionally. Drain chicken, reserving marinade.

2. Grill chicken on the rack of an uncovered grill directly over medium coals for 12 to 15 minutes or until chicken is tender and no longer pink (170°F), turning once and brushing with marinade halfway through grilling. Discard any remaining marinade.
Makes 4 servings.

Nutrition Facts per serving: 177 cal., 6 g total fat (1 g sat. fat), 66 mg chol., 179 mg sodium, 2 g carbo., 0 g fiber, 26 g pro. Daily Values: 9% vit. C, 1% calcium, 5% iron

Chicken and Pea Pods

Prep: 10 min. • Cook: 14 min.

- 4 skinless, boneless chicken breast halves (about 1¼ pounds)
- 2 teaspoons lemon-pepper seasoning
- 3 tablespoons butter or margarine
- 2 cups fresh sugar snap peas

1. Sprinkle both sides of chicken breast halves with 1½ teaspoons of seasoning. In a large skillet cook chicken in 2 tablespoons of the butter over medium heat for 12 to 14 minutes or until chicken is tender and no longer pink (170°F), turning once. Remove chicken from skillet; keep warm. Add remaining butter to skillet. Stir in peas and remaining seasoning. Cook and stir over medium heat for 2 to 3 minutes or until peas are crisp-tender. Transfer chicken to a serving platter. Spoon peas over chicken.
Makes 4 servings.

Nutrition Facts per serving: 259 cal., 11 g total fat (6 g sat. fat), 107 mg chol., 716 mg sodium, 5 g carbo., 1 g fiber, 34 g pro. Daily Values: 27% vit. A, 19% vit. C, 6% calcium, 9% iron

Pesto Chicken with Squash

Start to Finish: 15 min.

- 4 skinless, boneless chicken breast halves (about 1¼ pounds)
- 1 tablespoon olive oil or cooking oil
- 2 cups finely chopped zucchini and/or yellow summer squash
- 2 tablespoons purchased basil pesto
- 2 tablespoons finely shredded Asiago or Parmesan cheese

1. In a large nonstick skillet cook chicken in hot oil over medium heat for 4 minutes. Turn chicken; add zucchini. Cook for 4 to 6 minutes more or until chicken is tender and no longer pink (170°F) and squash is crisp-tender, stirring squash gently once or twice. Transfer chicken and squash to 4 dinner plates. Spread pesto over chicken; sprinkle with cheese.
Makes 4 servings.

Nutrition Facts per serving: 186 cal., 10 g total fat (2 g sat. fat), 55 mg chol., 129 mg sodium, 2 g carbo., 1 g fiber, 23 g pro. Daily Values: 4% vit. A, 10% vit. C, 7% calcium, 5% iron

Golden Skillet Chicken

Start to Finish: 20 min.

4   skinless, boneless chicken breast halves
    (about 1¼ pounds)
1   10¾-ounce can condensed golden
    mushroom soup
¾   cup reduced-sodium chicken broth
½   of an 8-ounce tub cream cheese with
    chives and onion
8   ounces angel hair pasta or thin spaghetti,
    cooked and drained

1. Place each chicken breast half, boned side
up, between 2 pieces of plastic wrap. Pound
lightly until ¼ inch thick. Discard plastic wrap.

2. Heat a large nonstick skillet over medium-
high heat for 1 minute. Add chicken; cook for 4 to
5 minutes or until chicken is tender and no longer
pink (170°F), turning once. (If necessary, cook
half the chicken at a time.) Remove chicken from
skillet; keep warm.

3. Add soup, broth, and cream cheese to hot
skillet. Cook and stir over medium heat until
mixture is heated through. Serve chicken and
sauce over hot cooked pasta.

Makes 4 servings.

Nutrition Facts per serving: 520 cal., 14 g total fat
(8 g sat. fat), 113 mg chol., 906 mg sodium, 51 g carbo.,
2 g fiber, 43 g pro. Daily Values: 17% vit. A, 2% vit. C,
6% calcium, 16% iron

Skillet Chicken Alfredo

Start to Finish: 20 min.

1   10-ounce package frozen broccoli or
    asparagus spears
12 ounces skinless, boneless chicken breast
    halves or turkey breast tenderloins
1   tablespoon cooking oil
1   10- or 12-ounce container Alfredo pasta
    sauce
4   English muffins or bagels, split and toasted

1. Cook broccoli according to package
directions; drain and keep warm. Meanwhile,
cut chicken crosswise into ½-inch strips. In a
large skillet cook chicken in hot oil over
medium-high heat for 3 to 4 minutes or until
tender and no longer pink (170°F). Drain fat.
Stir in pasta sauce. Simmer for 2 to 3 minutes or
until sauce is heated through. Place toasted
muffin or bagel halves on plates. Arrange
broccoli spears on top. Spoon chicken and
sauce over all.

Makes 4 servings.

Nutrition Facts per serving: 497 cal., 28 g total fat
(1 g sat. fat), 85 mg chol., 573 mg sodium, 33 g carbo.,
4 g fiber, 30 g pro. Daily Values: 27% vit. A, 51% vit. C,
14% calcium, 14% iron

Mustard-Puff Chicken

Prep: 5 min. • Broil: 9 min.

4   skinless, boneless chicken breasts halves
        (about 1¼ pounds)
⅓   cup mayonnaise or salad dressing
1   tablespoon Dijon-style mustard
1   tablespoon sliced green onion
       Dash ground red pepper

1. Place chicken on the unheated rack of a broiler pan. Broil 4 to 5 inches from the heat for 5 minutes. Meanwhile, in a small bowl stir together remaining ingredients. Turn chicken; brush liberally with mayonnaise mixture. Broil for 4 to 6 minutes more or until chicken is tender and no longer pink (170°F).
Makes 4 servings.

Nutrition Facts per serving: 265 cal., 17 g total fat
(2 g sat. fat), 72 mg chol., 182 mg sodium, 1 g carbo.,
0 g fiber, 27 g pro. Daily Values: 1% vit. A, 2% vit. C,
2% calcium, 5% iron

Buttermilk Pan-Fried Chicken

Prep: 5 minutes • Cook: 10 minutes

¾   cup fine dry bread crumbs
½   of a 0.7-ounce package dry Italian salad
        dressing mix (2½ teaspoons)
½   cup buttermilk
4   skinless, boneless chicken breast halves
        (about 1¼ pounds)
2   tablespoons cooking oil

1. In a shallow dish combine bread crumbs and salad dressing mix. Pour buttermilk into a small bowl. Dip chicken breast halves into buttermilk; coat with bread crumb mixture. Heat oil in a large nonstick skillet over medium heat. Arrange chicken in skillet so that pieces don't touch. Reduce heat to medium low. Cook, uncovered, for 10 to 12 minutes or until chicken is tender and no longer pink (170°F), turning once to brown evenly. Transfer to a serving platter.
Makes 4 servings.

Nutrition Facts per serving: 289 cal., 10 g total fat
(2 g sat. fat), 83 mg chol., 822 mg sodium, 13 g carbo.,
1 g fiber, 35 g pro. Daily Values: 1% vit. A, 3% vit. C,
9% calcium, 10% iron

Italian Grilled Chicken

Prep: 10 min. • Marinate: 24 hours
Grill: 12 min.

8   skinless, boneless chicken breast halves
      (about 2½ pounds)
¾   cup bottled Italian salad dressing

1. Place chicken in a self-sealing plastic bag set in a large bowl. Pour dressing over chicken. Close bag and turn chicken to coat well. Marinate in the refrigerator for 24 hours, turning occasionally. Drain chicken, reserving marinade.

2. Grill chicken on the rack of an uncovered grill directly over medium coals for 8 minutes, brushing occasionally with marinade. Turn chicken and grill for 4 to 5 minutes more or until chicken is tender and no longer pink (170°F). **Makes 8 servings.**

Nutrition Facts per serving: 232 cal., 12 g total fat (2 g sat. fat), 66 mg chol., 235 mg sodium, 2 g carbo., 0 g fiber, 26 g pro. Daily Values: 1% vit. A, 2% vit. C, 2% calcium, 4% iron

Chicken Phyllo Bundles

Prep: 30 min. • Bake: 25 min.

4   skinless, boneless chicken breast halves
      (about 1¼ pounds)
      Freshly ground black pepper
1   5-ounce container semisoft cheese with
      French onions, garlic, and herb or
      garden vegetables
8   sheets frozen phyllo dough, thawed
⅓   cup butter, melted

1. Place each chicken breast half, boned side up, between 2 pieces of plastic wrap. Pound lightly until about ¼ inch thick. Discard plastic wrap. Sprinkle chicken with pepper. Divide cheese into 4 pieces; form into balls. Place a cheese ball in the center of each piece of chicken. Fold in the sides and roll up.

2. Evenly stack 8 phyllo dough sheets on a work surface. Cut the stack into 12-inch squares; discard trimmings.

3. Generously brush one square with butter. Place another square on top; brush with butter. Keep the remaining 6 squares of phyllo covered with plastic wrap to prevent drying.

4. Place a chicken breast, seam side down, on the buttered sheets. Gather up the phyllo to form a bundle, twisting top slightly to hold it together. Transfer to a foil-lined baking sheet. Repeat with the remaining phyllo squares and chicken breasts. Bake in a 375°F oven for 25 to 30 minutes or until phyllo is golden and chicken is tender (170°F).
Makes 4 servings.

Nutrition Facts per serving: 548 cal., 32 g total fat (19 g sat. fat), 158 mg chol., 424 mg sodium, 21 g carbo., 1 g fiber, 38 g pro. Daily Values: 13% vit. A, 2% vit. C, 5% calcium, 12% iron

Stuffed Chicken Breasts

Prep: 25 min. • Cook: 14 min.

- 4   skinless, boneless chicken breast halves (about 1¼ pounds)
- 4   ounces feta cheese with peppercorn, feta cheese with garlic and herb, or feta cheese, crumbled
- ½   of a 7-ounce jar roasted red sweet peppers, drained and cut into strips (½ cup)
- 1   tablespoon olive oil
- ¼   cup chicken broth

1. Place each chicken breast half, boned side up, between 2 pieces of plastic wrap. Pound lightly until ¼ inch thick. Discard plastic wrap.

2. Sprinkle chicken with cheese. Place roasted pepper strips in the center of each breast. Fold in sides and roll up, pressing the edges to seal. Secure with toothpicks.

3. In a large nonstick skillet cook chicken in hot oil over medium heat about 5 minutes, turning to brown all sides. Add broth. Bring to boiling; reduce heat. Simmer, covered, for 7 to 8 minutes or until chicken is tender and no longer pink (170°F). Spoon juices over chicken.
Makes 4 servings.

Nutrition Facts per serving: 265 cal., 11 g total fat
(5 g sat. fat), 107 mg chol., 449 mg sodium, 2 g carbo.,
0 g fiber, 37 g pro. Daily Values: 3% vit. A, 77% vit. C,
15% calcium, 7% iron

Cheesy Mediterranean Chicken

Prep: 20 min. • Cook: 25 min.

- 4   skinless, boneless chicken breast halves (about 1¼ pounds)
- 4   oil-packed dried tomato halves, drained and cut into strips
- 2   ounces mascarpone cheese or feta cheese
- 4   teaspoons snipped fresh oregano, basil, tarragon, or parsley or ½ teaspoon dried oregano, basil, tarragon, or parsley, crushed
- 2   tablespoons olive oil

1. Place each chicken breast half, boned side up, between 2 sheets of plastic wrap. Pound lightly until ¼ inch thick. Discard plastic wrap.

2. On each breast, layer some of the tomatoes, cheese, and herb. Fold narrow ends over filling; fold in sides. Roll up each breast half from a short side. Secure with toothpicks.

3. In a medium skillet cook chicken in hot oil over medium-low heat about 25 minutes or until tender and no longer pink (170°F), turning to brown evenly.
Makes 4 servings.

Nutrition Facts per serving: 257 cal., 17 g total fat
(6 g sat. fat), 77 mg chol., 114 mg sodium, 2 g carbo.,
0 g fiber, 25 g pro. Daily Values: 1% vit. A, 11% vit. C,
1% calcium, 5% iron

Florentine Chicken

Start to Finish: 45 min.

1   12-ounce package frozen spinach soufflé
4   skinless, boneless chicken breast halves
      (about 1¼ pounds)
1   4-ounce can sliced mushroom stems and
      pieces, drained
½   cup shredded cheddar cheese (2 ounces)

1. Run warm water over spinach soufflé for a few seconds to loosen it from the pan. Remove soufflé from pan and divide into 4 squares. Place each chicken breast half, boned side up, between 2 pieces of plastic wrap. Pound the chicken lightly until ¼ inch thick. Discard plastic wrap.

2. Place chicken pieces in a greased 3-quart rectangular baking dish. Top each piece with some of the mushrooms and 1 portion of soufflé. Bake in a 400°F oven for 20 minutes. Sprinkle shredded cheese on top of each piece. Bake about 5 minutes more or until chicken is tender and no longer pink (170°F) and the cheese is melted.
Makes 4 servings.

Nutrition Facts per serving: 331 cal., 14 g total fat
(5 g sat. fat), 187 mg chol., 642 mg sodium, 8 g carbo.,
1 g fiber, 41 g pro. Daily Values: 30% vit. A, 4% vit. C,
20% calcium, 10% iron

Apricot-Cranberry Chicken

Prep: 1 hour • Bake: 25 min.

6   skinless, boneless chicken breast halves
      (about 2 pounds)
1½   cups herb-seasoned stuffing mix
½   cup apricot jam
⅓   cup dried cranberries
¼   cup butter or margarine, melted

1. Place each chicken breast half, boned side up, between 2 pieces of plastic wrap. Pound lightly until about ⅛ inch thick. Discard plastic wrap. Set chicken aside.

2. In a medium bowl combine stuffing mix, ⅓ cup of the jam, ¼ cup of the cranberries, and 3 tablespoons of the butter. Stir until moistened; set aside.

3. For glaze, in a small bowl, stir together the remaining jam, cranberries, and melted butter. Set glaze aside. Place some of stuffing mixture on each chicken piece. Fold in sides and roll up. Secure with toothpicks. Place chicken rolls in a greased 3-quart rectangular baking dish. Bake, uncovered, in a 400°F oven for 15 minutes. Brush glaze mixture over chicken. Bake for 10 to 15 minutes more or until chicken is tender and no longer pink (170°F).
Makes 6 servings.

Nutrition Facts per serving: 393 cal., 11 g total fat
(6 g sat. fat), 109 mg chol., 374 mg sodium, 35 g carbo.,
2 g fiber, 37 g pro. Daily Values: 7% vit. A, 6% vit. C,
4% calcium, 10% iron

Sweet Ginger Stir-Fry

Prep: 10 min. • Cook: 8 min.

12 ounces skinless, boneless chicken breast
      halves or skinless, boneless chicken
      thighs
 2 tablespoons cooking oil
 2 cups loose-pack frozen mixed vegetables
 ½ cup purchased sweet ginger stir-fry sauce
 2 cups hot cooked rice

1. Cut chicken into 1-inch pieces; set aside. In a wok or large skillet heat oil over medium-high heat. Add vegetables; cook and stir for 3 minutes or until vegetables are crisp-tender. Remove vegetables from wok. Add chicken to hot wok. (Add more oil if necessary.) Cook and stir for 3 to 4 minutes or until chicken is no longer pink. Push chicken from center of the wok. Add sauce to center of the wok. Cook and stir until bubbly. Return cooked vegetables to wok; heat through. Serve over hot cooked rice. **Makes 4 servings.**

Nutrition Facts per serving: 382 cal., 9 g total fat
(1 g sat. fat), 49 mg chol., 879 mg sodium, 50 g carbo.,
3 g fiber, 24 g pro. Daily Values: 70% vit. A, 12% vit. C,
4% calcium, 13% iron

Ranch-Style Chicken Strips

Prep: 15 min. • Bake: 12 min.

      Nonstick cooking spray
 2 cups crushed cornflakes
 2 tablespoons snipped fresh basil or
      1 teaspoon dried basil, crushed
 1 8-ounce bottle buttermilk ranch salad
      dressing
12 ounces skinless, boneless chicken breast
      halves, cut into thin strips

1. Lightly coat a 15×10×1-inch baking pan with cooking spray; set aside. In a shallow dish combine the cornflakes and basil. In another dish place ½ cup of the dressing. Dip chicken strips into dressing, roll in crumb mixture to coat. Arrange strips in prepared pan. Bake in a 425°F oven for 12 to 15 minutes or until chicken is tender and no longer pink (170°F). Serve with remaining dressing.
Makes 4 servings.

Nutrition Facts per serving: 543 cal., 32 g total fat
(5 g sat. fat), 54 mg chol., 928 mg sodium, 38 g carbo.,
0 g fiber, 24 g pro. Daily Values: 1% vit. A, 2% vit. C,
1% calcium, 43% iron

Chile-Lime Chicken Skewers

Prep: 20 min. • Broil: 10 min.

1 **pound skinless, boneless chicken breasts**
2 **limes**
1½ **teaspoons ground ancho chile pepper**
1 **teaspoon garlic-herb seasoning**

1. Cut chicken into 1-inch strips. Place chicken strips in a shallow dish; set aside. Finely shred enough peel from one of the limes to measure 1 teaspoon (chill lime and use another time). Cut remaining lime into wedges and set aside. For rub, combine lime peel and remaining ingredients. Using your fingers, rub into the chicken.

2. On 4 long metal skewers thread chicken accordion-style, leaving ¼ inch between pieces. Place skewers on the unheated rack of a broiler pan. Broil 4 to 5 inches from heat for 10 to 12 minutes or until chicken is no longer pink. Serve with lime wedges.
Makes 4 servings.

Nutrition Facts per serving: 132 cal., 2 g total fat (0 g sat. fat), 66 mg chol., 62 mg sodium, 1 g carbo., 0 g fiber, 26 g pro. Daily Values: 5% vit. A, 10% vit. C, 1% calcium, 4% iron

Barbecued Chicken Pizza

Prep: 20 min. • Bake: 19 min.

1 **10-ounce package refrigerated pizza dough**
½ **of a 32-ounce container shredded cooked chicken in barbecue sauce (about 2 cups)**
1 **8-ounce package shredded four-cheese pizza blend**
¼ **cup snipped fresh cilantro**

1. In a greased 15×10×1-inch baking pan unroll pizza dough. Using your hands, press dough into a 12×10-inch rectangle. Build up the edges slightly. Bake dough in a 425°F oven for 7 minutes. Remove from oven.

2. Spread chicken evenly over hot crust. Sprinkle with cheese and cilantro. Bake for 12 to 15 minutes more or until lightly brown. Cut into wedges.
Makes 6 servings.

Nutrition Facts per serving: 324 cal., 13 g total fat (6 g sat. fat), 39 mg chol., 683 mg sodium, 33 g carbo., 1 g fiber, 20 g pro. Daily Values: 13% vit. C, 19% calcium, 9% iron

Mushroom-Tomato-Pesto Pizza

Prep: 15 min. • Bake: 10 min.

1   12-inch Italian bread shell (Boboli)
½   cup purchased dried tomato pesto
1   cup shredded four-cheese pizza blend
1   6-ounce package refrigerated Italian-
      seasoned cooked chicken breast strips
1½   cups sliced mushrooms

1. Place bread shell in a 12-inch pizza pan. Spread pesto over bread shell. Sprinkle with half of the cheese. Top with the chicken pieces and mushrooms. Sprinkle with the remaining cheese. Bake in a 400°F oven for 10 to 15 minutes or until cheese is golden and bubbly.
Makes 4 servings.

Nutrition Facts per serving: 585 cal., 24 g total fat (8 g sat. fat), 55 mg chol., 1,382 mg sodium, 64 g carbo., 4 g fiber, 33 g pro. Daily Values: 8% vit. A, 8% vit. C, 40% calcium, 26% iron

Fast Chicken Fettuccine

Start to Finish: 20 min.

1   9-ounce package refrigerated red sweet
      pepper fettuccine
¼   of a 7-ounce jar oil-packed dried tomato
      strips or pieces (¼ cup)
1   large zucchini or yellow summer squash,
      halved lengthwise and sliced (about
      2 cups)
8   ounces skinless, boneless chicken breast
      strips for stir-fry
½   cup finely shredded Parmesan, Romano, or
      Asiago cheese (2 ounces)

1. Cut pasta in half. Cook according to package directions; drain. Return pasta to hot pan.

2. Meanwhile, drain tomato strips, reserving 2 tablespoons oil from jar; set aside. In a large skillet cook and stir zucchini in 1 tablespoon reserved oil over medium-high heat for 2 to 3 minutes or until crisp-tender. Remove from skillet. Add remaining reserved oil to skillet. Add chicken; cook and stir for 2 to 3 minutes or until no longer pink. Add zucchini, chicken, tomato strips, and cheese to cooked pasta; toss gently to combine.
Makes 4 servings.

Nutrition Facts per serving: 394 cal., 15 g total fat (5 g sat. fat), 113 mg chol., 231 mg sodium, 39 g carbo., 3 g fiber, 26 g pro. Daily Values: 10% vit. A, 29% vit. C, 16% calcium, 13% iron

Tequila-Lime Chicken

Start to Finish: 15 min.

1   9-ounce package refrigerated fettuccini
1   lime
1   10-ounce container refrigerated regular or
      light Alfredo sauce
¼   cup tequila or milk
1   9-ounce package refrigerated grilled
      chicken breast strips

1. Cook fettuccini according to package directions; drain. Meanwhile, finely shred enough peel from lime to equal 1 teaspoon. Cut lime into wedges and set aside. In a medium saucepan heat and stir Alfredo sauce, peel, and tequila just to boiling. Stir in chicken strips; heat through. Toss sauce with hot fettuccini Serve with lime wedges.

Makes 4 servings.

Nutrition Facts per serving: 528 cal., 24 g total fat
(1 g sat. fat), 123 mg chol., 853 mg sodium, 39 g carbo.,
2 g fiber, 11 g pro. Daily Values: 1% vit. A, 1% vit. C,
1% calcium, 15% iron

Sweet Chicken Tostadas

Start to Finish: 20 min.

8   tostada shells
½   cup dairy sour cream
1   cup purchased fruit salsa
1½ cups chopped cooked chicken
1   cup shredded Monterey Jack cheese with
      jalapeño peppers (4 ounces)

1. Spread one side of each tostada shell with sour cream, spreading to edges. Spread salsa evenly on top of sour cream on each tostada. Top each tostada with chicken and cheese.

2. Place 4 of the tostadas on a large baking sheet. Place on a broiler rack 4 to 5 inches from the heat. Broil for 1 to 1½ minutes or until cheese is melted. Repeat with remaining tostadas. Serve warm.

Makes 4 servings.

Nutrition Facts per serving: 511 cal., 26 g total fat
(12 g sat. fat), 89 mg chol., 488 mg sodium, 42 g carbo.,
4 g fiber, 27 g pro. Daily Values: 12% vit. A, 27% calcium,
7% iron

Thai Chicken Pasta

Start to Finish: 20 min.

8   ounces dried angel hair pasta

3   cups frozen cooked chicken breast strips, thawed

1   14-ounce can unsweetened coconut milk

1   teaspoon Thai seasoning

¼   cup roasted peanuts

1. Cook pasta according to package directions; drain well. Return pasta to pan; keep warm.

2. Meanwhile, in a large skillet combine the chicken strips, coconut milk, and seasoning. Cook and stir over medium heat until mixture is heated through. Pour hot chicken mixture over cooked pasta in pan. Toss gently to coat. Transfer to a serving platter or bowl. Sprinkle with peanuts.

Makes 4 servings.

Nutrition Facts per serving: 644 cal., 31 g total fat (19 g sat. fat), 93 mg chol., 236 mg sodium, 47 g carbo., 2 g fiber, 42 g pro. Daily Values: 1% vit. A, 3% calcium, 23% iron

Chopped Cooked Chicken

Time- and simplicity-conscious recipes often call for cooked chicken. If you don't have leftovers, you can buy a deli-roasted chicken. One average bird yields 1½ to 2 cups chopped chicken. Another option includes poaching chicken breasts. In a large skillet bring 12 ounces of boneless chicken breasts and 1½ cups water to boiling; reduce heat. Simmer, covered, for 12 to 15 minutes. Drain well. Twelve ounces of breasts yield about 2 cups cubed cooked chicken.

Cheesy Corn and Chicken Turnovers

Prep: 25 min. • Bake: 15 min.

1   15-ounce package folded refrigerated unbaked piecrust (2 crusts)

1   11-ounce can whole kernel corn with sweet peppers, drained

2   cups chopped cooked chicken

1   cup shredded cheddar cheese (4 ounces)

1   10¾-ounce can condensed cream of chicken and herbs or cream of mushroom soup

1. Let piecrusts stand according to package directions. In a medium bowl combine corn, chicken, cheese, and soup. Unfold piecrusts according to package directions. On a lightly floured surface, roll each piecrust into a 13-inch circle. Cut each piecrust into quarters. Spoon about ½ cup chicken mixture along one straight side of each triangle, about ¾ inch from edge. Brush edges of triangle with a little water. Fold other straight side of triangle over the filling. Seal with a fork. Prick the top of pastry several times with a fork. Repeat with remaining pastry and filling. Place wedges on a large greased baking sheet. Bake in a 400°F oven for 15 minutes or until pastry is golden brown.

Makes 4 servings.

Nutrition Facts per serving: 862 cal., 47 g total fat (21 g sat. fat), 118 mg chol., 1,625 mg sodium, 73 g carbo., 3 g fiber, 33 g pro. Daily Values: 13% vit. A, 2% vit. C, 23% calcium, 7% iron

Five-Spice Chicken

Prep: 15 min. • Bake: 15 min.

⅓ cup bottled hoisin sauce
1 to 1½ teaspoons five-spice powder
Orange juice
1 1½- to 2-pound hot deli-cooked
rotisserie chicken
2 3-ounce package ramen noodles

1. In a small bowl stir together hoisin sauce, five-spice powder, and enough orange juice (1 to 2 tablespoons) to thin mixture for brushing. Brush about half of the mixture over entire chicken. Place chicken on a rack in a shallow roasting pan.

2. Bake, uncovered, in a 400°F oven for 15 to 18 minutes or until heated through (165°F) and glazed. Stir 1 to 2 tablespoons additional orange juice into remaining hoisin mixture until easy to drizzle. Place hoisin mixture in a small saucepan; heat through. Discard seasoning packets from ramen noodles. Cook and drain noodles according to package directions.

3. To serve, carve the chicken. Arrange chicken slices and ramen noodles on 4 dinner plates. Spoon half of the sauce over chicken; pass remaining sauce.
Makes 4 servings.

Nutrition Facts per serving: 429 cal., 13 g total fat (4 g sat. fat), 115 mg chol., 491 mg sodium, 43 g carbo., 1 g fiber, 29 g pro. Daily Values: 3% vit. A, 3% vit. C, 3% calcium, 15% iron

Chicken Alfredo Pot Pies

Prep: 20 min. • Bake: 12 min.

½ of a 15-ounce package folded refrigerated
unbaked piecrust (1 crust)
3 cups frozen mixed vegetable blend
3 cups cubed cooked chicken
1 10-ounce carton refrigerated Alfredo sauce
(about 1 cup)
½ teaspoon dried sage, marjoram, or
thyme, crushed

1. Let piecrust stand according to package directions. In a large skillet cook vegetables in a small amount of boiling water for 5 minutes; drain. Return to skillet. Stir in remaining ingredients. Cook and stir until bubbly. Divide mixture among four 10-ounce casseroles or custard cups.

2. On a lightly floured surface, roll crust into a 13-inch round. Cut four 5-inch circles and place on top of the casseroles. Press edges of pastry firmly against sides of casseroles. Cut slits in the top for steam to escape. Place casseroles in a foil-lined shallow baking pan. Bake in a 450°F oven for 12 to 15 minutes or until pastry is golden brown.
Makes 4 servings.

Nutrition Facts per serving: 709 cal., 41 g total fat (19 g sat. fat), 143 mg chol., 596 mg sodium, 45 g carbo., 4 g fiber, 38 g pro. Daily Values: 105% vit. A, 16% vit. C, 14% calcium, 13% iron

Honey-Chicken Sandwiches

Start to Finish: 20 min.

3   tablespoons honey
2   teaspoons snipped fresh thyme or
        ½ teaspoon dried thyme, crushed
1   small red onion, halved and thinly sliced
        (⅓ cup)
12 ounces thinly sliced cooked chicken, halved
        crosswise
4   purchased croissants, halved horizontally
        and toasted

1. In a medium skillet combine honey, thyme, and red onion. Cook and stir over medium-low heat until warm (do not boil). Stir in chicken; heat through. Serve in croissants.
Makes 4 servings.

Nutrition Facts per serving: 445 cal., 18 g total fat
(8 g sat. fat), 118 mg chol., 498 mg sodium, 40 g carbo.,
2 g fiber, 29 g pro. Daily Values: 7% vit. A, 2% vit. C,
4% calcium, 13% iron

Quick Chicken Tortilla Bake

Prep: 15 min. • Bake: 45 min.

2   10¾-ounce cans reduced-sodium
        condensed cream of chicken soup
1   10-ounce can diced tomatoes with green
        chiles, undrained
12 6- or 7-inch corn tortillas, cut into thin
        bite-size strips
3   cups cubed cooked chicken
1   cup shredded cheese with Mexican-style
        seasoning (4 ounces)

1. In a medium bowl combine soup and undrained tomatoes. Set aside. Sprinkle one-third of the tortilla strips over the bottom of an ungreased 3-quart rectangular baking dish. Layer half of the chicken over tortilla strips; spoon half of the soup mixture on top. Repeat layers. Top with remaining tortilla strips.

2. Bake, covered, in a 350°F oven about 40 minutes or until bubbly around edges and center is hot. Uncover and sprinkle with cheese. Bake 5 minutes more or until cheese is melted.
Makes 8 servings.

Nutrition Facts per serving: 291 cal., 10 g total fat
(4 g sat. fat), 64 mg chol., 658 mg sodium, 28 g carbo.,
2 g fiber, 22 g pro. Daily Values: 14% vit. A, 32% vit. C,
16% calcium, 8% iron

Chunky Chicken Chili

Start to Finish: 20 min.

12   ounces skinless, boneless chicken thighs
      Nonstick cooking spray
1½   cups frozen pepper and onion stir-fry
      vegetables
2   15-ounce cans chili beans with spicy chili
      gravy, undrained
¾   cup salsa
      Crushed tortilla chips (optional)

1. Cut chicken into bite-size pieces. Coat an unheated large saucepan with cooking spray. Add chicken and frozen vegetables. Cook and stir over medium-high heat until chicken is brown. Stir in undrained chili beans and salsa. Bring to boiling; reduce heat. Simmer, uncovered, about 7 minutes or until chicken is no longer pink. If desired, top with crushed tortilla chips.
Makes 4 servings.

Nutrition Facts per serving: 321 cal., 5 g total fat (1 g sat. fat), 68 mg chol., 712 mg sodium, 38 g carbo., 13 g fiber, 29 g pro. Daily Values: 19% vit. A, 22% vit. C, 9% calcium, 20% iron

> **Purchasing Ground Chicken or Turkey**
> Ground chicken or turkey may be a lighter alternative to ground beef in many recipes. However, much of the ground poultry available is made from white and dark meat—as well as the high-fat skin. To make sure your ground poultry is as lean as possible, purchase ground breast meat only, often labeled "diet lean." If it's not visible in the meat case, ask your butcher to grind some breast meat for you.

Chicken-Rice Soup

Start to Finish: 25 min.

1   6¼- or 6¾-ounce package quick-cooking
      long grain and wild rice mix
5   cups water
½   pound ground raw chicken or ground
      raw turkey
1   12-ounce can evaporated milk, chilled
2   tablespoons all-purpose flour

1. In a 3-quart saucepan combine the rice mix with seasoning packet and the water. Bring to boiling. Drop the chicken by small spoonfuls into the boiling mixture (about 36 pieces). Reduce heat. Simmer, covered, for 5 minutes.

2. Gradually stir chilled milk into flour until smooth; add to boiling mixture. Cook and stir until slightly thickened and bubbly. Cook and stir for 1 minute more.
Makes 6 servings.

Nutrition Facts per serving: 242 cal., 8 g total fat (3 g sat. fat), 17 mg chol., 546 mg sodium, 30 g carbo., 0 g fiber, 14 g pro. Daily Values: 3% vit. A, 2% vit. C, 16% calcium, 9% iron

Turkey Breast with Raspberry Salsa

Prep: 10 min. • Grill: 1¼ hours

- ⅓ cup seedless raspberry jam
- 1 tablespoon Dijon-style mustard
- 1 teaspoon finely shredded orange peel
- ½ cup mild salsa
- 1 2- to 2½-pound turkey breast half

1. In a small bowl stir together jam, mustard, and orange peel. Stir 3 tablespoons of mixture into salsa. Cover both mixtures and chill.

2. Skin turkey breast, if desired. Insert an oven-safe meat thermometer into the center of turkey breast. In a covered grill arrange preheated coals around a drip pan. Test for medium heat above pan. Place turkey, bone side down, on grill over drip pan. Cover and grill for 1¼ to 2 hours or until turkey is no longer pink (170°F), brushing occasionally with reserved jam mixture. Remove turkey from grill and cover with foil. Let stand for 15 minutes before slicing; serve with salsa mixture.

Makes 8 servings.

Nutrition Facts per serving: 149 cal., 3 g total fat (1 g sat. fat), 46 mg chol., 147 mg sodium, 11 g carbo., 0 g fiber, 20 g pro. Daily Values: 19% vit. A, 8% vit. C, 1% calcium, 7% iron

Turkey Steaks with Grilled Pineapple

Prep: 15 min. • Grill: 8 min.

- 2 8-ounce turkey breast tenderloins, halved horizontally
- ½ teaspoon salt
- ¼ teaspoon freshly ground black pepper
- ¾ cup barbecue sauce
- 1 small pineapple, cored and cut into 8 spears

1. Sprinkle both sides of turkey steaks with salt and pepper. Brush one side of steaks with ¼ cup barbecue sauce. Arrange steaks, sauce side down, on the rack of an uncovered grill. Grill directly over medium-high coals for 4 to 5 minutes. Brush with another ¼ cup sauce; turn and grill 4 to 5 minutes more or until no longer pink (170°F).

2. Meanwhile, grill pineapple spears for 3 minutes. Turn spears; brush with remaining barbecue sauce. Grill for 3 minutes more or until heated through.

Makes 4 servings.

Nutrition Facts per serving: 222 cal., 3 g total fat (1 g sat. fat), 68 mg chol., 728 mg sodium, 20 g carbo., 2 g fiber, 28 g pro. Daily Values: 9% vit. A, 35% vit. C, 4% calcium, 12% iron

Turkey Nuggets and Sweet Potatoes

Prep: 15 min. • Roast: 20 min.

3   tablespoons olive oil

2   teaspoons snipped fresh rosemary

2   medium sweet potatoes, peeled and cut
      into bite-size pieces (3 cups)

12 ounces turkey breast tenderloin, cut into
      bite-size pieces

⅓   cup finely crushed stone-ground wheat
      crackers (8 to 10)

1. In a medium mixing bowl combine oil and rosemary. Toss potatoes in oil mixture; transfer to a 15×10×1-inch baking pan. Toss turkey with the remaining oil mixture in bowl. Add crushed crackers to turkey; toss to coat. Add to potatoes in pan. Arrange in a single layer. Roast, uncovered, in a 400°F oven for 20 minutes or until turkey and potatoes are tender and turkey is no longer pink.
Makes 4 servings.

Nutrition Facts per serving: 327 cal., 13 g total fat
(2 g sat. fat), 51 mg chol., 102 mg sodium, 30 g carbo.,
4 g fiber, 22 g pro. Daily Values: 405% vit. A, 30% vit. C,
4% calcium, 11% iron

Turkey Tenderloin with Black Bean and Corn Salsa

Start to Finish: 25 min.

2   turkey breast tenderloins, halved
      horizontally (1 pound)
      Salt and black pepper

¼   cup red jalapeño jelly

1¼ cups purchased black bean and corn salsa

2   tablespoons snipped fresh cilantro

1. Place turkey on the unheated rack of a broiler pan. Season with salt and pepper. Broil 4 to 5 inches from heat for 5 minutes. Meanwhile, in a small saucepan melt jelly. Remove 2 tablespoons of the jelly. Turn turkey and brush with the 2 tablespoons jelly. Broil 4 to 6 minutes more or until no longer pink (170°F). Transfer turkey to a serving plate. Spoon remaining jelly over turkey; cover and keep warm. In a small saucepan heat salsa; spoon over turkey. Sprinkle with cilantro.
Makes 4 servings.

Nutrition Facts per serving: 196 cal., 2 g total fat
(1 g sat. fat), 66 mg chol., 377 mg sodium, 16 g carbo.,
1 g fiber, 27 g pro. Daily Values: 8% vit. A, 11% vit. C,
3% calcium, 11% iron

Turkey with Onion-Cilantro Relish

Prep: 5 min. • Grill: 15 min.

½ cup chopped onion

¼ cup cilantro sprigs

⅛ teaspoon each salt and black pepper

2 turkey breast tenderloins, halved
    horizontally (about 1 pound)

3 tablespoons lime juice or lemon juice

1. In a blender container or food processor bowl combine onion, cilantro, salt, and pepper; cover and blend or process until mixture is finely chopped.

2. Dip turkey in lime juice. Grill on the rack of an uncovered grill directly over medium coals for 7 minutes. Turn and brush with lime juice. Spoon onion mixture over turkey. Grill for 8 to 11 minutes more or until turkey is no longer pink (170°F).
Makes 4 servings.

Nutrition Facts per serving: 141 cal., 2 g total fat
(1 g sat. fat), 68 mg chol., 130 mg sodium, 3 g carbo.,
1 g fiber, 27 g pro. Daily Values: 6% vit. A, 10% vit. C,
3% calcium, 8% iron

Nutty Turkey Tenderloins

Prep: 15 min. • Bake: 18 min.

2 turkey breast tenderloins, halved
    horizontally (about 1 pound)

¼ cup creamy Dijon-style mustard blend

1 cup corn bread stuffing mix

½ cup finely chopped pecans

2 tablespoons butter, melted

1. Brush turkey generously with the mustard blend. In a shallow dish combine the stuffing mix and pecans; dip turkey in stuffing mixture to coat both sides. Place in a shallow baking pan. Drizzle with melted butter. Bake, uncovered, in a 375°F oven for 18 to 20 minutes or until turkey is no longer pink (170°).
Makes 4 servings.

Nutrition Facts per serving: 395 cal., 21 g total fat
(5 g sat. fat), 84 mg chol., 566 mg sodium, 21 g carbo.,
1 g fiber, 30 g pro. Daily Values: 5% vit. A, 3% calcium,
13% iron

Polenta with Turkey Sausage Florentine

Start to Finish: 25 min.

1 9- or 10-ounce package frozen
    creamed spinach
8 ounces uncooked bulk turkey sausage
½ of a 16-ounce tube refrigerated cooked
    polenta with wild mushrooms, cut into
    ¾-inch slices
1 tablespoon olive oil
2 tablespoons sliced almonds or
    pine nuts, toasted

1. Cook spinach according to package directions. Meanwhile, in a medium skillet cook sausage until brown. Drain fat. In the same skillet cook polenta slices in hot oil for 3 minutes on each side or until golden. Transfer polenta to serving plates.

2. Stir cooked sausage into hot creamed spinach; heat through. Spoon over polenta. Sprinkle with nuts.
Makes 2 servings.

Nutrition Facts per serving: 607 cal., 41 g total fat (8 g sat. fat), 119 mg chol., 1,586 mg sodium, 33 g carbo., 6 g fiber, 28 g pro. Daily Values: 51% vit. A, 10% vit. C, 20% calcium, 17% iron

Turkey Chili with a Twist

Start to Finish: 20 min.

12 ounces uncooked bulk turkey Italian
     sausage or ground turkey
2   15-ounce cans chili beans with chili gravy
1   cup bottled salsa with lime
1   15-ounce can golden hominy, drained
⅔   cup water
⅓   cup sliced green onions

1. In a large saucepan cook sausage until brown. Stir in undrained chili beans, salsa, hominy, and water. Heat through. Sprinkle with green onions.
Makes 4 to 5 servings.

Nutrition Facts per serving: 470 cal., 11 g total fat (3 g sat. fat), 45 mg chol., 1,897 mg sodium, 64 g carbo., 16 g fiber, 28 g pro. Daily Values: 8% vit. A, 21% vit. C, 12% calcium, 20% iron

Easy Turkey-Pesto Pot Pie

Prep: 15 min. • Bake: 15 min.

1   18-ounce jar turkey gravy
¼   cup purchased basil or dried tomato pesto
3   cups cubed cooked turkey
1   16-ounce package loose-pack frozen peas
      and carrots
1   7-ounce package refrigerated
      breadsticks (6)

1. In a large saucepan combine gravy and pesto;
stir in turkey and vegetables. Bring to boiling,
stirring frequently. Divide mixture evenly among
six 8-ounce au gratin dishes. Unroll and separate
breadsticks. Arrange a breadstick on top of each
dish. Bake in a 375°F oven for 15 minutes or until
breadsticks are golden.
Makes 6 servings.

Nutrition Facts per serving: 372 cal., 14 g total fat
(2 g sat. fat), 59 mg chol., 988 mg sodium, 30 g carbo.,
3 g fiber, 30 g pro. Daily Values: 136% vit. A, 12% vit. C,
4% calcium, 17% iron

Turkey and Spinach Muffins with Hollandaise

Start to Finish: 20 min.

1   10-ounce package frozen chopped spinach
1   1-ounce package hollandaise sauce mix
4   English muffins, split and toasted
8   ounces sliced cooked smoked turkey or
      chicken breast
1   tablespoon cooking oil

1. Cook spinach according to package
directions; drain well. Prepare hollandaise
sauce according to package directions; cover
and keep warm. Place 2 muffin halves on each
of 4 dinner plates.

2. In a skillet cook turkey slices in hot oil over
medium heat for 1 minute or until heated
through. Spoon spinach over muffins; top with
turkey slices. Spoon hollandaise over turkey.
Makes 4 servings.

Nutrition Facts per serving: 267 cal., 7 g total fat
(1 g sat. fat), 29 mg chol., 1,117 mg sodium, 34 g carbo.,
4 g fiber, 17 g pro. Daily Values: 104% vit. A, 16% vit. C,
17% calcium, 17% iron

Turkey-Avocado Quesadillas

Prep: 10 min. • Cook: 4 min.

- 3   7- or 8-inch flour tortillas
- 3   tablespoons bottled peppercorn ranch salad dressing
- 1   cup bite-size pieces cooked turkey breast or one 5-ounce can chunk-style turkey, drained
- 1   avocado, halved, pitted, peeled, and sliced
- ¾   cup shredded Monterey Jack cheese (3 ounces)

1. Spread one side of each tortilla with salad dressing. Arrange turkey and avocado slices over half of each tortilla. Sprinkle cheese over turkey and avocado. Fold in half, pressing gently (tortillas will be full).

2. On a large nonstick griddle cook quesadillas over medium heat for 2 minutes per side or until lightly brown and cheese melts.
Makes 3 servings.

Nutrition Facts per serving: 437 cal., 29 g total fat
(9 g sat. fat), 69 mg chol., 481 mg sodium, 20 g carbo.,
3 g fiber, 26 g pro. Daily Values: 12% vit. A, 7% vit. C,
26% calcium, 15% iron

Quick Turkey Tetrazzini

Prep: 20 min. • Bake: 15 min.

-      Nonstick cooking spray
- 6   ounces spaghetti
- 1   19-ounce can ready-to-serve chunky creamy chicken with mushroom soup
- 6   ounces cooked turkey breast, chopped (about 1 cup)
- ½   cup finely shredded Parmesan cheese (2 ounces)
- 2   tablespoons sliced almonds

1. Lightly coat a 2-quart square baking dish with cooking spray; set aside. Cook spaghetti according to the package directions; drain and return to pan. Add soup, turkey, and half of the cheese; heat through. Transfer spaghetti mixture to baking dish. Sprinkle with almonds and remaining cheese. Bake in a 425°F oven for 12 to 15 minutes or until top is golden.
Makes 4 servings.

Nutrition Facts per serving: 413 cal., 13 g total fat
(5 g sat. fat), 59 mg chol., 752 mg sodium, 43 g carbo.,
2 g fiber, 28 g pro. Daily Values: 9% vit. A, 2% vit. C,
16% calcium, 13% iron

Turkey Calzones

Prep: 30 min. • Bake: 18 min.

12 ounces boneless cooked turkey breast,
      chopped (about 2¼ cups)
 2 cups chopped fresh spinach
 1 cup shredded four-cheese pizza blend
      (4 ounces)
 1 8-ounce can pizza sauce
 2 10-ounce packages refrigerated pizza
      dough

1. In a large bowl combine turkey, spinach, cheese, and ½ cup of the sauce. On a lightly floured surface, roll 1 package of pizza dough into a 12×10-inch rectangle. Cut into three 10×4-inch rectangles.

2. Place about ½ cup of the turkey mixture onto half of each rectangle to within about 1 inch of edge. Moisten edges of dough with water and fold over, forming a square. Press with a fork to seal edges. Prick tops of calzones with a fork; place on a lightly greased baking sheet. Repeat with remaining dough and turkey mixture. Bake in a 375°F oven about 18 minutes or until golden brown. Serve with remaining pizza sauce.
Makes 6 servings.

Nutrition Facts per serving: 344 cal., 10 g total fat
(3 g sat. fat), 57 mg chol., 1,338 mg sodium, 41 g carbo.,
2 g fiber, 23 g pro. Daily Values: 23% vit. A, 24% vit. C,
13% calcium, 23% iron

Turkey Sub with Orange Mayonnaise

Start to Finish: 15 min.

 1 orange
 ½ cup mayonnaise or salad dressing
 4 sourdough rolls or one 8-ounce loaf
      baguette-style French bread, cut
      crosswise into quarters
 8 to 12 ounces thinly sliced cooked peppered
      turkey or cooked smoked turkey
 4 slices Swiss or provolone cheese (3 or
      4 ounces)

1. Finely shred 1 teaspoon of peel from the orange. Cut the orange in half; squeeze 2 tablespoons juice from orange halves. Discard seeds and remaining orange. For citrus mayonnaise, stir together mayonnaise, orange juice, and orange peel.

2. Split rolls horizontally; toast, if desired. Spread citrus mayonnaise on cut sides of each roll. Place bottom halves of rolls on a serving platter, mayonnaise side up. Layer turkey slices and cheese on rolls. Top with remaining halves of rolls, mayonnaise side down. Cover and store any remaining citrus mayonnaise in the refrigerator for up to 3 days.
Makes 4 servings.

Nutrition Facts per serving: 436 cal., 30 g total fat
(7 g sat. fat), 61 mg chol., 1,123 mg sodium, 21 g carbo.,
1 g fiber, 21 g pro. Daily Values: 5% vit. A, 8% vit. C,
24% calcium, 12% iron

Raspberry-Smoked Turkey Pockets

Start to Finish: 15 min.

8	ounces smoked turkey breast, cut into thin strips
2	cups shredded romaine or spinach
¾	cup raspberries or sliced strawberries
¼	cup bottled raspberry vinaigrette salad dressing
2	large pita rounds, split

1. In a large bowl gently toss together turkey strips, romaine, raspberries, and vinaigrette until combined. Divide mixture among pita halves. **Makes 4 servings.**

Nutrition Facts per serving: 192 cal., 6 g total fat (1 g sat. fat), 25 mg chol., 935 mg sodium, 24 g carbo., 3 g fiber, 13 g pro. Daily Values: 15% vit. A, 21% vit. C, 4% calcium, 9% iron

Hoisin-Sauced Cornish Hens

Prep: 15 min. • Bake: 1¼ hours

2	1- to 1½-pound Cornish game hens
½	cup hoisin sauce
¼	cup raspberry vinegar or red wine vinegar
¼	cup orange juice
1	to 2 teaspoons chili paste

1. Rinse insides of hens; pat dry. Using a sharp knife or kitchen shears, halve hens lengthwise. Place hens, breast side up, on a rack in a shallow roasting pan. Cover loosely with foil. Roast in a 375°F oven about 30 minutes.

2. Meanwhile, in a small bowl stir together remaining ingredients. Brush some of the mixture over hens. Roast, uncovered, 45 to 60 minutes more or until hens are no longer pink (180°F), brushing with remaining hoisin mixture occasionally. **Makes 4 servings.**

Nutrition Facts per serving: 371 cal., 23 g total fat (5 g sat. fat), 120 mg chol., 2,223 mg sodium, 6 g carbo., 0 g fiber, 38 g pro. Daily Values: 13% vit. C, 5% iron

Orange Roughy with Lemon Butter

Start to Finish: 15 min.

1½	pounds fresh or frozen orange roughy, cod, or haddock fillets
2	tablespoons butter or margarine, melted
1	to 2 tablespoons lemon juice
	Salt and black pepper
	Snipped fresh parsley

1. Thaw fish, if frozen. Rinse fish; pat dry. Cut into 6 serving-size pieces, if necessary. Place fillets on the greased rack of an unheated broiler pan. Tuck under any thin edges to make even thickness. Measure thickness of fish. Combine butter and lemon juice; brush over fillets. Sprinkle with salt and pepper.

2. Broil fish 4 inches from the heat for 4 to 6 minutes per ½-inch thickness or until fish flakes easily when tested with a fork, brushing occasionally with lemon-butter mixture. Sprinkle with parsley.
Makes 6 servings.

Nutrition Facts per serving: 115 cal., 5 g total fat (3 g sat. fat), 33 mg chol., 210 mg sodium, 0 g carbo., 0 g fiber, 17 g pro. Daily Values: 5% vit. A, 3% vit. C, 4% calcium, 1% iron

Steamed Fish with Veggies

Prep: 15 min. • Cook: 6 min.

2	6-ounce fresh or frozen orange roughy or other fish fillets
	Whole fresh basil leaves
2	teaspoons shredded fresh ginger
1	cup thinly sliced sweet peppers
8	ounces fresh asparagus spears

1. Thaw fish, if frozen. Rinse fish; pat dry. Using a sharp knife, make bias cuts about ¾ inch apart into the fish fillets. (Do not cut completely through fish.) Tuck basil leaves into each cut. Rub fillets with ginger.

2. Place peppers and asparagus in a steamer basket. Place fish on top of vegetables. Place basket into a large, deep saucepan or wok over 1 inch of boiling water. Cover and steam for 6 to 8 minutes or until fish flakes easily with a fork.
Makes 2 servings.

Nutrition Facts per serving: 254 cal., 2 g total fat (0 g sat. fat), 37 mg chol., 61 mg sodium, 36 g carbo., 3 g fiber, 21 g pro. Daily Values: 15% vit. A, 77% vit. C, 3% calcium, 9% iron

Simple Salsa Fish

Start to Finish: 15 min.

1   pound fresh or frozen skinless orange
    roughy or red snapper fillets, ½ to
    1 inch thick
⅓   cup salsa
1   clove garlic, minced
1   14-ounce can vegetable broth
1   cup quick-cooking couscous

1. Thaw fish, if frozen. Rinse fish; pat dry. Set
aside. In a small bowl, combine salsa and garlic;
set aside. In a saucepan bring the broth to
boiling. Stir in couscous; cover and remove
from heat. Let stand for 5 minutes or until liquid
is absorbed.

2. Place fish on the greased unheated rack of a
broiler pan. Broil about 4 inches from the heat
until fish flakes easily when tested with a fork
(allow 4 to 6 minutes per ½-inch thickness of
fish). Turn 1-inch-thick fillets over halfway
through broiling. Spoon salsa mixture over fish;
broil about 1 minute more or until salsa is
heated through. Serve fish on couscous mixture.
Makes 4 servings.

Nutrition Facts per serving: 295 cal., 3 g total fat
(0 g sat. fat), 42 mg chol., 549 mg sodium, 39 g carbo.,
7 g fiber, 30 g pro. Daily Values: 4% vit. A, 12% vit. C,
4% calcium, 7% iron

Fish Fillets with Yogurt Dressing

Start to Finish: 45 min.

1   pound fresh or frozen skinless cod, orange
    roughy, or other fish fillets, ½ to 1 inch
    thick
⅔   cup bottled poppy seed salad dressing
3   tablespoons thinly sliced green onions
1   teaspoon snipped fresh thyme or
        ¼ teaspoon dried thyme, crushed
½   cup plain yogurt

1. Thaw fish, if frozen. Rinse fish; pat dry. Cut
into 4 serving-size pieces, if necessary. For
marinade, in a large bowl combine ½ cup of the
dressing, 2 tablespoons of the green onions,
and half of the thyme. Add fish. Turn to coat.
Cover and marinate in the refrigerator for 20 to
30 minutes. Drain fillets; discard marinade.

2. Measure thickness of the fish. Place fish in a
greased 2-quart rectangular baking dish, tucking
under any thin edges. Bake fish, uncovered, in a
450°F oven until fish flakes easily with a fork
(allow 4 to 6 minutes per ½-inch thickness of
fish). Transfer to a serving platter.

3. Meanwhile, for sauce, in a small bowl
combine yogurt, remaining salad dressing,
green onion, and thyme. Serve with fish.
Makes 4 servings.

Nutrition Facts per serving: 182 cal., 9 g total fat
(2 g sat. fat), 55 mg chol., 201 mg sodium, 3 g carbo.,
0 g fiber, 22 g pro. Daily Values: 2% vit. A, 3% vit. C,
7% calcium, 3% iron

Lime-Poached Mahi Mahi

Prep: 10 min. • Cook: 8 min.

4   6-ounce fresh or frozen mahi mahi or
     catfish fillets, ½ to ¾ inch thick
2   teaspoons seasoned pepper
1   tablespoon olive oil
⅓   cup frozen margarita mix concentrate,
     thawed
2   cups hot cooked basmati or long grain rice

1. Skin fish, if necessary. Rinse fish; pat dry. Rub both sides of fish with seasoned pepper. In a large nonstick skillet cook fish in hot oil over medium-high heat for 1 to 2 minutes on each side or until lightly brown. Reduce heat to medium-low. Carefully add concentrate to skillet. Cook, covered, for 6 to 8 minutes or until fish flakes easily when tested with a fork. Serve fish and sauce with rice.
Makes 4 servings.

Nutrition Facts per serving: 336 cal., 5 g total fat (1 g sat. fat), 124 mg chol., 150 mg sodium, 41 g carbo., 0 g fiber, 34 g pro. Daily Values: 6% vit. A, 7% vit. C, 3% calcium, 16% iron

Basmati Rice
Among the rainbow of rices is a family known as the aromatics. Jasmine (from Thailand), basmati (India), Texmati (Texas), and wild rice pecan (Louisiana) are all long grain, aromatic rices prized for their nutty flavor and sweet aroma. Aromatic rices go nicely with Asian-, Indian-, and Caribbean-style foods.

Almond Walleye

Start to Finish: 20 min.

4   8- to 10-ounce fresh or frozen walleye pike
     fillets or other fish fillets
½   cup all-purpose flour
¼   cup ground almonds (1 ounce)
¼   teaspoon each salt and black pepper
¼   cup olive oil

1. Thaw fish, if frozen. Rinse fish; pat dry. In a shallow pan or dish stir together flour, almonds, salt, and pepper. Coat fish with flour mixture. In a large skillet, cook 2 of the fillets in 2 tablespoons hot oil over medium heat for 4 to 6 minutes on each side or until coating is golden and fish flakes easily when tested with a fork. Remove from skillet; keep warm. Repeat with remaining fillets and oil.
Makes 4 servings.

Nutrition Facts per serving: 423 cal., 20 g total fat (3 g sat. fat), 194 mg chol., 261 mg sodium, 12 g carbo., 1 g fiber, 46 g pro. Daily Values: 3% vit. A, 27% calcium, 22% iron

Sesame-Seared Tuna

Prep: 10 min. • Cook: 8 min.

4   **6-ounce fresh or frozen tuna fillets, about ¾ inch thick**
1   **tablespoon olive oil**
⅓   **cup hoisin sauce**
3   **tablespoons orange juice**
1   **tablespoon sesame seeds, toasted**

1. Rinse fish; pat dry. In a large skillet cook fish in hot oil over medium-high heat about 4 minutes on each side or until tuna flakes easily when tested with a fork (tuna can be slightly pink in the center).

2. Meanwhile, in a small saucepan stir together the hoisin sauce and orange juice; heat through. To serve, drizzle sauce over fish. Sprinkle with sesame seeds.
Makes 4 servings.

Nutrition Facts per serving: 271 cal., 7 g total fat (1 g sat. fat), 76 mg chol., 297 mg sodium, 9 g carbo., 0 g fiber, 41 g pro. Daily Values: 5% vit. A, 12% vit. C, 4% calcium, 9% iron

Crunchy Catfish and Zucchini

Prep: 15 min. • Bake: 12 min.

1   **pound fresh or frozen catfish fillets**
1   **medium zucchini or yellow summer squash**
4   **cups cornflakes**
1   **cup bottled ranch salad dressing**
2   **teaspoons bottled hot pepper sauce**

1. Thaw fish, if frozen. Rinse fish; pat dry. Cut fish into 1-inch strips. Cut zucchini in half crosswise. Cut each half lengthwise into 6 wedges.

2. Place cornflakes in a large self-sealing plastic bag. Seal and crush slightly; set aside. In a large mixing bowl combine dressing and hot pepper sauce. Reserve half for dipping sauce; set aside. Add catfish and zucchini strips to remaining dressing in bowl; stir gently to coat.

3. Add one-third of the zucchini and fish to the bag with the crushed cornflakes. Seal; shake to coat. Place coated zucchini and fish in a single layer on a greased 15x10x1-inch baking pan. Repeat with remaining zucchini and fish.

4. Bake in a 425°F oven for 12 to 15 minutes or until fish flakes easily with a fork and crumbs are golden. Serve with reserved dipping sauce.
Makes 4 servings.

Nutrition Facts per serving: 545 cal., 40 g total fat (7 g sat. fat), 58 mg chol., 779 mg sodium, 24 g carbo., 0 g fiber, 20 g pro. Daily Values: 4% vit. A, 17% vit. C, 2% calcium, 7% iron

South-of-the-Border Snapper

Start to Finish: 20 min.

4   4-ounce fresh or frozen red snapper,
    orange roughy, sole, or cod fillets,
    about ½ inch thick
½   cup bottled chunky salsa
¾   cup shredded Monterey Jack and/or
    cheddar cheese

1. Thaw fish, if frozen. Rinse fish; pat dry.
Place fish in a greased 2-quart rectangular
baking dish, tucking under any thin edges.
Spoon salsa over fish and sprinkle with cheese.
Bake in a 425°F oven about 15 minutes or until
fish flakes easily when tested with a fork.
Makes 4 servings.

Nutrition Facts per serving: 177 cal., 5 g total fat
(3 g sat. fat), 56 mg chol., 277 mg sodium, 1 g carbo.,
0 g fiber, 29 g pro. Daily Values: 4% vit. A, 6% vit. C,
19% calcium, 2% iron

Snapper Veracruz

Prep: 15 min. • Bake: 30 min.

1¼ to 1½ pounds fresh or frozen skinless red
    snapper fillets or firm-textured
    whitefish fillets, such as catfish,
    ½ to ¾ inch thick
1   14½-ounce can Mexican-style stewed
    tomatoes, undrained
1   cup pitted ripe olives
2   tablespoons olive oil
1   10-ounce package seasoned yellow rice

1. Thaw fish, if frozen. Rinse fish; pat dry. Cut
into 4 serving-size pieces. In a large ovenproof
skillet combine undrained tomatoes and olives.
Top with fish fillets; drizzle with oil. Bake,
uncovered, in a 300°F oven for 15 minutes.
Spoon some of the tomato mixture over fish and
bake 15 minutes more or until fish flakes easily
with a fork.

2. Meanwhile, prepare rice according to package
directions. Serve fish and sauce with rice.
Makes 4 servings.

Nutrition Facts per serving: 566 cal., 19 g total fat
(3 g sat. fat), 52 mg chol., 1,466 mg sodium, 63 g carbo.,
3 g fiber, 36 g pro. Daily Values: 14% vit. A, 32% vit. C,
11% calcium, 28% iron

Beer-Battered Cod

Start to Finish: 35 min.

Cooking oil for deep-fat frying
6   4- to 6-ounce fresh or frozen cod fillets
2   cups self-rising flour
½   teaspoon each salt and black pepper
1   12-ounce can beer

1. In a heavy 3-quart saucepan or deep-fat fryer heat 2 inches of oil to 365°F.

2. Meanwhile, thaw fish, if frozen. Rinse fish; pat dry. In a large bowl stir together flour, salt, and pepper. Sprinkle both sides of fish with 2 tablespoons of the flour mixture. Add beer to remaining flour mixture and stir until combined. Dip fish pieces, one at a time, into the batter, coating well (batter will be thick).

3. Carefully lower fish into hot oil. Fry 1 or 2 pieces at a time for 4 to 6 minutes or until golden and fish flakes easily when tested with a fork. Drain on paper towels; keep warm in a 300°F oven while frying remaining fish.
Makes 4 servings.

Nutrition Facts per serving: 635 cal., 29 g total fat
(4 g sat. fat), 72 mg chol., 1,181 mg sodium, 50 g carbo.,
2 g fiber, 37 g pro. Daily Values: 1% vit. A, 3% vit. C,
24% calcium, 20% iron

Chilled Cod with Gazpacho Sauce

Prep: 25 min • Chill: 2 hours

8   ounces fresh or frozen cod, flounder, or
      orange roughy fillets, ½ inch thick
1   lemon, halved and sliced
¼   cup deli marinated cucumber salad or
      mixed vegetable salad, drained
¼   cup bottled chunky salsa
2   cups torn mixed salad greens

1. Thaw fish, if frozen. Rinse fish; pat dry. In a large skillet place a large steamer basket over ½ inch of boiling water. Reduce heat. Carefully place fish fillets in steamer basket. (If necessary, cut fish to fit.) Top with half of the lemon slices. Cover and steam fish about 6 minutes or until fish flakes easily when tested with a fork. Discard lemon slices. Remove fish from steamer basket. Cover and refrigerate for 2 to 4 hours.

2. Meanwhile, for sauce, cut up any large pieces of cucumbers. Stir together cucumber salad and salsa. Arrange greens on 2 dinner plates. Place half of the chilled fish on top of each plate of greens. Spoon salsa mixture over fish. Serve with remaining lemon slices.
Makes 2 servings.

Nutrition Facts per serving: 116 cal., 15 g total fat
(0 g sat. fat), 49 mg chol., 343 mg sodium, 5 g carbo.,
2 g fiber, 21 g pro. Daily Values: 54% vit. A, 9% vit. C,
4% calcium, 4% iron

Vegetable-Topped Fish

Start to Finish: 15 min.

- 1 pound fresh or frozen fish fillets
- 1 tablespoon butter or margarine, melted
- 1/8 teaspoon each salt and black pepper
- 1 8-ounce jar salsa (about 1 cup)
- 1 small yellow summer squash or zucchini, halved lengthwise and cut into 1/4-inch slices

1. Thaw fish, if frozen. Rinse fish; pat dry. Measure thickness of fish. Place fish in a greased shallow baking pan, tucking under any thin edges. Brush fish with melted butter. Sprinkle with salt and pepper. Bake, uncovered, in a 450°F oven until fish flakes easily when tested with a fork (allow 4 to 6 minutes per 1/2-inch thickness).

2. Meanwhile, in a small saucepan stir together salsa and squash. Bring to boiling; reduce heat. Simmer, covered, for 5 to 6 minutes or until squash is crisp-tender. Serve over fish.
Makes 4 servings.

Nutrition Facts per serving: 131 cal., 4 g total fat (0 g sat. fat), 48 mg chol., 403 mg sodium, 5 g carbo., 1 g fiber, 22 g pro. Daily Values: 10% vit. A, 21% vit. C, 4% calcium, 6% iron

Fish Fillets au Gratin

Prep: 10 min. • Bake: 23 min.

- 1 pound fresh or frozen skinless fish fillets, 3/4 inch thick
- 1/4 cup fine dry bread crumbs
- 2 teaspoons snipped fresh dill or 1/2 teaspoon dried dill
- 1/4 teaspoon lemon-pepper seasoning
- 1/2 cup shredded cheddar cheese (2 ounces)

1. Thaw fish, if frozen. Rinse fish; pat dry. Cut fish into 4 serving-size portions, if necessary. Place fillets in a greased shallow baking dish; set aside. In a small bowl stir together bread crumbs, dill, and seasoning. Spoon over fish.

2. Bake, uncovered, in a 400°F oven for 20 to 25 minutes or until fish flakes easily when tested with a fork. Sprinkle with cheese; bake for 3 to 5 minutes more or until cheese melts.
Makes 4 servings.

Nutrition Facts per serving: 169 cal., 6 g total fat (33 g sat. fat), 63 mg chol., 350 mg sodium, 4 g carbo., 0 g fiber, 24 g pro. Daily Values: 4% vit. A, 2% vit. C, 13% calcium, 5% iron

Fish with Black Bean Sauce

Prep: 15 min. • Cook: 12 min.

1½ **pounds fresh or frozen skinless sea bass or orange roughy fillets, cut into 6 portions**
1 **15-ounce can black beans, rinsed and drained**
3 **tablespoons teriyaki sauce**
2 **tablespoons hoisin sauce**
  Nonstick cooking spray
  Hot cooked rice

1. Thaw fish, if frozen. Rinse fish; pat dry. In a blender container or food processor bowl combine drained beans, teriyaki sauce, and hoisin sauce. Cover and blend or process until nearly smooth.

2. Lightly coat a 12-inch skillet with cooking spray; heat over medium-high heat. Carefully place fish portions in skillet and cook about 2 minutes on each side or until golden brown. Add bean mixture to fish. Bring to boiling; reduce heat. Simmer, covered, about 8 minutes or until fish flakes easily when tested with a fork. To serve, spoon sauce over fish and rice.
Makes 6 servings.

Nutrition Facts per serving: 276 cal., 3 g total fat (1 g sat. fat), 46 mg chol., 617 mg sodium, 35 g carbo., 4 g fiber, 28 g pro. Daily Values: 4% vit. A, 5% calcium, 12% iron

Maple-Hazelnut Salmon

Prep: 10 min. • Cook: 8 min.

8 **6- to 8-ounce fresh or frozen salmon fillets, about 1 inch thick**
  Salt and black pepper
½ **cup pure maple syrup or maple-flavored syrup**
¾ **cup chopped hazelnuts or pecans**
2 **tablespoons butter or margarine**

1. Thaw fish, if frozen. Rinse fish; pat dry. Arrange fish in a lightly greased 3-quart rectangular baking dish, turning under any thin edges. Sprinkle lightly with salt and pepper. Drizzle maple syrup over fish. Bake, uncovered, in a 450°F oven for 8 to 12 minutes or until fish flakes easily when tested with a fork.

2. Meanwhile, in a medium skillet cook and stir nuts in hot butter over medium heat for 2 to 4 minutes or until lightly toasted. Spoon nuts over fish.
Makes 8 servings.

Nutrition Facts per serving: 299 cal., 15 g total fat (4 g sat. fat), 39 mg chol., 204 mg sodium, 15 g carbo., 1 g fiber, 26 g pro. Daily Values: 7% vit. A, 3% calcium, 2% iron

Parmesan Baked Fish

Prep: 15 min. • Bake: 12 min.

4   4-ounce fresh or frozen skinless salmon
     fillets or other firm-textured fish fillets,
     ¾ to 1 inch thick
     Nonstick cooking spray
¼   cup light mayonnaise dressing or salad
     dressing
2   tablespoons grated Parmesan cheese
1   tablespoon snipped fresh chives or sliced
     green onion
1   teaspoon white wine Worcestershire sauce

1. Thaw fish, if frozen. Rinse fish; pat dry. Coat a
2-quart baking dish with cooking spray. Arrange
fillets in dish. In a small bowl stir together
remaining ingredients; spread over fillets. Bake,
uncovered, in a 450°F oven for 12 to 15 minutes
or until fish flakes easily when tested with a fork.
Makes 4 servings.

Nutrition Facts per serving: 252 cal., 16 g total fat
(3 g sat. fat), 77 mg chol., 200 mg sodium, 2 g carbo.,
0 g fiber, 25 g pro. Daily Values: 5% vit. A, 1% vit. C,
4% calcium, 3% iron

Salmon with Basil Mayonnaise

Start to Finish: 20 min.

4   5- to 6-ounce fresh or frozen skinless
     salmon fillets
2   tablespoons crumbled firm-textured bread
¼   cup mayonnaise or salad dressing
3   tablespoons purchased basil pesto
1   tablespoon grated Parmesan cheese

1. Thaw fish, if frozen. Rinse fish; pat dry.
Place bread crumbs in a shallow baking pan.
Broil 4 inches from heat for 1 to 2 minutes or
until lightly toasted, stirring once. Set aside.

2. Measure thickness of fish. Place fish on the
greased unheated rack of a broiler pan, tucking
under any thin edges. Broil 4 inches from heat
for 4 to 6 minutes per ½-inch thickness or until
fish flakes easily with a fork. Turn 1-inch-thick
fillets once halfway through broiling.

3. Meanwhile, in a small bowl stir together the
mayonnaise and pesto; set aside. Combine the
toasted bread crumbs and cheese. Spoon
mayonnaise mixture over fish. Sprinkle with
crumb mixture. Broil 1 to 2 minutes more or
until crumbs are lightly browned.
Makes 4 servings.

Nutrition Facts per serving: 363 cal., 24 g total fat
(3 g sat. fat), 84 mg chol., 309 mg sodium, 5 g carbo.,
0 g fiber, 31 g pro. Daily Values: 6% vit. A, 4% calcium,
7% iron

Sweet Mustard Halibut

Start to Finish: 20 min.

- 1   to 1¼ pounds fresh or frozen halibut steaks, ¾ inch thick
- ½   cup bottled chunky salsa
- 2   tablespoons honey
- 2   tablespoons Dijon-style mustard

1. Thaw fish, if frozen. Rinse fish; pat dry. Arrange steaks in a greased shallow 2-quart baking dish. Bake, uncovered, in a 450°F oven about 6 minutes or until fish flakes easily when tested with a fork. Drain liquid from fish.

2. Meanwhile, in a small bowl stir together salsa and honey. Spread mustard over fish; spoon salsa mixture on top of mustard; bake 2 to 3 minutes more or until salsa is heated through.
Makes 4 servings.

Nutrition Facts per serving: 176 cal., 4 g total fat
(0 g sat. fat), 36 mg chol., 362 mg sodium, 11 g carbo.,
0 g fiber, 24 g pro. Daily Values: 8% vit. A, 15% vit. C,
4% calcium, 8% iron

Dilly Salmon Fillets

Prep: 25 min. • Grill: 5 min.

- 4   6-ounce fresh or frozen skinless salmon fillets, ½ to ¾ inch thick
- 3   tablespoons lemon juice
- 2   tablespoons snipped fresh dill
- 2   tablespoons mayonnaise or salad dressing
- 2   teaspoons Dijon-style mustard

1. Thaw fish, if frozen. Rinse fish; pat dry. Place in a shallow dish. In a small bowl combine lemon juice and half of the dill; pour over fish. Let stand at room temperature for 10 minutes. Meanwhile, stir together remaining dill, mayonnaise, and mustard. Set aside.

2. In a grill with a cover arrange heated coals around a drip pan. Test for medium heat above pan. Place the fish on the lightly greased grill rack over the drip pan. Cover and grill for 3 minutes. Turn fish; spread with mayonnaise mixture. Cover and grill 2 to 6 minutes more or until fish flakes easily when tested with a fork.
Makes 4 servings.

Nutrition Facts per serving: 211 cal., 11 g total fat
(2 g sat. fat), 35 mg chol., 204 mg sodium, 1 g carbo.,
0 g fiber, 25 g pro. Daily Values: 4% vit. A, 8% vit. C,
1% calcium, 7% iron

Foil-Wrapped Salmon

Prep: 20 min. • Bake: 35 min.

4   fresh or frozen salmon steaks, about
      ¾ inch thick, or four 6- to 8-ounce
      center-cut salmon fillets
1   pound fresh asparagus
      Nonstick cooking spray
1   20-ounce package refrigerated
      sliced potatoes
6   tablespoons butter, cut into 12 pieces
4   teaspoons lemon, basil, and thyme
      seasoning blend or 2 teaspoons
      lemon-pepper seasoning

1. Thaw fish, if frozen. Rinse fish; pat dry. Snap off and discard woody bases of asparagus.

2. Tear off four 18-inch squares of heavy-duty aluminum foil. Lightly coat one side of each piece of foil with cooking spray. Divide fish, asparagus, potatoes, butter, and seasoning evenly among pieces of foil.

3. Bring up two opposite edges of foil; seal with a double fold. Fold ends to enclose fish and vegetables, leaving space for steam to build. Place packets, seam side up, on a baking sheet.

4. Bake in a 350°F oven for 35 to 40 minutes or until fish flakes easily when tested with a fork. Open packets carefully to allow steam to escape.
Makes 4 servings.

Nutrition Facts per serving: 506 cal., 25 g total fat
(12 g sat. fat), 137 mg chol., 804 mg sodium, 30 g carbo.,
2 g fiber, 39 g pro. Daily Values: 19% vit. A, 41% vit. C,
4% calcium, 13% iron

Herb-Crusted Salmon with Roasted Pepper Cream

Prep: 25 min. • Bake: 20 min.

4   6-ounce fresh or frozen skinless, boneless
      salmon fillets
3   tablespoons honey-Dijon mustard
3   tablespoons seasoned fine dry bread
      crumbs
½   cup drained, chopped roasted red sweet
      peppers
1   cup whipping cream

1. Thaw fish, if frozen. Rinse fish; pat dry. Use 2 tablespoons of the mustard to coat one side of each fillet. Sprinkle with bread crumbs. Place fish, crumb-side up, in a greased 3-quart rectangular baking dish. Bake, uncovered, in a 400°F oven for 20 to 25 minutes or until crumbs are golden and fish flakes easily when tested with a fork.

2. Meanwhile, in a medium saucepan, combine remaining mustard, the peppers, and cream. Bring to boiling; reduce heat. Boil gently, uncovered, for 15 minutes or until reduced to 1 cup. Serve over fish.
Makes 4 servings.

Nutrition Facts per serving: 576 cal., 32 g total fat
(15 g sat. fat), 227 mg chol., 359 mg sodium, 11 g carbo.,
0 g fiber, 57 g pro. Daily Values: 24% vit. A, 86% vit. C,
8% calcium, 14% iron

Asian-Glazed Salmon

Prep: 15 min. • Broil: 8 min.

1	**1-pound fresh or frozen skinless salmon fillet, 1 inch thick**
1/3	**cup packed brown sugar**
2	**tablespoons soy sauce**
1	**tablespoon Dijon-style mustard**
3	**tablespoons rice vinegar**

1. Thaw fish, if frozen. For glaze, combine brown sugar, soy sauce, and mustard. Set aside 2 tablespoons of the brown sugar mixture for sauce.

2. Rinse fish; pat dry. Cut into 4 serving-size pieces. Place fish on the greased unheated rack of a broiler pan. Broil 4 inches from the heat for 8 to 12 minutes or until fish flakes easily when tested with a fork, carefully turning once halfway through broiling time and brushing with glaze during the last 2 to 3 minutes of broiling time.

3. For sauce, stir together vinegar and reserved brown sugar mixture until sugar is dissolved. Serve with fish.
Makes 4 servings.

Nutrition Facts per serving: 214 cal., 4 g total fat
(1 g sat. fat), 59 mg chol., 733 mg sodium, 19 g carbo.,
0 g fiber, 24 g pro. Daily Values: 2% vit. A, 4% calcium,
8% iron

Mustard-Glazed Halibut Steaks

Prep: 10 min. • Grill: 8 min.

4	**6-ounce fresh or frozen halibut steaks, 1 inch thick**
2	**tablespoons butter or margarine**
2	**tablespoons lemon juice**
1	**tablespoon Dijon-style mustard**
2	**teaspoons snipped fresh basil or 1/2 teaspoon dried basil, crushed**

1. Thaw fish, if frozen. Rinse fish; pat dry. In a small saucepan heat all remaining ingredients over low heat until melted. Brush both sides of steaks with mustard mixture.

2. Grill steaks on the greased rack of an uncovered grill directly over medium coals for 8 to 12 minutes or until fish flakes easily when tested with a fork, turning once and brushing occasionally with mustard mixture.
Makes 4 servings.

Nutrition Facts per serving: 243 cal., 10 g total fat
(4 g sat. fat), 70 mg chol., 254 mg sodium, 1 g carbo.,
0 g fiber, 36 g pro. Daily Values: 14% vit. A, 5% vit. C,
6% calcium, 9% iron

Swordfish with Cucumber Sauce

Prep: 10 min. • Grill: 8 min.

2   fresh or frozen swordfish or halibut steaks,
      ¾ inch thick (1 pound)
⅓   cup plain low-fat yogurt
¼   cup finely chopped cucumber
1   teaspoon snipped fresh mint or dill or
      ¼ teaspoon dried mint, crushed, or
      dried dill
    Nonstick cooking spray

1. Thaw fish, if frozen. Rinse fish; pat dry. Cut each steak in half. For sauce, in a small bowl stir together yogurt, cucumber, and mint. Cover and chill until serving time.

2. Coat an unheated grill rack with cooking spray. Grill steaks on the prepared rack over medium-hot coals for 6 to 9 minutes or until fish is lightly browned. Turn and grill 2 to 3 minutes more or until fish flakes easily when tested with a fork. Serve fish with sauce. **Makes 4 servings.**

Nutrition Facts per serving: 149 cal., 5 g total fat
(1 g sat. fat), 44 mg chol., 116 mg sodium, 2 g carbo.,
0 g fiber, 24 g pro. Daily Values: 3% vit. A, 3% vit. C,
4% calcium, 6% iron

Browned Butter Salmon

Prep: 20 min. • Broil: 8 min.

4   fresh or frozen salmon or halibut steaks,
      1 inch thick (about 1½ pounds)
    Salt and black pepper
2   tablespoons butter
2   tablespoons pure maple syrup or maple-
      flavored syrup
1   teaspoon finely shredded orange peel

1. Thaw fish, if frozen. Rinse fish; pat dry. Sprinkle both sides of steaks with salt and pepper; set aside. In a small saucepan cook butter over medium heat for 3 minutes or until golden brown, stirring occasionally. Remove from heat. Cool 10 minutes. Stir in the maple syrup and orange peel (mixture may thicken).

2. Place fish on the greased unheated rack of a foil-lined broiler pan. Spread both sides of fish with the browned butter mixture. Broil 4 inches from the heat for 5 minutes. Using a wide spatula, carefully turn fish over. Broil for 3 to 7 minutes more or until fish flakes easily when tested with a fork. **Makes 4 servings.**

Nutrition Facts per serving: 277 cal., 12 g total fat
(5 g sat. fat), 105 mg chol., 322 mg sodium, 7 g carbo.,
0 g fiber, 34 g pro. Daily Values: 8% vit. A, 1% vit. C,
3% calcium, 8% iron

Pistachio-Salmon Nuggets

Start to Finish: 50 min.

1   **pound fresh or frozen skinless salmon fillets, 1 inch thick**
2   **tablespoons water**
2   **tablespoons soy sauce**
1   **tablespoon grated fresh ginger**
2   **tablespoons cooking oil**
1   **tablespoon finely chopped pistachio nuts**

1. Thaw fish, if frozen. Rinse fish; pat dry. Cut fish into bite-size pieces. Place fish in a self-sealing plastic bag set in a shallow dish. For marinade, combine water, soy sauce, ginger, and 1 tablespoon of the oil in a small bowl. Pour marinade over fish. Seal bag. Marinate at room temperature for 30 minutes, turning occasionally.

2. Drain fish, discard marinade. Heat remaining oil in a large nonstick skillet. Cook and gently stir half of the fish pieces over medium heat for 3 to 5 minutes or until fish flakes easily with a fork. Remove from skillet and place on paper towels. Repeat with remaining fish; remove and place on paper towels. Transfer to a serving platter and sprinkle with nuts.
Makes 4 servings.

Nutrition Facts per serving: 267 cal., 17 g total fat
(3 g sat. fat), 70 mg chol., 514 mg sodium, 1 g carbo.,
0 g fiber, 26 g pro. Daily Values: 4% vit. A, 1% calcium,
3% iron

Salmon-Potato Cakes

Prep: 20 min. • Cook: 8 min.

1   **pound fresh or frozen skinless salmon fillets**
3   **cups frozen shredded hash brown potatoes, thawed**
2   **slightly beaten eggs**
1   **tablespoon seafood seasoning**
2   **tablespoons butter or margarine**

1. Thaw fish, if frozen. Rinse fish; pat dry. In a large skillet cook fish, covered, in a small amount of boiling water for 6 to 9 minutes or until fish flakes easily when tested with a fork. Place fish in a large bowl and flake with a fork; cool slightly.

2. Add potatoes, eggs, and seasoning to fish; stir gently to combine. Shape mixture into 6 patties. In a 12-inch skillet cook patties in hot butter over medium heat for 4 minutes per side or until browned and heated through.
Makes 6 servings.

Nutrition Facts per serving: 235 cal., 9 g total fat
(4 g sat. fat), 121 mg chol., 466 mg sodium, 19 g carbo.,
1 g fiber, 19 g pro. Daily Values: 7% vit. A, 11% vit. C,
3% calcium, 10% iron

Smoked Salmon Pizza

Prep: 10 min. • Bake: 11 min.

1   16-ounce Italian bread shell (Boboli)
2   medium tomatoes, very thinly sliced
4   ounces sliced provolone cheese
3   ounces thinly sliced smoked salmon
        (lox-style)
½   cup crumbled semisoft goat cheese or
        garlic-and-herb feta cheese

1. Place bread shell on a baking sheet. Arrange tomatoes, provolone cheese, and salmon on top. Sprinkle with goat cheese. Bake in a 400°F oven for 11 to 13 minutes or until heated through.
Makes 6 to 8 servings.

Nutrition Facts per serving: 316 cal., 12 g total fat (5 g sat. fat), 24 mg chol., 899 mg sodium, 35 g carbo., 2 g fiber, 18 g pro. Daily Values: 8% vit. A, 13% vit. C, 24% calcium, 12% iron

Smoked Salmon Pasta

Prep: 10 min. • Cook: 12 min.

8   ounces bow tie or mini lasagna pasta
1   cup whipping cream
½   teaspoon seafood seasoning
8   ounces smoked salmon, flaked, with skin
        and bones removed, if present
½   cup drained roasted red sweet peppers, cut
        into bite-size strips

1. In a large saucepan cook pasta according to package directions. Meanwhile, in a medium saucepan heat cream and seasoning over medium heat until bubbly. Continue to cook, uncovered, for 5 minutes or until thickened, stirring occasionally. Stir in salmon and pepper strips; heat through. Drain pasta; return to pan. Add salmon mixture. Toss to coat.
Makes 4 to 6 servings.

Nutrition Facts per serving: 489 cal., 26 g total fat (14 g sat. fat), 95 mg chol., 552 mg sodium, 45 g carbo., 2 g fiber, 19 g pro. Daily Values: 19% vit. A, 86% vit. C, 5% calcium, 13% iron

Tuna and Noodles

Start to Finish: 20 min.

1   12-ounce package dried egg noodles
    (6 cups)
1   10¾-ounce can condensed cream of
    celery soup
6   ounces American cheese, cubed, or process
    Swiss cheese slices, torn
½   cup milk
1   12-ounce can solid white tuna (water-
    pack), drained

1. In a 4-quart Dutch oven cook noodles according to package directions; drain. In the same pan combine soup, cheese, and milk. Cook and stir over medium heat until bubbly. Stir tuna into soup mixture. Gently stir in noodles. Cook for 2 to 3 minutes more until heated. **Makes 4 to 6 servings.**

Nutrition Facts per serving: 645 cal., 23 g total fat (11 g sat. fat), 162 mg chol., 1,476 mg sodium, 68 g carbo., 3 g fiber, 40 g pro. Daily Values: 17% vit. A, 1% vit. C, 36% calcium, 23% iron

Tuna Muffin Melt

Start to Finish: 19 min.

1   5-ounce jar cream cheese spread with
    olives and pimiento or American
    cheese spread
1   6½-ounce can tuna, drained and broken
    into chunks
3   English muffins, split and toasted
6   slices tomato, halved
    Pimiento-stuffed olives, quartered or
    sliced (optional)

1. In a bowl combine ⅓ cup of the cheese spread and the tuna. Spread tuna mixture onto muffin halves. Place halves on the unheated rack of a broiler pan. Broil 4 inches from the heat about 3 minutes or until sandwiches are heated through.

2. Top each muffin half with 2 tomato half slices and a spoonful of the remaining cheese spread. Broil about 1 minute more or until heated through. If desired, top with olives. **Makes 3 servings.**

Nutrition Facts per serving: 367 cal., 12 g total fat (7 g sat. fat), 61 mg chol., 1,235 mg sodium, 33 g carbo., 2 g fiber, 32 g pro. Daily Values: 18% vit. A, 1% vit. C, 46% calcium, 16% iron

Tuna Salad with a Twist

Start to Finish: 15 min.

1   12-ounce can chunk white tuna (water-
      pack), drained
1/3 cup bottled creamy Italian salad dressing
1/3 cup finely chopped fresh or drained,
      canned pineapple
4   Boston lettuce leaves
2   sourdough, sesame, or plain bagels, halved
      and toasted

1. In a medium bowl combine drained tuna,
dressing, and pineapple. Place lettuce leaves
on toasted bagel halves. Spoon tuna mixture
over the lettuce leaves.
Makes 4 servings.

Nutrition Facts per serving: 276 cal., 10 g total fat
(2 g sat. fat), 38 mg chol., 902 mg sodium, 22 g carbo.,
1 g fiber, 24 g pro. Daily Values: 5% vit. A, 6% vit. C,
4% calcium, 9% iron

Shrimp with Basil on Linguine

Prep: 20 min. • Cook: 2 min.

1   pound fresh or frozen peeled, deveined
      medium shrimp (1½ pounds in shell)
6   ounces spinach linguine or fettuccine
2   teaspoons snipped fresh basil or tarragon
      or 1 teaspoon dried basil or tarragon,
      crushed
2   tablespoons butter or margarine

1. Thaw shrimp, if frozen. Rinse shrimp; pat
dry. Prepare linguine according to package
directions. In a large skillet cook shrimp and
basil in hot butter over medium-high heat for
2 to 3 minutes or until shrimp turn opaque,
stirring frequently. Serve warm over linguine.
Makes 4 servings.

Nutrition Facts per serving: 332 cal., 9 g total fat
(4 g sat. fat), 189 mg chol., 231 mg sodium, 33 g carbo.,
1 g fiber, 29 g pro. Daily Values: 9% vit. A, 3% vit. C,
7% calcium, 21% iron

Shrimp with Honey-Ginger Sauce

Prep: 20 min. • Broil: 3 min.

1½ pounds fresh or frozen large shrimp
      in shells
3   tablespoons honey
¼   teaspoon ground ginger
½   cup dairy sour cream or plain low-fat
      yogurt
      Salt and black pepper

1. Thaw shrimp, if frozen. In a small bowl stir together honey and ginger. Reserve 2 tablespoons of the honey mixture; set aside. For Honey-Ginger Sauce, stir sour cream into remaining honey mixture; set aside.

2. Peel and devein shrimp. Rinse and pat dry. Thread shrimp onto 4 long metal skewers. Place shrimp kabobs on the greased unheated rack of a broiler pan. Brush reserved honey mixture onto shrimp. Sprinkle with salt and pepper. Broil 4 inches from the heat for 3 to 5 minutes or until shrimp turn opaque, turning skewers halfway through broiling time. Serve with Honey-Ginger Sauce.
Makes 4 servings.

Nutrition Facts per serving: 250 cal., 7 g total fat (4 g sat. fat), 226 mg chol., 293 mg sodium, 15 g carbo., 0 g fiber, 30 g pro. Daily Values: 9% vit. A, 5% vit. C, 10% calcium, 20% iron

Capellini with Shrimp and Pesto

Start to Finish: 20 min.

12   ounces fresh or frozen peeled,
      deveined shrimp
8   ounces dried tomato-flavored or plain
      angel hair pasta (capellini), fettuccine,
      or linguine
      Nonstick cooking spray
2   medium yellow summer squash and/or
      zucchini, cut into ½-inch chunks
      (about 2 cups)
⅓   cup purchased basil pesto
1   medium Roma tomato, chopped

1. Thaw shrimp, if frozen. Rinse shrimp; pat dry. Cook pasta according to package directions. Drain and keep warm.

2. Meanwhile, coat an unheated large nonstick skillet with cooking spray. Heat skillet over medium-high heat. Add shrimp; cook and stir for 2 minutes. Add squash; cook and stir about 2 minutes more or until shrimp turn opaque and squash is crisp-tender. Remove from heat. Add pesto; toss gently to coat. Serve shrimp mixture over pasta; sprinkle with tomato.
Makes 4 servings.

Nutrition Facts per serving: 246 cal., 12 g total fat (3 g sat. fat), 135 mg chol., 305 mg sodium, 14 g carbo., 2 g fiber, 23 g pro. Daily Values: 16% vit. A, 35% vit. C, 17% calcium, 20% iron

Sweet-and-Sour Shrimp

Start to Finish: 15 min.

- ³/₄ **pound fresh or frozen peeled, deveined shrimp**
- ¹/₃ **cup bottled stir-fry sauce**
- ¹/₄ **cup pineapple-orange juice**
  Nonstick cooking spray
- 3 **cups assorted fresh stir-fry vegetables**

1. Thaw shrimp, if frozen. Rinse shrimp; pat dry. In a small bowl, combine stir-fry sauce and juice.

2. Coat an unheated nonstick wok or large skillet with cooking spray. (Add oil, if necessary, during cooking.) Heat wok or skillet over medium-high heat. Add vegetables; cook and stir for 3 to 5 minutes or until crisp-tender. Remove from wok. Add shrimp; cook and stir for 2 to 3 minutes or until shrimp turn opaque. Push shrimp to side of wok.

3. Add sauce mixture to wok. Stir in vegetables; heat through.
Makes 4 servings.

Nutrition Facts per serving: 119 cal., 1 g total fat (0 g sat. fat), 131 mg chol., 666 mg sodium, 11 g carbo., 2 g fiber, 17 g pro. Daily Values: 63% vit. A, 108% vit. C, 4% calcium, 16% iron

Peppy Asparagus-Shrimp Toss

Start to Finish: 20 min.

- 8 **ounces asparagus, trimmed and cut into bite-size pieces**
- 3 **cups cooked brown rice, chilled**
- 8 **ounces peeled, deveined cooked shrimp**
- 3 **tablespoons chopped oil-packed dried tomatoes, drained**
- 2 **tablespoons sweet-hot mustard**

1. In a saucepan cook asparagus, covered, in a small amount of boiling water for 3 to 6 minutes or until crisp-tender; drain. Rinse under cold water; drain again. In a large bowl toss together asparagus and remaining ingredients.
Makes 4 servings.

Nutrition Facts per serving: 306 cal., 7 g total fat (1 g sat. fat), 111 mg chol., 205 mg sodium, 42 g carbo., 5 g fiber, 20 g pro. Daily Values: 7% vit. A, 28% vit. C, 6% calcium, 21% iron

Curried Coconut Shrimp

Start to Finish: 30 minutes

1   pound fresh or frozen large shrimp in shells
     (14 to 16 count)
1   cup uncooked jasmine rice
1   15¼-ounce can tropical fruit salad or
     pineapple chunks
1   teaspoon red curry paste
1   cup unsweetened coconut milk

1. Thaw shrimp, if frozen. Prepare rice according to package directions; set aside. Meanwhile, peel and devein the shrimp. Rinse and pat dry; set aside. Drain liquid from fruit, reserving ½ cup. Set liquid and fruit aside.

2. In a large nonstick skillet cook and stir shrimp and curry paste over medium–high heat for 3 to 4 minutes or until shrimp turn opaque. Remove from skillet; set aside. Add coconut milk and reserved liquid from fruit to the skillet. Bring to boiling; reduce heat. Simmer, uncovered, for 5 to 7 minutes until mixture is slightly thickened and reduced to about 1 cup.

3. Divide hot cooked rice among 4 shallow bowls. Arrange shrimp on top of the rice and spoon the sauce over shrimp. Top each serving with fruit.
Makes 4 servings.

Nutrition Facts per serving: 463 cal., 17 g total fat
(13 g sat. fat), 151 mg chol., 263 mg sodium, 55 g carbo.,
2 g fiber, 24 g pro. Daily Values: 4% vit. A, 55% vit. C,
11% calcium, 31% iron

Mediterranean Shrimp and Couscous

Start to Finish: 15 min.

1   14½-ounce can diced tomatoes with garlic
     and onion, undrained
¾ cup water
1   5.6-ounce package toasted pine nut
     couscous mix
12 ounces peeled, deveined medium shrimp
     (1 pound in shells)
½ cup golden raisins

1. In a large skillet bring undrained tomatoes, water, and seasoning packet from the couscous mix to boiling. Stir in shrimp; cook over high heat for 2 to 3 minutes or until shrimp turn opaque. Stir in couscous and raisins. Remove from heat. Cover. Let stand for 5 minutes or until liquid is absorbed.
Makes 4 servings.

Nutrition Facts per serving: 338 cal., 4 g total fat
(1 g sat. fat), 129 mg chol., 967 mg sodium, 53 g carbo.,
6 g fiber, 25 g pro. Daily Values: 3% vit. A, 16% vit. C,
7% calcium, 22% iron

Shrimp and Coconut Soup

Start to Finish: 15 min.

8   ounces fresh or frozen peeled, deveined
    small shrimp
2   14-ounce cans chicken broth
4   ounces dried angel hair pasta or vermicelli,
    broken into 2-inch pieces
1   tablespoon curry powder
1   cup unsweetened coconut milk

1. Thaw shrimp, if frozen. Rinse shrimp; pat
dry. In a large saucepan bring chicken broth to
boiling. Add pasta and curry powder; return to
boiling. Boil gently for 3 minutes. Add shrimp;
cook for 2 to 3 minutes or until shrimp turn
opaque and pasta is tender. Stir in coconut
milk; heat through.
Makes 3 servings.

Nutrition Facts per serving: 411 cal., 21 g total fat
(15 g sat. fat), 115 mg chol., 1,292 mg sodium, 33 g carbo.,
2 g fiber, 24 g pro. Daily Values: 3% vit. A, 4% vit. C,
7% calcium, 35% iron

Shrimp and Scallop Skewers

Start to Finish: 60 min.

12   large fresh or frozen shrimp in shells (8 to
     12 ounces)
12   large fresh or frozen sea scallops
2/3 cup bottled Italian salad dressing
2   medium sweet peppers, cut into 1½-inch
     pieces

1. Thaw shrimp and scallops, if frozen. Peel and
devein shrimp. Rinse shrimp and scallops; pat
dry. In a self-sealing plastic bag set in a shallow
dish combine ½ cup of the dressing, the shrimp,
and scallops. Close bag. Marinate in refrigerator
for 30 minutes to 2 hours. Drain; discard
marinade. Soak sixteen 10-inch wooden skewers
in water for 30 minutes, or use 10-inch metal
skewers. Cook peppers in boiling water for
2 minutes; drain.

2. Alternately thread shrimp, scallops, and
peppers on the skewers, using 2 skewers side by
side for each kabob. Grill directly over medium
coals about 12 minutes or until shrimp and
scallops are opaque, turning once. Before
serving, brush kabobs with remaining dressing.
Makes 4 servings.

Nutrition Facts per serving: 174 cal., 8 g total fat
(1 g sat. fat), 76 mg chol., 264 mg sodium, 7 g carbo.,
1 g fiber, 18 g pro. Daily Values: 66% vit. A, 163% vit. C,
4% calcium, 7% iron

Buttery Bay Scallops

Start to Finish: 10 min.

3/4 pound fresh or frozen bay scallops
1   clove garlic, minced
1/8 teaspoon dried tarragon, crushed
2   tablespoons butter or margarine
     Salt and black pepper

1. Thaw scallops, if frozen. Rinse scallops; pat dry. In a skillet cook garlic and tarragon in hot butter over medium heat for 1 minute. Remove from heat. Add scallops. Sprinkle lightly with salt and pepper. Cook over medium heat about 4 minutes or just until opaque, turning occasionally.
Makes 3 or 4 servings.

Nutrition Facts per serving: 173 cal., 9 g total fat (5 g sat. fat), 59 mg chol., 362 mg sodium, 3 g carbo., 0 g fiber, 19 g pro. Daily Values: 7% vit. A, 5% vit. C, 3% calcium, 2% iron

Scallop Fried Rice

Start to Finish: 45 min.

8   ounces fresh or frozen bay scallops
1/4 cup Thai ginger sauce or stir-fry sauce
     Nonstick cooking spray
1   egg
2   green onions, thinly bias-sliced
1   10-ounce package frozen rice with peas
         and mushrooms, thawed

1. Thaw scallops, if frozen. Rinse scallops; pat dry. In a small bowl stir together scallops and ginger sauce. Cover and marinate in the refrigerator for 30 minutes.

2. Coat a wok or large skillet with cooking spray. Heat over medium-high heat. Crack egg into hot wok. Cook and stir for 1 minute or until egg is cooked through (should look like scrambled egg). Remove egg from wok.

3. Add scallops with sauce and green onions to wok. Cook and stir about 2 minutes or until scallops are opaque. Add thawed rice mixture and cooked egg to wok. Stir all ingredients together. Cook and stir 2 minutes more or until heated through.
Makes 2 servings.

Nutrition Facts per serving: 362 cal., 5 g total fat (1 g sat. fat), 144 mg chol., 1,502 mg sodium, 48 g carbo., 2 g fiber, 26 g pro. Daily Values: 7% vit. A, 14% vit. C, 7% calcium, 15% iron

French Omelet

Start to Finish: 7 min.

2 **eggs**
1 **tablespoon water**
⅛ **teaspoon salt**
   Dash black pepper
   Nonstick cooking spray

1. In a bowl combine eggs, water, salt, and pepper. Using a fork, beat until combined but not frothy. Coat an unheated 8- or 10-inch nonstick skillet with flared sides with cooking spray.

2. Add egg mixture to skillet; cook over medium heat. As eggs set, run a spatula around the edge of the skillet, lifting eggs so uncooked portion flows underneath. When eggs are set but still shiny, remove from heat. Fold omelet in half. Transfer to a warm plate.
Makes 1 serving.

Nutrition Facts per serving: 152 cal., 11 g total fat (3 g sat. fat), 426 mg chol., 393 mg sodium, 1 g carbo., 0 g fiber, 13 g pro. Daily Values: 19% vit. A, 4% vit. C, 9% iron

French Omelet Fillings

Much of the beauty of the classic omelet is its versatility. Delicious plain, it is even better filled. Try one or a combination of these quick fillings sprinkled on top of the omelet before it is folded and slid out of the pan. Try grated or soft cheeses, fresh herbs, roasted red pepper strips, cooked chicken, ham, prosciutto, olives, capers, salsa, fresh tomato, spinach, or steamed asparagus.

Oven Omelets with Pesto

Start to Finish: 35 min.

2 **cups desired frozen vegetables**
3 **tablespoons purchased basil pesto**
   Nonstick cooking spray
3 **cups refrigerated or frozen egg product, thawed, or 12 eggs**
¼ **cup water**
⅛ **teaspoon each salt and black pepper**

1. Cook vegetables according to package directions. Drain. Cut up any large pieces. Stir in pesto. Meanwhile, coat a 15×10×1-inch baking pan with cooking spray; set aside.

2. In a mixing bowl combine egg product, water, salt, and pepper. Using a fork or rotary beater, beat until combined but not frothy. Place prepared pan on center oven rack. Pour egg mixture into pan. Bake, uncovered, in a 400°F oven about 8 minutes or until mixture is set but still has a shiny surface.

3. Cut baked eggs into six 5-inch squares. Invert omelet squares onto warm serving plates. Spoon cooked vegetables on half of each omelet; fold other half over, forming a triangle.
Makes 6 servings.

Nutrition Facts per serving: 142 cal., 7 g total fat (2 g sat. fat), 4 mg chol., 290 mg sodium, 5 g carbo., 1 g fiber, 15 g pro. Daily Values: 15% vit. A, 9% vit. C, 11% calcium, 15% iron

Spinach and Feta Omelet

Start to Finish: 25 min.

4   cups chopped fresh spinach
6   large eggs
1   tablespoon butter or margarine
½   cup crumbled feta cheese (2 ounces)

1. In a medium saucepan cook spinach, covered, in a small amount of salted, boiling water for 3 to 4 minutes or until tender. Drain spinach thoroughly. In a medium bowl beat eggs well. Add drained spinach; beat until combined.

2. Heat half of the butter in a 7- or 8- inch omelet pan or skillet with flared sides over medium-high heat. Pour half of the egg mixture into pan. As eggs set, run a spatula around the edge of the skillet, lifting eggs so uncooked portion flows underneath. Cook until top of omelet is set but still shiny. Turn omelet; sprinkle with half of the cheese. Cook 2 minutes more until cheese is melted.

3. Transfer omelet to a warm serving plate; roll up omelet. Cover and keep warm in a 300°F oven while using remaining ingredients to make a second omelet.
Makes 2 servings.

Nutrition Facts per serving: 357 cal., 27 g total fat (13 g sat. fat), 679 mg chol., 639 mg sodium, 3 g carbo., 6 g fiber, 25 g pro. Daily Values: 94% vit. A, 25% vit. C, 26% calcium, 37% iron

Potatoes 'n' Eggs

Start to Finish: 10 min.

1   cup frozen loose-pack diced hash brown
        potatoes with onion and peppers
1   8-ounce carton refrigerated or frozen egg
        product, thawed, or 4 eggs
⅛   teaspoon salt
2   tablespoons shredded cheddar cheese
2   tablespoons salsa

1. In a 1-quart microwave-safe casserole microwave potatoes, covered, on 100 percent power (high) for 3 to 5 minutes or until tender, stirring once.

2. In a small mixing bowl beat together eggs and salt; add to potatoes. Microwave, uncovered, on high for 1 to 3 minutes or until almost set, pushing cooked egg to center after 1 minute, then every 15 seconds. Top with cheese; let stand for 1 minute. Serve with salsa.
Makes 2 servings.

Nutrition Facts per serving: 147 cal., 3 g total fat (1 g sat. fat), 7 mg chol., 488 mg sodium, 16 g carbo., 0 g fiber, 14 g pro. Daily Values: 10% vit. A, 13% vit. C, 9% calcium, 13% iron

Minted Pea-Egg Salad

Prep: 15 min. • Chill: 4 to 24 hours

1	tablespoon fat-free mayonnaise dressing or salad dressing
1/2	teaspoon snipped fresh mint or thyme or 1/8 teaspoon dried mint or thyme, crushed
2/3	cup frozen peas
1	hard-cooked egg, chopped
1/4	cup chopped celery

1. In a medium bowl stir together mayonnaise dressing and mint. Add remaining ingredients. Cover and refrigerate for 4 to 24 hours.
Makes 1 serving.

Nutrition Facts per serving: 165 cal., 6 g total fat (2 g sat. fat), 212 mg chol., 308 mg sodium, 17 g carbo., 5 g fiber, 11 g pro. Daily Values: 20% vit. A, 32% vit. C, 6% calcium, 13% iron

Mediterranean Couscous with Tofu

Prep: 10 min. • Cook: 5 min.

1	5.7-ounce package Mediterranean curry- or roasted-garlic-flavored couscous mix
1/2	of a 12- to 16-ounce package extra-firm tofu (fresh bean curd), well drained
1	tablespoon olive oil
1/2	cup sliced, pitted ripe olives or sliced, pitted Greek black olives
1/2	cup crumbled feta cheese or finely shredded Parmesan cheese

1. Prepare couscous according to package directions, except omit oil. Meanwhile, cut tofu into 1/2-inch cubes. Pat dry with clean, white paper towels. In a large skillet cook and stir tofu in hot oil over medium-high heat for 5 to 7 minutes or until tofu is browned. Stir tofu and olives into couscous. Transfer to a serving dish. Top with cheese.
Makes 4 servings.

Nutrition Facts per serving: 259 cal., 10 g total fat (4 g sat. fat), 17 mg chol., 763 mg sodium, 33 g carbo., 3 g fiber, 11 g pro. Daily Values: 6% vit. A, 3% vit. C, 14% calcium, 11% iron

Sweet Beans and Noodles

Start to Finish: 30 min.

8	ounces dried linguine pasta
1 1/2	cups frozen sweet soybeans (edamame)
1	cup purchased shredded carrot
1	10-ounce container purchased Alfredo sauce
2	teaspoons snipped fresh rosemary

1. Cook pasta according to package directions, adding soybeans and carrot during the last 10 minutes. Drain and return to pan. Add Alfredo sauce and rosemary; toss to combine. Heat through.
Makes 4 servings.

Nutrition Facts per serving: 544 cal., 27 g total fat (1 g sat. fat), 35 mg chol., 280 mg sodium, 57 g carbo., 5 g fiber, 20 g pro. Daily Values: 173% vit. A, 24% vit. C, 12% calcium, 19% iron

Black Bean and Corn Quesadillas

Start to Finish: 20 min.

2   cups shredded four-cheese Mexican-style blend (8 ounces)
8   8-inch flour tortillas
1½ cups bottled black bean and corn salsa
1   medium avocado, seeded, peeled, and chopped
    Dairy sour cream

1. Sprinkle ¼ cup cheese over half of each tortilla. Top with 1 tablespoon salsa. Divide avocado among tortillas. Fold tortillas in half, pressing gently.

2. Heat a large skillet over medium-high heat for 2 minutes; reduce heat to medium. Cook quesadillas, two at a time, for 2 to 3 minutes or until lightly brown and cheese is melted, turning once. Remove quesadillas from skillet; place on a baking sheet. Keep warm in a 300°F oven. Repeat with remaining quesadillas. Cut into wedges. Serve with sour cream and remaining salsa.
Makes 4 servings.

Nutrition Facts per serving: 512 cal., 33 g total fat (14 g sat. fat), 55 mg chol., 940 mg sodium, 38 g carbo., 4 g fiber, 18 g pro. Daily Values: 13% vit. A, 17% vit. C, 42% calcium, 16% iron

Chipotle-Bean Enchiladas

Prep: 25 min. • Bake: 30 min.

10 6-inch corn tortillas
1   15-ounce can pinto beans or black beans, rinsed and drained
1   tablespoon chopped chipotle pepper in adobo sauce
2   cups shredded four-cheese Mexican-style blend (8 ounces)
2   10-ounce cans enchilada sauce

1. Stack tortillas; wrap tightly in foil. Bake in a 350°F oven for 10 minutes or until warm. Meanwhile, for filling, combine beans, chipotle, 1 cup of the cheese, and ½ cup of the enchilada sauce. Spoon about ¼ cup filling onto one edge of each tortilla. Roll up each tortilla. Arrange tortillas, seam side down, in a greased 2-quart rectangular baking dish. Top with remaining sauce. Bake, covered, in a 350°F oven for 25 minutes or until heated through. Sprinkle with remaining cheese. Bake, uncovered, about 5 minutes more until cheese melts.
Makes 5 servings.

Nutrition Facts per serving: 487 cal., 19 g total fat (8 g sat. fat), 40 mg chol., 1,091 mg sodium, 63 g carbo., 14 g fiber, 23 g pro. Daily Values: 137% vit. A, 2% vit. C, 36% calcium, 40% iron

Chipotle Chile Peppers
A chipotle chile is a dried, smoked jalapeño that's milder than a fresh jalapeño and has a smoky, almost chocolatey flavor. In addition to the dried form, they also come canned in adobo sauce—a mixture of ground chiles, herbs, and vinegar. They're available at local supermarkets or Hispanic food markets.

Tortilla Lasagna

Prep: 10 min. • Bake: 35 min.

1 7-ounce package Spanish rice mix
1 11-ounce can whole kernel corn with sweet peppers
2 15-ounce cans black beans
10 6-inch corn tortillas
2 cups shredded Monterey Jack cheese with jalapeño peppers (8 ounces)

1. Prepare the rice according to package directions, except substitute undrained corn for 1/2 cup of the liquid. In a medium bowl slightly mash undrained beans.

2. Place 5 tortillas in the bottom of a greased 3-quart rectangular baking dish, overlapping and placing slightly up the sides of the dish (cut tortillas as necessary to fit). Spoon beans evenly over tortillas. Sprinkle with 1 cup of the cheese. Top with the remaining tortillas. Spoon cooked rice over tortillas.

3. Bake, covered, in a 400°F oven for 30 minutes. Uncover and sprinkle with remaining cheese. Bake 5 minutes more or until cheese is melted. Let stand for 10 minutes before serving.
Makes 8 servings.

Nutrition Facts per serving: 406 cal., 12 g total fat (7 g sat. fat), 34 mg chol., 1,101 mg sodium, 60 g carbo., 11 g fiber, 20 g pro. Daily Values: 11% vit. A, 12% vit. C, 33% calcium, 20% iron

Black Bean Cakes

Prep: 10 min. • Cook: 8 min.

1 15-ounce can black beans with cumin and chili spices or black beans, undrained
1 cup bottled salsa
2 tablespoons lime juice
1 8 1/2-ounce package or 1/2 of a 15-ounce package corn bread and muffin mix
   Nonstick cooking spray
1/2 cup dairy sour cream Mexican-style dip

1. In a medium bowl slightly mash undrained beans. Stir in 1/2 cup of the salsa and the lime juice. Stir in corn bread mix just until moistened.

2. Coat a large nonstick skillet or griddle with cooking spray; heat skillet over medium heat. For each cake, spoon about 1/4 cup batter into hot skillet. Use the back of a spoon to spread batter into a 4-inch circle. Cook for 1 to 2 minutes on each side or until browned. Repeat with remaining batter. Serve with remaining salsa and sour cream dip.
Makes 4 servings.

Nutrition Facts per serving: 429 cal., 12 g total fat (5 g sat. fat), 1 mg chol., 1,314 mg sodium, 65 g carbo., 11 g fiber, 12 g pro. Daily Values: 18% vit. A, 11% vit. C, 11% calcium, 21% iron

Spicy Simmered Beans and Vegetables

Prep: 10 min. • Cook: 15 min.

1   16-ounce package frozen Brussels sprouts, cauliflower, and carrot vegetable blend

1   16-ounce jar Indian-style cooking sauce (or one 15-ounce can tomato sauce plus 1 teaspoon curry powder and ¼ teaspoon ground red pepper)

1   15-ounce can garbanzo beans, rinsed and drained

2   cups hot cooked rice

1   tablespoon snipped fresh cilantro

1. In a large skillet combine vegetables, sauce, and beans. Bring to boiling; reduce heat. Simmer, covered, for 15 minutes or until vegetables are crisp-tender, stirring occasionally. Serve over rice and sprinkle with cilantro.
Makes 4 servings.

Nutrition Facts per serving: 360 cal., 6 g total fat
(0 g sat. fat), 0 mg chol., 831 mg sodium, 63 g carbo.,
10 g fiber, 12 g pro. Daily Values: 46% vit. A, 89% vit. C,
11% calcium, 24% iron

Lentil-Vegetable Turnovers

Prep: 25 min. • Bake: 25 min.

1   15-ounce package folded refrigerated unbaked piecrust (2 crusts)

1   9-ounce jar mango chutney (¾ cup)

2   teaspoons curry paste

2   cups frozen loose-pack whole potatoes, broccoli, carrots, baby corn, and red pepper, thawed and chopped

1   cup cooked lentils

1. Let piecrusts stand at room temperature according to package directions. In a medium bowl stir together the chutney and curry paste. Add vegetables and lentils; stir to coat.

2. Line a large baking sheet with foil; grease foil. Cut each piecrust in half, forming 4 semicircles. Place one-fourth of the lentil mixture in the center of each piece of pastry. Brush the edges with a little water. Fold dough in half over the filling, press edges together, and crimp with a fork to seal. Place turnovers on the baking sheet. Prick each with a fork. Bake in a 375°F oven for 25 minutes or until golden. Serve warm.
Makes 4 servings.

Nutrition Facts per serving: 642 cal., 29 g total fat
(12 g sat. fat), 20 mg chol., 623 mg sodium, 88 g carbo.,
5 g fiber, 7 g pro. Daily Values: 36% vit. A, 41% vit. C,
3% calcium, 12% iron

Polenta with Mushroom Sauce and Cheese

Prep: 15 min. • Bake: 25 min.

Nonstick cooking spray
3 cups sliced fresh mushrooms (8 ounces)
1 15-ounce container refrigerated
    marinara sauce
1 16-ounce tube refrigerated cooked
    plain polenta
1/4 cup thinly sliced fresh basil
1 cup shredded Italian-style cheese blend
    (4 ounces)

1. Coat a large skillet with cooking spray. Heat over medium heat. Cook mushrooms for 5 to 7 minutes or until tender, stirring occasionally. Remove from heat and stir in sauce; set aside.

2. Cut polenta into 1/2-inch slices. Arrange in the bottom of a greased 2-quart square baking dish. Top with sliced basil. Sprinkle half the cheese over basil. Top with the sauce. Bake, uncovered, in a 350°F oven for 20 minutes or until heated through. Sprinkle with remaining cheese. Bake 5 minutes more or until cheese is melted.
Makes 6 servings.

Nutrition Facts per serving: 186 cal., 8 g total fat (3 g sat. fat), 13 mg chol., 684 mg sodium, 20 g carbo., 4 g fiber, 9 g pro. Daily Values: 12% vit. A, 1% vit. C, 16% calcium, 6% iron

Gardener's Pie

Prep: 15 min. • Bake: 45 min.

1 16-ounce package loose-pack frozen
    vegetable medley, thawed
1 11-ounce can condensed cheddar
    cheese soup
1/2 teaspoon dried thyme, crushed
1 20-ounce package refrigerated
    mashed potatoes
1 cup shredded smoked cheddar cheese
    (4 ounces)

1. In a 1 1/2-quart casserole, combine vegetables, soup, and thyme. Stir mashed potatoes to soften. Spread carefully over vegetable mixture to cover surface. Bake, covered, in a 350°F oven for 30 minutes. Uncover and bake 15 minutes more or until heated through, topping with cheese the last 5 minutes of baking.
Makes 4 servings.

Nutrition Facts per serving: 349 cal., 17 g total fat (8 g sat. fat), 39 mg chol., 1,031 mg sodium, 40 g carbo., 4 g fiber, 15 g pro. Daily Values: 95% vit. A, 43% vit. C, 28% calcium, 5% iron

Vegetable-Cheese Chowder

Start to Finish: 20 min.

- 1   16-ounce package loose-pack frozen
      broccoli, cauliflower, and carrots
- ½   cup water
- 2   cups milk
- ⅓   cup all-purpose flour
- 1   14-ounce can chicken broth
- 1   cup shredded smoked or regular Gouda
      cheese (4 ounces)

1. In a large saucepan combine vegetables and water. Bring to boiling; reduce heat. Simmer, covered, about 4 minutes or until vegetables are just tender. Do not drain.

2. Meanwhile, in a screw-top jar combine ⅔ cup of the milk and the flour; cover and shake well. Add to saucepan; add remaining milk and the chicken broth. Cook and stir until thickened and bubbly. Cook and stir for 1 minute more. Add cheese; cook and stir over low heat until cheese nearly melts.
Makes 4 servings.

Nutrition Facts per serving: 370 cal., 20 g total fat (13 g sat. fat), 81 mg chol., 942 mg sodium, 22 g carbo., 3 g fiber, 25 g pro. Daily Values: 162% vit. A, 72% vit. C, 52% calcium, 9% iron

Bread Bowl Potato Soup

Prep: 5 min. • Cook: 15 min.

- 1   14-ounce can reduced-sodium
      chicken broth
- 1   20-ounce package refrigerated diced
      potatoes with onions
- 1   cup milk
- 1   10-ounce package soy-based vegetarian
      smoked sausage, halved lengthwise and
      sliced
- 4   purchased bread bowls (optional)

1. In a large saucepan bring chicken broth to boiling. Add potatoes; return to boiling. Reduce heat. Simmer, covered, for 10 minutes or until potatoes are very tender. Remove from heat. Cool slightly.

2. Place half of the potato mixture in a food processor bowl or blender container. Cover and process or blend until almost smooth, leaving some pieces of potato. Remove to a large bowl. Repeat with remaining potato mixture. Return all to saucepan. Stir in milk and sausage. Heat through. If desired, serve in bread bowls.
Makes 4 servings.

Nutrition Facts per serving: 724 cal., 11 g total fat (2 g sat. fat), 5 mg chol., 2,401 mg sodium, 121 g carbo., 10 g fiber, 32 g pro. Daily Values: 3% vit. A, 27% vit. C, 23% calcium, 33% iron

Pasta Stir-Fry

Start to Finish: 25 min.

- 1   9-ounce package refrigerated cheese-
         filled tortellini
- 1   16-ounce package fresh cut or frozen
         stir-fry vegetables, such as broccoli,
         pea pods, carrots, and celery
- 1   tablespoon cooking oil
- ¾   cup peanut or garlic stir-fry sauce
- ¼   cup chopped unsalted cashews or peanuts

1. Cook pasta according to package directions. Drain and set aside. In a wok or large skillet cook and stir vegetables in hot oil for 3 to 5 minutes (7 to 8 minutes for frozen vegetables) or until crisp-tender. Add pasta and stir-fry sauce; toss to coat. Heat through. Sprinkle with cashews. **Makes 4 servings.**

Nutrition Facts per serving: 304 cal., 10 g total fat (3 g sat. fat), 10 mg chol., 1,842 mg sodium, 48 g carbo., 5 g fiber, 16 g pro. Daily Values: 81% vit. A, 56% vit. C, 14% calcium, 9% iron

Tortellini with Roasted Peppers

Start to Finish: 20 min.

- 1   9-ounce package refrigerated cheese-
         filled tortellini
- 1   4-ounce jar roasted red sweet peppers
- ½   cup refrigerated light Alfredo sauce
- ½   cup thinly sliced fresh basil
- ½   teaspoon coarsely ground black pepper

1. Cook pasta according to package directions; drain. Meanwhile, drain sweet peppers; cut into strips. In a large saucepan heat Alfredo sauce. Stir in drained pasta. Reduce heat; add sweet peppers. Simmer for 5 minutes, stirring often. Stir in half of the basil. To serve, sprinkle with remaining basil and the black pepper. **Makes 3 servings.**

Nutrition Facts per serving: 362 cal., 12 g total fat (5 g sat. fat), 61 mg chol., 710 mg sodium, 50 g carbo., 1 g fiber, 16 g pro. Daily Values: 19% vit. A, 113% vit. C, 13% calcium, 14% iron

Linguine with Gorgonzola Sauce

Start to Finish: 20 min.

- 1   9-ounce package refrigerated linguine
- 1   pound asparagus, cut into bite-size pieces
- 1   cup half-and-half or light cream
- ½   cup crumbled Gorgonzola or other blue
         cheese (2 ounces)
- 2   tablespoons chopped walnuts, toasted

1. Cook pasta according to package directions, adding asparagus to the water with pasta; drain. Return pasta and asparagus to pan.

2. Meanwhile, in a medium saucepan combine half-and-half and cheese. Bring to boiling over medium heat; reduce heat. Simmer, uncovered, for 3 minutes. Pour sauce over pasta mixture; toss gently to coat. Transfer to a warm serving dish. Sprinkle with nuts. **Makes 3 servings.**

Nutrition Facts per serving: 478 cal., 22 g total fat (10 g sat. fat), 62 mg chol., 365 mg sodium, 54 g carbo., 2 g fiber, 19 g pro. Daily Values: 22% vit. A, 40% vit. C, 19% calcium, 12% iron

Pesto and Cheese Tomato Melt

Prep: 10 min. • Broil: 2 min.

¼ cup purchased basil pesto

2 tablespoons chopped nuts

4 1-inch slices sourdough French bread,
   toasted

¼ cup oil-packed dried tomatoes, drained
   and chopped

1 cup shredded mozzarella cheese (4 ounces)

1. In a small bowl stir together pesto and nuts.
Spread over toasted bread slices. Top with
tomatoes and cheese. Place on a baking sheet.
Broil 4 inches from the heat for 2 to 3 minutes or
until cheese melts.
Makes 2 servings.

Nutrition Facts per serving: 587 cal., 34 g total fat
(6 g sat. fat), 36 mg chol., 918 mg sodium, 44 g carbo.,
2 g fiber, 25 g pro. Daily Values: 15% vit. A, 23% vit. C,
56% calcium, 15% iron

Brie Sandwiches with Greens

Prep: 10 min. • Cook: 7 min.

2 tablespoons butter or margarine

2 cloves garlic, minced

6 cups fresh spinach leaves

8 ounces cold Brie, cut into ⅛-inch slices

8 slices firm-textured whole grain bread

1. In a large skillet melt 1 tablespoon of the
butter. Add garlic; cook for 30 seconds. Add
spinach. Cook over medium heat, tossing until
spinach begins to wilt. Set aside.

2. Divide cheese among 4 slices of the bread.
Top with spinach mixture. Cover with remaining
bread slices. Lightly spread the outside of each
sandwich with remaining butter.

3. In a large skillet cook half of the sandwiches
over medium-low heat for 7 to 9 minutes or
until golden brown, turning once. Repeat with
remaining sandwiches.
Makes 4 servings.

Nutrition Facts per serving: 405 cal., 27 g total fat
(12 g sat. fat), 57 mg chol., 771 mg sodium, 25 g carbo.,
7 g fiber, 18 g pro. Daily Values: 67% vit. A, 8% vit. C, 25%
calcium, 24% iron

Cashew-Vegetable Stir-Fry

Prep: 5 min. • Cook: 6 min.

1   16-ounce package frozen stir-fry
     vegetables

1   tablespoon cooking oil

$1/3$ cup bottled stir-fry sauce

3   cups hot cooked rice

$3/4$ cup dry roasted cashews

1. In a large skillet cook and stir vegetables in hot oil for 5 minutes or until crisp-tender. Add sauce; cook and stir 1 to 2 minutes more until heated through. Serve over rice. Top with nuts.
Makes 4 servings.

Nutrition Facts per serving: 393 cal., 16 g total fat (3 g sat. fat), 0 mg chol., 720 mg sodium, 54 g carbo., 4 g fiber, 9 g pro. Daily Values: 44% vit. A, 30% vit. C, 7% calcium, 21% iron

Asian Noodle Bowl

Start to Finish: 25 min.

8   ounces dry buckwheat soba noodles, udon
     noodles, or vermicelli noodles

2   cups vegetable broth

$1/2$ cup bottled peanut sauce

2   cups Chinese-style frozen stir-fry
     vegetables

$1/2$ cup dry roasted peanuts, chopped

1. Cook noodles according to package directions. Drain but do not rinse. Set aside. In the same pan, combine broth and peanut sauce. Bring to boiling. Stir in frozen vegetables and cooked noodles. Return to boiling; reduce heat. Simmer for 2 to 3 minutes or until vegetables are heated through. Divide noodles and broth among 4 bowls. Sprinkle with peanuts.
Makes 4 servings.

Nutrition Facts per serving: 403 cal., 15 g total fat (2 g sat. fat), 0 mg chol., 1,326 mg sodium, 59 g carbo., 4 g fiber, 15 g pro. Daily Values: 3% calcium, 10% iron

Fresh Tomato Pizza with Pesto

Start to Finish: 15 min.

- ½ cup purchased pesto
- 1 16-ounce Italian bread shell (Boboli)
- 3 medium ripe tomatoes, thinly sliced
- 1 2¼-ounce can sliced, pitted ripe olives, drained (about ⅔ cup)
- 2 cups shredded Monterey Jack or mozzarella cheese (8 ounces)

1. Spread pesto over bread shell. Place on a large pizza pan or baking sheet. Arrange tomato slices on top. Sprinkle with olives and cheese. Bake in a 425°F oven for 10 to 15 minutes or until cheese melts. Cut into wedges.
Makes 4 servings.

Nutrition Facts per serving: 776 cal., 48 g total fat
(11 g sat. fat), 60 mg chol., 1,265 mg sodium, 60 g carbo.,
4 g fiber, 32 g pro. Daily Values: 28% vit. A, 29% vit. C,
70% calcium, 22% iron

Portobellos Florentine

Prep: 15 min. • Bake: 20 min.

- 4 portobello mushrooms (about 5 inches in diameter)
- ½ cup purchased basil pesto
- 1 cup finely chopped fresh spinach leaves or ½ of a 10-ounce package frozen chopped spinach, thawed and well drained
- ½ cup ricotta cheese
- 2 medium Roma tomatoes, chopped

1. Remove and discard stems from mushrooms, if present. Spread stem sides of mushroom caps with half of the pesto. Place caps, stem side up, in a shallow baking pan.

2. In a small bowl combine remaining pesto, spinach, and cheese. Divide spinach mixture among mushroom caps. Bake, uncovered, in a 350°F oven about 20 minutes or until mushrooms are tender and filling is heated through. Sprinkle with tomatoes.
Makes 4 servings.

Nutrition Facts per serving: 260 cal., 19 g total fat
(5 g sat. fat), 21 mg chol., 269 mg sodium, 11 g carbo.,
5 g fiber, 11 g pro. Daily Values: 22% vit. A, 17% vit. C,
20% calcium, 8% iron

Squash with Wild Rice and Plums

Prep: 20 min. • Bake: 50 min.

2   1- to 1½-pound acorn squash
5   tablespoons bottled balsamic vinaigrette
      salad dressing
1   6-ounce package long grain and wild rice
      blend with seasoning packet
3   ounces dried plums, snipped (½ cup)
⅓   cup chopped pecans

1. Halve each squash lengthwise. Scrape out and discard seeds. Brush cut sides of squash with 1 tablespoon of the vinaigrette. Place squash halves, cut side down, in a greased 3-quart baking dish. Bake in a 375°F oven for 40 minutes or until squash is tender.

2. Meanwhile, prepare rice according to package directions, except stir in plums when water begins to boil.

3. Remove squash from oven; carefully turn cut side up. Spoon cooked rice mixture into each squash half, mounding as necessary. Drizzle filling and squash with remaining vinaigrette. Sprinkle pecans over filling. Bake, uncovered, for 10 minutes more.
Makes 4 servings.

Nutrition Facts per serving: 428 cal., 16 g total fat
(2 g sat. fat), 0 mg chol., 1,016 mg sodium, 69 g carbo.,
6 g fiber, 9 g pro. Daily Values: 184% vit. A, 44% vit. C,
9% calcium, 19% iron

Couscous and Pine Nut-Stuffed Peppers

Prep: 15 min. • Cook: 5 min. • Bake: 25 min.

1   5.6-ounce package pine nut couscous mix
½   cup purchased shredded carrot
2   large sweet peppers
½   cup shredded Italian-style cheese blend
      (2 ounces)
1½ cups purchased olive pasta sauce

1. Prepare couscous mix according to package directions, except omit oil and add the shredded carrot with the couscous.

2. Meanwhile, cut peppers in half lengthwise; remove seeds and membranes. Cook pepper halves in boiling water for 5 minutes. Drain on paper towels. Place peppers, cut side up, in a 2-quart rectangular baking dish. Spoon cooked couscous mixture into pepper halves.

3. Bake, covered, in a 350°F oven for 20 to 25 minutes or until filling is heated through and peppers are tender. Sprinkle cheese over peppers. Bake, uncovered, 5 minutes more or until cheese is melted. Meanwhile, in a small saucepan heat the pasta sauce. Serve peppers with sauce.
Makes 4 servings.

Nutrition Facts per serving: 259 cal., 6 g total fat
(3 g sat. fat), 10 mg chol., 801 mg sodium, 42 g carbo.,
7 g fiber, 11 g pro. Daily Values: 150% vit. A, 205% vit. C,
10% calcium, 6% iron

Chiles Rellenos

Prep: 50 min. • Cook: 6 min.

6   fresh poblano chiles
2   cups shredded cheddar cheese (8 ounces)
1   cup all-purpose flour
4   eggs
1½ cups cooking oil

1. Place whole chiles on a foil-lined baking sheet. Bake in a 425°F oven for 20 to 25 minutes or until skins are bubbly and brown. Wrap chiles in foil; seal. Let stand for 20 to 30 minutes or until cool enough to handle. Make a slit in each chile from top to the bottom. Remove seeds.

2. Fill chiles with cheese. Secure chiles with wooden toothpicks, if necessary. Coat chiles with some of the flour. Whisk eggs in a bowl. Dip chiles into the beaten eggs. Coat evenly with remaining flour. In a heavy skillet heat the oil to 365°F. Fry chiles, a few at a time, for 3 to 4 minutes or until golden, turning once. Drain on paper towels; serve warm.
Makes 6 servings.

Nutrition Facts per serving: 359 cal., 21 g total fat (10 g sat. fat), 181 mg chol., 282 mg sodium, 24 g carbo., 1 g fiber, 18 g pro. Daily Values: 28% vit. A, 413% vit. C, 32% calcium, 23% iron

Spicy Pasta and Broccoli

Start to Finish: 25 min.

12 ounces orecchiette or medium shell pasta
      (about 4 cups)
2   tablespoons extra virgin olive oil
3   cups chopped Broccolini or broccoli florets
1   cup chicken broth with Italian herbs
¼   to ½ teaspoon crushed red pepper

1. Cook pasta according to package directions; drain. Return pasta to pan. Drizzle 1 tablespoon of the oil over pasta; toss to coat. Cover and keep warm.

2. Meanwhile, in a large skillet cook and stir Broccolini in remaining oil over medium-high heat for 3 minutes. Add broth and red pepper. Bring to boiling; reduce heat. Simmer, covered, for 2 to 3 minutes more until Broccolini is crisp-tender. Combine pasta and Broccolini mixture; toss to mix.
Makes 4 servings.

Nutrition Facts per serving: 404 cal., 9 g total fat (1 g sat. fat), 0 mg chol., 214 mg sodium, 67 g carbo., 4 g fiber, 14 g pro. Daily Values: 19% vit. A, 77% vit. C, 5% calcium, 18% iron

Creamy Lemon Pasta

Start to Finish: 15 min.

9   ounces refrigerated or 6 ounces dried
       fettuccine
½   cup whipping cream
¾   cup freshly grated Parmesan cheese
1   teaspoon finely shredded lemon peel
       Salt and black pepper

1. Cook pasta according to package directions. Drain well. Add cream, half of the cheese, and the lemon peel. Toss gently to coat. Transfer to a serving dish and top with remaining cheese. Season to taste with salt and pepper.
Makes 3 servings.

Nutrition Facts per serving: 489 cal., 24 g total fat
(15 g sat. fat), 170 mg chol., 529 mg sodium, 47 g carbo.,
2 g fiber, 20 g pro. Daily Values: 18% vit. A, 2% vit. C,
30% calcium, 10% iron

Summer Spaghetti

Start to Finish: 20 min.

2   cups mixed vegetables, such as sliced
       yellow summer squash, halved baby
       sunburst squash, chopped carrots, and
       sliced green onions
8   ounces spaghetti
2   tablespoons olive oil
¼   cup finely shredded Asiago or
       Parmesan cheese
⅛   teaspoon freshly ground black pepper

1. Place vegetables in a colander. Cook pasta according to package directions. Pour over vegetables in colander; drain. Transfer pasta and vegetable mixture to a serving bowl. Drizzle with oil, tossing to coat. Sprinkle with cheese and pepper.
Makes 4 servings.

Nutrition Facts per serving: 320 cal., 10 g total fat
(6 g sat. fat), 24 mg chol., 152 mg sodium, 48 g carbo.,
3 g fiber, 10 g pro. Daily Values: 135% vit. A, 19% vit. C,
7% calcium, 12% iron

SAUCES & MORE

Chapter five

Spanish Olive Rub

Start to Finish: 10 min.

- ½ cup pimiento-stuffed green olives
- 3 cloves garlic, chopped
- 1 tablespoon capers, drained
- 1½ teaspoons finely shredded orange peel
- ½ teaspoon black pepper

1. In a blender container or food processor bowl combine all ingredients. Cover and blend or process until chunky. Rub evenly over meat. Cook as desired.
Makes enough for 1 pound of beef, pork, or lamb.

Horseradish-Pepper Rub

Start to Finish: 10 min.

- 2 tablespoons cream-style prepared horseradish
- 4 cloves garlic, minced
- 1 tablespoon pink and black peppercorns, cracked, or cracked black pepper
- ½ teaspoon salt

1. In a small bowl stir together all ingredients. Rub evenly onto meat. Cook as desired.
Makes enough for 6 pounds of beef or lamb.

BBQ Rub

Start to Finish: 5 min.

- 2 tablespoons barbecue seasoning
- 1 tablespoon garlic powder
- 1 teaspoon onion salt
- ½ teaspoon celery seeds, ground
- ¼ teaspoon ground red pepper

1. In a small bowl stir together all ingredients. Rub evenly onto meat. Cook as desired.
Makes enough for 4 pounds of beef, pork, or lamb.

Chili and Spice Rub

Start to Finish: 10 min.

- ¼ cup chili powder
- 1 teaspoon dried oregano, crushed
- 1 teaspoon ground cumin
- 1 teaspoon salt
- 4 cloves garlic, minced

1. In a small bowl stir together all ingredients. Rub evenly onto meat. Cook as desired.
Makes enough for 3 to 4 pounds of pork or beef.

Three-Herb Rub

Start to Finish: 5 min.

- ½ teaspoon salt
- ½ teaspoon dried thyme, crushed
- ½ teaspoon dried rosemary, crushed
- ½ teaspoon dried savory, crushed
- ¼ teaspoon black pepper

1. In a small bowl stir together all ingredients. Rub evenly onto meat. Cook as desired.
Makes enough for 2½ pounds of beef, pork, chicken, or turkey.

Chipotle Rub

Start to Finish: 10 min.

- 1 teaspoon ground coriander
- ¼ teaspoon paprika
- ¼ to ½ teaspoon ground black pepper
- 1 small dried chipotle pepper, seeded and crushed, or ⅛ to ¼ teaspoon ground red pepper

1. In a small bowl stir together all ingredients. Rub evenly onto meat. Cook as desired.
Makes enough for 2½ pounds of pork, chicken, or turkey.

Curry Rub

Prep: 5 min. • Marinate: 2 hours

- ⅓ cup sugar
- 2 teaspoons paprika
- 1 teaspoon black pepper
- 1 teaspoon curry powder
- ½ teaspoon salt

1. In a small bowl stir together all ingredients. Rub evenly onto meat. Cover and refrigerate for at least 2 hours or up to 6 hours. Cook as desired.
Makes enough for 4 pounds of pork, chicken, or turkey.

Beer Marinade

Prep: 10 min. • Marinate: 4 to 24 hours

1   cup beer (measured after foam has
      subsided) or apple cider
2   tablespoons brown sugar
1   tablespoon Worcestershire sauce
2   teaspoons chili powder
1   clove garlic, minced

1. In a small bowl stir together all ingredients. Pour over meat; turn to coat. Marinate in the refrigerator for 4 to 24 hours, turning occasionally. Drain, discarding marinade. Cook as desired.
Makes enough for 3 pounds of beef or pork.

Espresso Marinade

Prep: 10 min. • Marinate: 2 to 24 hours

1   medium onion, chopped
½   cup bottled steak sauce or hickory-
      flavored barbecue sauce
¼   to ⅓ cup strong brewed espresso or coffee
2   tablespoons Worcestershire sauce

1. In a small bowl stir together all ingredients. Pour over meat; turn to coat. Marinate in the refrigerator for at least 2 hours or up to 24 hours. Drain meat, discarding marinade. Cook as desired.
Makes enough for 1½ pounds of beef, chicken, or turkey.

Citrus-Honey Marinade

Prep: 10 min. • Marinate: 1 hour

¼   cup orange juice
2   tablespoons lemon juice
2   tablespoons Dijon-style mustard
2   tablespoons honey
1   tablespoon soy sauce

1. In a small bowl stir together all ingredients. Pour over meat, poultry, or fish; turn to coat. Marinate in the refrigerator for 1 hour, turning occasionally. Drain, reserving marinade. Cook as desired. Brush reserved marinade on meat halfway through cooking.
Makes enough for 1 pound of pork, ham, chicken, turkey, or fish.

Broiling Made Easy

Broiling is a good, no-hassle substitute for grilling. There's just one downside—having to scrub the broiler pan. Here's a tip to eliminate that unpleasant job. Line the drip pan and the slotted rack of the broiler pan with foil before you start. Cut slots through the foil to correspond with slots or holes in the rack of the broiler pan so fat and meat juices can drip through. Now, anything that sticks stays on the foil, not the pan—so just toss it.

Lemon-Rosemary Marinade

Prep: 10 min. • Marinate: 2 to 24 hours

1/3 cup bottled vinegar-and-oil salad dressing
1 teaspoon finely shredded lemon peel
1 tablespoon lemon juice
1 teaspoon snipped fresh rosemary or
   1/4 teaspoon dried rosemary, crushed
1 teaspoon snipped fresh thyme or
   1/4 teaspoon dried thyme, crushed

1. In a small bowl stir together all ingredients. Pour over meat, poultry, or fish; turn to coat. Marinate in the refrigerator for 2 hours for fish, at least 3 hours or up to 24 hours for meat, turning occasionally. Drain, discarding marinade. Cook as desired.
Makes enough for 1 pound of pork, chicken, turkey, or fish.

Savory-Balsamic Marinade

Prep: 10 min. • Marinate: 2 to 4 hours

1/4 cup balsamic vinegar
1 tablespoon snipped fresh savory or
   1 teaspoon dried savory, crushed
1/2 teaspoon black pepper

1. In a small bowl stir together all ingredients. Pour over meat, poultry, or fish; turn to coat. Marinate in the refrigerator for up to 2 hours for fish, up to 4 hours for meat, turning once. Drain, discarding marinade. Cook as desired.
Makes enough for 1 pound of beef, pork, lamb, chicken, turkey, or fish.

Sherry Marinade

Prep: 10 min. • Marinate: 30 minutes

2 tablespoons cooking oil
2 tablespoons dry sherry
2 tablespoons stone-ground mustard
1 tablespoon honey
1 1/2 teaspoons soy sauce

1. In a small bowl stir together all ingredients. Pour over meat or seafood; turn to coat. Marinate in the refrigerator for 30 minutes. Drain, discarding marinade. Cook as desired.
Makes enough for 1 pound of pork, ham, fish, or shellfish.

Mustard

Mustard is a culinary magic-maker. Having a variety of mustards in your pantry makes quick, flavorful cooking as easy as opening a jar. There are herb mustards, fruit mustards, nut mustards, spirit mustards, cheese-flavored mustards, and Dijon-style. Use mustard in marinades and sauces; as a rub, dip, or glaze for grilled meats; or to flavor roasted chicken or potatoes. Stir together a few tablespoons of mustard with a little olive oil, minced garlic, and fresh or dried herbs, and toss with chicken pieces or potato chunks before roasting.

Seafood Marinade

Prep: 10 min. • Marinate: 2 hours

3   tablespoons lemon juice

2   tablespoons olive oil

2   teaspoons snipped fresh oregano or
        tarragon or ½ teaspoon dried oregano
        or tarragon, crushed

¼   teaspoon dry mustard

¼   teaspoon salt and ⅛ teaspoon black pepper

1. In a small bowl stir together all ingredients. Pour over shellfish or fish; turn to coat. Marinate in the refrigerator for at least 2 hours or up to 3 hours, turning occasionally. Drain, discarding marinade. Cook as desired.
Makes enough for 2 pounds of seafood.

Currant Sauce

Start to Finish: 10 min.

¼   cup currant jelly

3   tablespoons catsup

1   tablespoon vinegar

⅛   teaspoon ground cinnamon
        Dash ground cloves

1. In a small saucepan stir together all ingredients. Cook and stir just until boiling. Serve with beef, pork, ham, chicken, or turkey.
Makes about ½ cup.

Nutrition Facts per tablespoon: 33 cal., 0 g total fat
(0 g sat. fat), 0 mg chol., 69 mg sodium, 8 g carbo., 0 g fiber,
0 g pro. Daily Values: 1% vit. A, 2% vit. C

Easy Plum-Mustard Sauce

Start to Finish: 10 min.

1   18-ounce jar red plum jam

2   tablespoons honey mustard or Dijon-style
        mustard

⅛   teaspoon black pepper

1. In a small saucepan heat and stir jam over medium-low heat until jam is melted and bubbly. Stir in mustard and pepper. Serve warm with ham, turkey, or pork.
Makes about 1½ cups.

Nutrition Facts per 2 tablespoons: 123 cal., 0 g total fat
(0 g sat. fat), 0 mg chol., 16 mg sodium, 30 g carbo.,
0 g fiber, 0 g pro. Daily Values: 6% vit. C, 1% calcium, 1% iron

Raspberry Piquant Sauce

Start to Finish: 15 min.

- 3 tablespoons bottled chili sauce
- 2 tablespoons seedless raspberry
       spreadable fruit
- 1 tablespoon orange juice or apple juice
- 1½ teaspoons brown mustard or spicy brown
       mustard

1. In a small saucepan stir together all ingredients. Cook and stir over low heat until spreadable fruit is melted. Serve with beef, pork, ham, chicken, or turkey.
Makes about ⅓ cup.

Nutrition Facts per tablespoon: 29 cal., 0 g total fat
(0 g sat. fat), 0 mg chol., 141 mg sodium, 7 g carbo.,
1 g fiber, 0 g pro. Daily Values: 1% vit. A, 5% vit. C, 1% iron

Mustard-Horseradish Sauce

Start to Finish: 5 min.

- 1 tablespoon Dijon-style mustard
- ⅓ cup dairy sour cream, mayonnaise, or
       salad dressing
- 1 green onion, finely chopped
- 1 to 2 teaspoons prepared horseradish

1. In a small bowl stir together all ingredients. Serve with beef, pork, lamb, chicken, or turkey.
Makes about ½ cup.

Nutrition Facts per tablespoon: 20 cal., 2 g total fat
(1 g sat. fat), 4 mg chol., 16 mg sodium, 1 g carbo., 0 g fiber,
0 g pro. Daily Values: 1% vit. A, 1% vit. C, 1% calcium

Cranberry-Chipotle Sauce

Start to Finish: 20 min.

- 1 8-ounce can jellied cranberry sauce
- ⅓ cup apricot or peach preserves or apricot or
       peach spreadable fruit
- ¼ cup chopped onion
- 1 tablespoon lemon juice or cider vinegar
- 1 canned chipotle pepper in adobo sauce or
       1 jalapeño pepper, seeded and chopped

1. In a small saucepan stir together all ingredients. Bring to boiling, stirring constantly; reduce heat. Simmer, uncovered, for 5 minutes, stirring occasionally.

2. To use, brush pork or chicken with some of the sauce during the last 10 minutes of cooking. If desired, reheat and pass additional sauce. Cover and store any remaining sauce in the refrigerator for up to 2 weeks.
Makes 1½ cups.

Nutrition Facts per ¼ cup: 112 cal., 0 g total fat
(0 g sat. fat), 0 mg chol., 43 mg sodium, 28 g carbo.,
1 g fiber, 0 g pro. Daily Values: 7% vit. C, 1% calcium, 1% iron

Honey-Peach Sauce

Start to Finish: 25 min.

4   medium peaches, peeled (if desired), or
       nectarines, pitted
2   tablespoons lemon juice
2   tablespoons honey
½   teaspoon cracked black pepper
1   to 2 teaspoons snipped fresh thyme or ¼ to
       ½ teaspoon dried thyme, crushed

1. Cut up 3 of the peaches. In a blender container or food processor bowl combine cut-up fruit, lemon juice, honey, and pepper. Cover and blend or process until smooth. Transfer mixture to a small saucepan. Bring to boiling; reduce heat. Simmer, uncovered, about 15 minutes or until slightly thickened, stirring occasionally.

2. Meanwhile, finely chop remaining peach; stir into sauce with thyme. Brush sauce onto pork, chicken, or turkey during the last 15 minutes of cooking. Heat remaining sauce until bubbly.
Makes about 1¾ cups.

Nutrition Facts per ¼ cup: 70 cal., 0 g total fat
(0 g sat. fat), 0 mg chol., 0 mg sodium, 19 g carbo., 1 g fiber,
0 g pro. Daily Values: 4% vit. A, 8% vit. C

Lime Hollandaise Sauce

Start to Finish: 15 min.

½   cup butter (no substitutes)
3   beaten egg yolks
1   tablespoon water
1   tablespoon lime juice
⅛   teaspoon salt

1. Cut butter into thirds; bring to room temperature. In the top of a double boiler, combine egg yolks, water, lime juice, and salt. Add a piece of the butter. Place over boiling water (upper pan should not touch water). Cook, stirring rapidly with a whisk, until butter melts and sauce begins to thicken. Add remaining butter, a piece at a time, stirring constantly until melted. Continue to cook and stir about 2 minutes more or until sauce thickens. Immediately remove from heat. If sauce is too thick or curdles, immediately whisk in 1 to 2 tablespoons hot water. Serve with fish, shellfish, or vegetables.
Makes ¾ cup.

Nutrition Facts per 2 tablespoons: 164 cal., 18 g total fat
(10 g sat. fat), 147 mg chol., 203 mg sodium, 0 g carbo.,
0 g fiber, 2 g pro. Daily Values: 30% vit. A, 1% vit. C,
1% calcium, 2% iron

Lemon Sauce

Start to Finish: 10 min.

¼   cup mayonnaise or salad dressing
2   tablespoons dairy sour cream
1   tablespoon snipped fresh Italian parsley
1   teaspoon finely shredded lemon peel
1   teaspoon lemon juice

1. In a small bowl stir together all ingredients. Serve with fish or shellfish.
Makes about ⅓ cup.

Nutrition Facts per tablespoon: 90 cal., 10 g total fat
(2 g sat. fat), 9 mg chol., 66 mg sodium, 1 g carbo., 0 g fiber,
0 g pro. Daily Values: 2% vit. A, 3% vit. C, 1% calcium, 1% iron

Pear-Chutney Salsa

Start to Finish: 10 min.

- ½ cup bottled chunky salsa
- 3 tablespoons chutney, large pieces cut up
- 1 medium pear, peeled, cored, and chopped (1 cup)
- ½ cup chopped, seeded, peeled cucumber
- 2 tablespoons slivered almonds, toasted

1. In a medium bowl stir together salsa, chutney, pear, and cucumber. Serve immediately or cover and chill until serving time. Before serving, stir in almonds. Serve with pork, ham, or chicken.
Makes 2 cups.

Nutrition Facts per tablespoon: 12 cal., 0 g total fat (0 g sat. fat), 0 mg chol., 10 mg sodium, 2 g carbo., 0 g fiber, 0 g pro. Daily Values: 2% vit. A, 2% vit. C

Strawberry Salsa

Start to Finish: 10 min.

- ¼ cup apricot jam or preserves
- ¼ teaspoon ground cinnamon
- 2 cups chopped fresh strawberries

1. In a medium bowl combine jam and cinnamon; stir in strawberries. Let stand a few minutes to blend flavors. Serve over waffles, pancakes, French toast, or hot cereal, or stir into yogurt.
Makes 2 cups.

Nutrition Facts per ½ cup: 78 cal., 0 g total fat (0 g sat. fat), 0 mg chol., 7 mg sodium, 19 g carbo., 2 g fiber, 1 g pro. Daily Values: 71% vit. C, 2% calcium, 2% iron

Pico de Gallo

Prep: 10 min. • Chill: 2 hours

- 2 ripe medium tomatoes, peeled and finely chopped
- 2 tablespoons finely chopped red onion
- 2 tablespoons snipped fresh cilantro
- ⅛ teaspoon salt
- Dash sugar

1. In a bowl stir together all ingredients. Cover and chill for at least 2 hours or overnight. Serve with tortilla chips.
Makes: 1¼ cups.

Nutrition Facts per tablespoon: 3 cal., 0 g total fat (0 g sat. fat), 0 mg chol., 16 mg sodium, 1 g carbo., 0 g fiber, 0 g pro. Daily Values: 4% vit. C

Skinless and Seedless Tomatoes
If you want your salsa or Pico de Gallo free of tomato skins and seeds, here's an easy way to take care of both. Make a shallow X on the bottom of the tomato, then place it on a slotted spoon. Dip it into boiling water for 15 seconds and rinse with cold water. Use a paring knife to gently pull on the peel where the skin has split. It will slip off easily. To remove seeds, cut the tomato in half crosswise. Holding one half over a bowl, use tip of spoon to remove the seeds.

Fresh Ginger Relish

Prep: 5 min. • Chill: 4 hours

- 1/3 cup peeled, minced fresh ginger
- 2   tablespoons finely chopped red sweet
        pepper
- 2   tablespoons cider vinegar
- 2   tablespoons orange juice
- 1   to 2 teaspoons brown sugar

1. In a small bowl stir together all ingredients. Cover and chill for at least 4 hours. Store in the refrigerator for up to 1 week. Serve with beef, pork, lamb, chicken, turkey, or fish.
Makes 1/2 cup.

Nutrition Facts per 2 tablespoons: 14 cal., 0 g total fat
(0 g sat. fat), 0 mg chol., 2 mg sodium, 3 g carbo., 0 g fiber,
0 g pro. Daily Values: 6% vit. A, 22% vit. C, 1% iron

Zucchini-Tomato Relish

Prep: 5 min. • Chill: 24 hours

- 1   cup chopped tomato
- 1   cup chopped zucchini
- 2   teaspoons olive oil
- 1   teaspoon balsamic vinegar
- 1   clove garlic, minced

1. In a small bowl stir together all ingredients. Cover and chill for up to 24 hours. Serve with beef, pork, or chicken.
Makes about 2 cups.

Nutrition Facts per 1/2 cup: 9 cal., 1 g total fat
(0 g sat. fat), 0 mg chol., 1 mg sodium, 1 g carbo., 0 g fiber,
0 g pro. Daily Values: 2% vit. A, 5% vit. C

Cranberry-Apple-Orange Relish

Prep: 20 min. • Chill: 8 hours

- 4   medium tart apples, cored
- 2   cups fresh cranberries
- 2   small navel oranges, peeled and sectioned
- 1   to 1 1/2 cups sugar

1. Using a food processor coarsely chop apples, cranberries, and oranges, one-fourth at a time. In a large bowl combine the fruit and sugar. Cover and chill for at least 8 hours. Stir before serving. Serve with pork, ham, chicken, or turkey.
Makes 5 cups.

Nutrition Facts per 1/4 cup: 59 cal., 0 g total fat
(0 g sat. fat), 0 mg chol., 3 mg sodium, 16 g carbo., 2 g fiber,
0 g pro. Daily Values: 10% vit. C, 1% calcium, 1% iron

Pineapple-Mint Relish

Prep: 10 min. • Chill: 1 hour

1   cup pineapple chunks (juice-pack), drained
½   cup lightly packed fresh mint leaves
1   tablespoon coarse-grain brown mustard

1. In a blender container or food processor bowl combine all ingredients. Cover and blend or process just until combined. Cover and chill for at least 1 hour or up to 24 hours. Serve with chicken, pork, or lamb.
Makes 1 cup.

Nutrition Facts per ¼ cup: 29 cal., 0 g total fat
(0 g sat. fat), 0 mg chol., 35 mg sodium, 7 g carbo., 0 g fiber,
0 g pro. Daily Values: 14% vit. C, 2% calcium, 8% iron

Mango-Habañero Mojo

Start to Finish: 15 min.

2   ripe mangoes, peeled, pitted, and chopped
½   cup Chardonnay or other dry white wine
2   tablespoons orange juice
½   of a fresh habañero or Scotch bonnet
     pepper, seeded and finely chopped

1. In a blender container or food processor bowl combine mangoes, wine, and orange juice. Cover and blend or process until smooth. Strain through a medium-fine mesh strainer to remove fruit pulp. Stir in habañero pepper. Cover and chill until ready to serve. Serve with fish or chicken.
Makes 4 servings.

Nutrition Facts per serving: 93 cal., 0 g total fat
(0 g sat. fat), 0 mg chol., 4 mg sodium, 19 g carbo., 2 g fiber,
1 g pro. Daily Values: 41% vit. A, 77% vit. C, 1% calcium,
2% iron

Roasted Garlic Mayonnaise

**Prep: 10 min. • Bake: 45 min.
Chill: 3 hours**

1   medium bulb garlic
2   teaspoons olive oil
½   cup light mayonnaise dressing or
     salad dressing
     Milk (optional)

1. Peel away outer skin from garlic. Cut off the pointed top portion with a knife, leaving bulb intact but exposing individual cloves. Place in a small baking dish; drizzle with oil. Cover and bake in a 325°F oven for 45 to 60 minutes or until cloves are very soft. Cool slightly.

2. Press to remove garlic from individual cloves. Mash garlic with tines of a fork. Stir together garlic paste and mayonnaise dressing. Thin mixture with a little milk, if necessary. Cover and chill for at least 3 hours. Use as a spread for roast beef or pork sandwiches.
Makes ½ cup.

Nutrition Facts per teaspoon: 21 cal., 2 g total fat
(0 g sat. fat), 2 mg chol., 30 mg sodium, 1 g carbo., 0 g fiber,
0 g pro.

Handling Chile Peppers

Hot peppers such as jalapeños, habañeros, and serranos contain fiery oils that enliven your cooking but can burn your skin and eyes. When working with fresh hot peppers, wear rubber or disposable plastic gloves. If your bare hands touch the peppers, wash your hands and nails well with soap and water. If you get some of the oil in your eyes, flush with cool water.

Lime Mayonnaise

Start to Finish: 10 min.

⅓ cup mayonnaise or salad dressing
1 teaspoon Dijon-style mustard
½ teaspoon finely shredded lime peel
1 teaspoon lime juice

1. In a small bowl stir together all ingredients. Cover and chill for up to 24 hours. Serve with beef, pork, lamb, chicken, turkey, or fish. **Makes ⅓ cup.**

Nutrition Facts per tablespoon: 106 cal., 12 g total fat (2 g sat. fat), 9 mg chol., 89 mg sodium, 1 g carbo., 0 g fiber, 0 g pro. Daily Values: 1% vit. A, 1% vit. C, 1% iron

Herbed Mayonnaise

Prep: 10 min. • Chill: 1 hour

½ cup mayonnaise or salad dressing
½ cup dairy sour cream
3 tablespoons snipped fresh dill
2 tablespoons snipped fresh parsley
1 clove garlic, minced

1. In a blender container or food processor bowl combine all ingredients. Cover and blend or process until almost smooth. Cover and chill for at least 1 hour or up to 24 hours. Serve with beef, pork, lamb, chicken, turkey, or fish. **Makes 1¼ cups.**

Nutrition Facts per tablespoon: 50 cal., 5 g total fat (1 g sat. fat), 5 mg chol., 34 mg sodium, 0 g carbo., 0 g fiber, 0 g pro. Daily Values: 1% vit. A, 1% vit. C, 1% calcium

Curry Mayonnaise

Start to Finish: 5 min.

¼ cup mayonnaise or salad dressing
¼ cup dairy sour cream
2 tablespoons frozen orange
    juice concentrate
¾ to 1 teaspoon curry powder
4 to 5 tablespoons fat-free milk

1. In a small bowl stir together mayonnaise, sour cream, orange juice concentrate, and curry powder. Stir in enough milk to make of drizzling consistency. Serve with chicken, turkey, or fish. **Makes ½ cup.**

Nutrition Facts per tablespoon: 73 cal., 7 g total fat (2 g sat. fat), 7 mg chol., 47 mg sodium, 3 g carbo., 0 g fiber, 1 g pro. Daily Values: 2% vit. A, 11% vit. C, 2% calcium, 1% iron

VEGGIES & SIDES

Chapter six

Lemony Herbed Asparagus

Start to Finish: 15 min.

1   **pound asparagus spears**
1   **tablespoon olive oil**
½   **teaspoon snipped fresh basil**
½   **teaspoon snipped fresh oregano**
1   **teaspoon lemon juice**

1. Snap off and discard woody bases from asparagus. Place asparagus in a steamer basket over simmering water. Steam, covered, for 5 to 8 minutes or until tender.

2. Meanwhile, stir together oil, basil, oregano, and lemon juice. Transfer asparagus to a serving platter. Drizzle with herb mixture.
Makes 4 servings.

Nutrition Facts per serving: 44 cal., 3 g total fat
(0 g sat. fat), 0 mg chol., 1 mg sodium, 3 g carbo., 1 g fiber,
1 g pro. Daily Values: 7% vit. A, 12% vit. C, 1% calcium,
3% iron

Asparagus with Citrus Mayonnaise

Start to Finish: 25 min.

1   **pound fresh asparagus spears or one**
      10-ounce package frozen asparagus
      spears
2   **tablespoons plain fat-free yogurt**
2   **tablespoons light mayonnaise dressing or**
      salad dressing
½   **teaspoon finely shredded orange peel**
      Dash ground red pepper

1. Snap off and discard woody bases from asparagus. In a medium saucepan cook fresh asparagus, covered, in a small amount of boiling water for 4 to 6 minutes or until crisp-tender. (Or cook frozen asparagus according to package directions.) Drain; keep warm. Meanwhile, in a small bowl stir together remaining ingredients. Spoon over hot asparagus.
Makes 4 servings.

Nutrition Facts per serving: 46 cal., 3 g total fat
(1 g sat. fat), 3 mg chol., 60 mg sodium, 3 g carbo., 2 g fiber,
2 g pro. Daily Values: 1% vit. A, 26% vit. C, 2% calcium,
2% iron

Green Beans and Bacon

Start to Finish: 30 min.

- 7 slices bacon
- 2 9-ounce packages frozen whole green beans, thawed
- 6 medium carrots, cut into 3- to 4-inch strips
- 2 tablespoons butter or margarine
- 2 cloves garlic, minced

1. In a large skillet cook bacon over medium heat for 8 to 10 minutes or until just crisp, turning occasionally. Remove bacon, reserving 2 tablespoons drippings in skillet; drain bacon on paper towels.

2. Add remaining ingredients to reserved drippings in skillet. Cook and stir over medium high heat about 5 minutes or until vegetables are crisp-tender. Transfer to a serving bowl. Crumble bacon; sprinkle over beans.
Makes 12 servings.

Nutrition Facts per serving: 67 cal., 4 g total fat (2 g sat. fat), 8 mg chol., 98 mg sodium, 6 g carbo., 2 g fiber, 2 g pro. Daily Values: 55% vit. A, 10% vit. C, 2% calcium, 4% iron

Tangy Green Beans

Prep: 10 min. • Cook: 14 min.

- ¾ pound fresh green beans, cut into bite-size pieces (about 2¼ cups)
- 2 tablespoons water
- 2 tablespoons butter or margarine
- ⅓ cup chopped walnuts
- ½ cup crumbled feta cheese or ½ cup mozzarella cheese cut into ½-inch cubes

1. In a microwave-safe baking dish or casserole combine green beans and water. Microwave, covered, on 100 percent power (high) for 12 to 14 minutes or until just tender, stirring once after 6 minutes. Drain. Cover and keep warm.

2. Place butter and walnuts in another baking dish. Microwave on 100 percent power (high) for 1½ to 2½ minutes or until butter is bubbly and just beginning to brown, stirring after 1 minute. Add walnut mixture and cheese to green beans in casserole; toss to combine.
Makes 4 servings.

Nutrition Facts per serving: 194 cal., 17 g total fat (7 g sat. fat), 33 mg chol., 277 mg sodium, 8 g carbo., 4 g fiber, 6 g pro. Daily Values: 17% vit. A, 20% vit. C, 14% calcium, 7% iron

Golden Green Bean Crunch

Prep: 15 min. • Bake: 30 min.

1   16-ounce package frozen French-cut green beans

1   10¾-ounce can condensed golden mushroom soup

1   8-ounce can sliced water chestnuts, drained (optional)

1   cup chow mein noodles or ½ of a 2.8-ounce can French-fried onions (about ¾ cup)

1. Cook frozen green beans according to package directions; drain well. In a 1½-quart casserole combine the green beans, soup, and, if desired, water chestnuts. Bake, uncovered, in a 350°F oven for 25 minutes or until bubbly around edges. Sprinkle with noodles. Bake for 5 minutes more or until heated through.
Makes 4 to 6 servings.

Nutrition Facts per serving: 188 cal., 6 g total fat
(1 g sat. fat), 3 mg chol., 719 mg sodium, 27 g carbo.,
5 g fiber, 5 g pro. Daily Values: 20% vit. A, 4% vit. C,
3% calcium, 9% iron

Green Beans with Shallot Sauce

Start to Finish: 25 min.

2   pounds green beans, trimmed

3   tablespoons butter (no substitutes)

1   cup chopped shallots

½   teaspoon salt

⅛   teaspoon freshly ground black pepper

1. Place green beans in a large steamer basket over simmering water. Steam, covered, for 7 to 10 minutes or until tender.

2. Meanwhile, in a 12-inch skillet melt 2 tablespoons of the butter over medium heat. Cook butter about 7 minutes or until lightly brown, stirring occasionally. Be careful not to burn. Transfer brown butter to a cup, scraping skillet with a rubber spatula.

3. In the same skillet melt remaining butter over medium heat. Add shallots; cook, covered, for 8 to 10 minutes or until lightly brown, stirring occasionally. Add green beans, reserved brown butter, salt, and pepper; heat through.
Makes 12 servings.

Nutrition Facts per serving: 57 cal., 3 g total fat
(2 g sat. fat), 8 mg chol., 133 mg sodium, 7 g carbo.,
2 g fiber, 2 g pro. Daily Values: 14% vit. A, 17% vit. C,
3% calcium, 5% iron

Baked Beets in Gingered Syrup

Prep: 20 min. • Bake: 1¾ hours

12	medium beets
2	cups cider vinegar
1	cup sugar
1	3- to 4-inch piece fresh ginger, peeled
½	teaspoon salt

1. Wash and trim beets, leaving root and 1 inch of stem intact. Place beets in a 3-quart casserole. Bake, covered, in a 325°F oven for 1¾ to 2 hours or until tender.

2. Meanwhile, for syrup, in a medium saucepan stir together remaining ingredients. Bring mixture to boiling; reduce heat. Cook, uncovered, about 10 minutes. Remove from heat. Discard ginger. Cool syrup.

3. Allow beets to cool slightly. Using paper towels, rub beets while still warm to remove skins. Trim stem and root ends. Halve or quarter beets; toss in prepared syrup. Serve beets with a slotted spoon. Serve warm, cold, or at room temperature.
Makes 8 to 12 servings.

Nutrition Facts per serving: 88 cal., 0 g total fat
(0 g sat. fat), 0 mg chol., 126 mg sodium, 23 g carbo.,
5 g fiber, 1 g pro. Daily Values: 11% vit. C, 2% calcium

Broccoli and Peppers

Prep: 10 min. • Cook: 8 min.

1	pound broccoli, cut into florets (3⅔ cups)
1	sweet pepper, cut into bite-size pieces
2	tablespoons butter or margarine
1	teaspoon finely shredded lemon peel
1	tablespoon lemon juice

1. Place broccoli and pepper in a steamer basket over simmering water. Steam, covered, for 8 to 12 minutes or until vegetables are crisp-tender. Arrange on a serving platter. Meanwhile, in a small saucepan melt butter. Stir in lemon peel and lemon juice. Drizzle over vegetables.
Makes 6 servings.

Nutrition Facts per serving: 63 cal., 4 g total fat
(3 g sat. fat), 11 mg chol., 62 mg sodium, 6 g carbo.,
3 g fiber, 2 g pro. Daily Values: 47% vit. A, 156% vit. C,
4% calcium, 4% iron

Cream of Broccoli Soup

Start to Finish: 20 min.

2   cups chopped broccoli

2   cups boiling water

3   tablespoons butter or margarine

¼   cup all-purpose flour

2   teaspoons instant chicken bouillon
      granules

2   cups half-and-half, light cream, or milk

1. In a large saucepan cook broccoli in the boiling water for 8 to 10 minutes or until very tender. Drain broccoli, reserving cooking liquid. (Add additional water, if necessary, to make 1½ cups.) In a blender container combine broccoli and the reserved cooking liquid. Cover and blend at low speed until smooth. Set aside.

2. In the same saucepan, melt butter. Stir in flour and bouillon. Add half-and-half all at once. Cook and stir over medium heat until thickened and bubbly. Cook and stir for 1 minute more. Stir in broccoli mixture; heat through.
Makes 6 to 8 servings.

Nutrition Facts per serving: 186 cal., 15 g total fat
(10 g sat. fat), 46 mg chol., 393 mg sodium, 9 g carbo.,
1 g fiber, 4 g pro. Daily Values: 20% vit. A, 40% vit. C,
10% calcium, 3% iron

Broccoli Corn Bread

Prep: 10 min. • Bake: 30 min.

1   8½-ounce package corn muffin mix

3   eggs

2   cups shredded cheddar cheese (8 ounces)

1   10-ounce package frozen chopped broccoli,
      thawed and well drained

½   cup chopped onion

1. In a large bowl combine corn muffin mix and eggs. Stir in remaining ingredients. Spoon into a greased 9×9×2-inch baking pan. Bake in a 350°F oven about 30 minutes or until a toothpick inserted near the center comes out clean. Serve corn bread warm.
Makes 16 servings.

Nutrition Facts per serving: 138 cal., 7 g total fat
(3 g sat. fat), 55 mg chol., 209 mg sodium, 12 g carbo.,
1 g fiber, 6 g pro. Daily Values: 11% vit. A, 12% vit. C,
12% calcium, 4% iron

Brussels Sprouts with Prosciutto

Start to Finish: 25 min.

1½ pounds fresh Brussels sprouts

3 ounces prosciutto or 3 slices crisp-cooked bacon, chopped

1 teaspoon finely shredded lemon peel

½ teaspoon salt

¼ teaspoon freshly ground black pepper

1. In a 4-quart Dutch oven cook Brussels sprouts, covered, in 3 quarts boiling water for 6 to 8 minutes or until just tender. Drain in colander and rinse with cold water to chill.

2. Thinly slice Brussels sprouts. Heat a 12-inch nonstick skillet for 1 minute over medium-high heat. Add Brussels sprouts; cook and stir for 2 to 3 minutes or until heated through. Stir in the prosciutto and remaining ingredients.
Makes 12 servings.

Nutrition Facts per serving: 38 cal., 1 g total fat
(0 g sat. fat), 5 mg chol., 301 mg sodium, 5 g carbo.,
2 g fiber, 4 g pro. Daily Values: 9% vit. A, 61% vit. C,
2% calcium, 5% iron

Glazed Brussels Sprouts

Prep: 5 min. • Cook: 10 min.

1 10-ounce package frozen Brussels sprouts

2 tablespoons mango chutney

1 tablespoon butter or margarine
Salt and freshly ground black pepper

1. Cook Brussels sprouts according to package directions; drain well. In the same saucepan heat chutney and butter over medium-low heat until butter melts. Return Brussels sprouts to chutney mixture in saucepan. Stir to coat. Season to taste with salt and pepper.
Makes 3 servings.

Nutrition Facts per serving: 110 cal., 4 g total fat
(3 g sat. fat), 11 mg chol., 159 mg sodium, 17 g carbo.,
4 g fiber, 4 g pro. Daily Values: 26% vit. A, 97% vit. C,
3% calcium, 5% iron

Glazed Carrot Coins

Prep: 10 min. • Cook: 10 min.

1½ **pounds medium carrots and/or parsnips,
      peeled and cut into ¼-inch slices**
 ¼ **cup packed brown sugar**
 2 **tablespoons olive oil**
 2 **tablespoons balsamic vinegar or
      white wine vinegar**
 1 **teaspoon cornstarch**

1. In a medium saucepan cook carrots, covered, in a small amount of boiling water for 7 to 9 minutes or until crisp-tender. Drain carrots; remove from pan.

2. In the same saucepan stir together remaining ingredients. Cook and stir over medium heat until slightly thickened. Add carrots; cook, uncovered, about 2 minutes more or until carrots are glazed, stirring frequently.
Makes 8 servings.

Nutrition Facts per serving: 91 cal., 4 g total fat (0 g sat. fat), 0 mg chol., 71 mg sodium, 15 g carbo., 3 g fiber, 1 g pro. Daily Values: 192% vit. A, 4% vit. C, 2% calcium, 5% iron

Honey-Ginger Carrots

Start to Finish: 15 min.

 1 **pound carrots, peeled and cut into
      ¼-inch slices (3 cups)**
 2 **tablespoons water**
 2 **tablespoons honey**
 1 **tablespoon butter or margarine**
 ⅛ **teaspoon ground ginger**

1. In a microwave-safe baking dish or casserole combine the carrots and water. Microwave, covered, on 100 percent power (high) for 7 to 9 minutes or until carrots are just tender, stirring once after 4 minutes. Drain.

2. Add remaining ingredients to baking dish. Cover; microwave for 1 to 2 minutes more. Stir to combine.
Makes 4 servings.

Nutrition Facts per serving: 98 cal., 3 g total fat (2 g sat. fat), 8 mg chol., 64 mg sodium, 18 g carbo., 3 g fiber, 1 g pro. Daily Values: 463% vit. A, 11% vit. C, 3% calcium, 3% iron

Sweet Saucy Carrots and Pecans

Start to Finish: 20 min.

- 1   **pound peeled baby carrots**
- 2   **tablespoons orange marmalade**
- 1   **tablespoon butter or margarine**
- ½   **teaspoon salt**
- 2   **tablespoons pecan pieces, toasted**

1. In a large saucepan cook carrots, covered, in a small amount of boiling water for 8 to 10 minutes or until crisp-tender. Drain. Return carrots to pan. Stir in orange marmalade, butter, and salt until carrots are coated. Top with pecans.
Makes 4 servings.

Nutrition Facts per serving: 124 cal., 6 g total fat (2 g sat. fat), 8 mg chol., 365 mg sodium, 19 g carbo., 4 g fiber, 2 g pro. Daily Values: 577% vit. A, 13% vit. C, 4% calcium, 4% iron

Cooking Apples

Some apples are best eaten out of hand; others lend themselves better to cooking and baking. To pick prime apples for cooking, consider one of these varieties: Cortland, Granny Smith, Golden Delicious, Newtown Pippin, Northern Spy, Rome Beauty, Stayman, Winesap, or York Imperial.

Glazed Parsnips and Apples

Prep: 10 min. • Cook: 10 min.

- 1   **pound parsnips, peeled and cut into**
  ¼-inch slices
- ¾   **cup apple cider or apple juice**
- 2   **tablespoons butter or margarine**
- 2   **tablespoons brown sugar**
- 2   **medium cooking apples, cored and thinly**
  sliced

1. In a large skillet cook parsnips, covered, in simmering apple cider for 7 to 8 minutes or until crisp-tender. Remove parsnips and any liquid from skillet; set parsnips and liquid aside.

2. In the same skillet combine butter and brown sugar. Cook, uncovered, over medium-high heat about 1 minute or until mixture begins to thicken. Add apples and undrained parsnips; cook, uncovered, for 2 minutes or until glazed, stirring frequently.
Makes 4 to 5 servings.

Nutrition Facts per serving: 206 cal., 7 g total fat (4 g sat. fat), 16 mg chol., 74 mg sodium, 38 g carbo., 7 g fiber, 1 g pro. Daily Values: 5% vit. A, 26% vit. C, 5% calcium, 5% iron

Corn on the Cob with Herb Butter

Prep: 15 min. • **Chill:** 1 hour • **Cook:** 5 min.

1   cup butter or margarine
1   tablespoon each snipped fresh thyme and
         marjoram or 2 tablespoons snipped
         fresh basil
16   ears of corn
         Salt and black pepper

1. Stir together butter and herb. Cover and chill for at least 1 hour or up to 24 hours before serving to allow flavors to blend.

2. Remove husks from corn. Scrub with a stiff brush to remove silks; rinse. Cook, covered, in enough boiling water to cover for 5 to 7 minutes or until tender. Serve with herb butter. Sprinkle with salt and pepper.
Makes 16 servings.

Nutrition Facts per serving: 185 cal., 13 g total fat (8 g sat. fat), 33 mg chol., 137 mg sodium, 17 g carbo., 2 g fiber, 3 g pro. Daily Values: 14% vit. A, 8% vit. C, 1% calcium, 3% iron

Parmesan Tossed Squash

Prep: 10 min. • **Cook:** 4 min.

1   medium zucchini, cut into 1/4-inch slices
1   medium yellow summer squash, cut into
         1/4-inch slices
2   tablespoons snipped fresh oregano or
         2 teaspoons dried oregano, crushed
2   tablespoons olive oil or cooking oil
1/4 cup finely shredded Parmesan cheese
         (1 ounce)

1. In a 1 1/2-quart microwave-safe casserole or baking dish combine zucchini, summer squash, oregano, and oil. Microwave, covered, on 100 percent power (high) for 4 to 6 minutes or until squash is just tender, stirring once after 2 minutes. Sprinkle cheese over vegetables; toss.
Makes 4 servings.

Nutrition Facts per serving: 101 cal., 9 g total fat (2 g sat. fat), 6 mg chol., 77 mg sodium, 3 g carbo., 1 g fiber, 3 g pro. Daily Values: 6% vit. A, 13% vit. C, 8% calcium, 2% iron

Summer Squash with Peppers

Prep: 15 min. • Roast: 15 min.

 2 pounds zucchini and/or yellow summer squash, cut into bite-size chunks
 1 sweet pepper, cut into strips
 2 tablespoons olive oil
 1½ teaspoons Greek-style or Mediterranean-style seasoning blend
 ¼ teaspoon ground black pepper

1. Place squash and sweet pepper strips in a large shallow roasting pan. Drizzle with oil; sprinkle with seasoning and black pepper; toss to coat. Roast, uncovered, in a 425°F oven for 15 minutes or until just tender, stirring once.
Makes 6 servings.

Nutrition Facts per serving: 66 cal., 5 g total fat (1 g sat. fat), 0 mg chol., 25 mg sodium, 6 g carbo., 2 g fiber, 2 g pro. Daily Values: 30% vit. A, 69% vit. C, 2% calcium, 4% iron

Roasted Zucchini

Prep: 10 min. • Roast: 30 min.

 2½ pounds small zucchini
 2 teaspoons olive oil or cooking oil
 ½ teaspoon salt
 ¼ teaspoon freshly ground black pepper

1. Cut zucchini in half crosswise; cut each half lengthwise into quarters. Toss with oil, salt, and pepper in large bowl. In a 15×10×1-inch baking pan arrange zucchini in a single layer. Roast in a 450°F oven for 30 minutes or until tender.
Makes 8 servings.

Nutrition Facts per serving: 29 cal., 1 g total fat (0 g sat. fat), 0 mg chol., 149 mg sodium, 4 g carbo., 2 g fiber, 2 g pro. Daily Values: 9% vit. A, 17% vit. C, 2% calcium, 3% iron

Herbed Zucchini

Prep: 8 min. • Cook: 5 min.

4   cups sliced zucchini (4 to 5 small)
2   teaspoons olive oil
1   tablespoon snipped fresh mint or basil or
        1 teaspoon dried mint or basil, crushed
¼   teaspoon salt and a dash black pepper
2   tablespoons finely shredded Parmesan or
        Romano cheese

1. In a large skillet combine zucchini, oil, dried herb (if using), salt, and pepper. Cook, uncovered, over medium heat about 5 minutes or until zucchini is crisp-tender, stirring occasionally. To serve, sprinkle with cheese and fresh herb (if using).
Makes 6 servings.

Nutrition Facts per serving: 33 cal., 2 g total fat (1 g sat. fat), 2 mg chol., 125 mg sodium, 2 g carbo., 1 g fiber, 2 g pro. Daily Values: 6% vit. A, 10% vit. C, 3% calcium, 3% iron

Cider Peas and Apples

Start to Finish: 15 min.

3   cups frozen peas
1   medium apple, cored and thinly sliced
⅓   cup apple cider or apple juice
1   teaspoon cornstarch

1. Place peas in a steamer basket over simmering water. Steam, covered, for 5 minutes. Add apple slices; steam for 2 to 4 minutes more or until apples are just tender.

2. Meanwhile, in a medium saucepan combine apple cider and cornstarch. Cook and stir until mixture is thickened and bubbly. Cook and stir for 2 minutes more. Add peas and apples, tossing gently to coat with sauce.
Makes 4 servings.

Nutrition Facts per serving: 102 cal., 0 g total fat (0 g sat. fat), 0 mg chol., 82 mg sodium, 21 g carbo., 4 g fiber, 5 g pro. Daily Values: 6% vit. A, 18% vit. C, 2% calcium, 10% iron

Herb-Yogurt Baked Tomatoes

Prep: 10 min. • Bake: 20 min.

2	large tomatoes, cored and halved crosswise
½	cup plain fat-free yogurt
2	teaspoons all-purpose flour
½	teaspoon dried marjoram, crushed
3	tablespoons grated Parmesan or Romano cheese

1. Place tomato halves, cut sides up, in an ungreased 2-quart square baking dish.

2. In a small bowl stir together yogurt, flour, and marjoram. Spoon yogurt mixture onto each tomato half. Sprinkle with cheese. Bake in a 375°F oven for 20 to 25 minutes or until tomatoes are heated through.
Makes 4 servings.

Nutrition Facts per serving: 53 cal., 1 g total fat
(1 g sat. fat), 4 mg chol., 76 mg sodium, 7 g carbo., 1 g fiber,
4 g pro. Daily Values: 10% vit. A, 25% vit. C, 11% calcium,
4% iron

Saffron Rice Baked Tomatoes

Prep: 30 min. • Bake: 30 min.

1	5-ounce package saffron-flavored yellow rice mix
6	large tomatoes (about 3 pounds)
¼	cup dried mixed fruit bits or golden raisins
¼	cup pine nuts
½	teaspoon dried oregano, crushed

1. Prepare rice mix according to package directions, except omit the oil or margarine. Meanwhile, cut a slice off the stem end of each tomato; reserve tops. With a spoon carefully scoop out pulp; chop. Measure 1½ cups of the chopped pulp; set it aside. Discard remaining pulp. Place tomatoes upside down on paper towels to drain.

2. In a medium bowl combine cooked rice mix, 1½ cups reserved tomato pulp, fruit bits, pine nuts, and oregano. Fill tomatoes with rice mixture. Cover with reserved tops. Place in a 2-quart rectangular baking dish. Spoon any remaining rice filling in the bottom of the baking dish around tomatoes. Bake, uncovered, in a 350°F oven for 30 to 40 minutes or until tomatoes and rice are heated through.
Makes 6 servings.

Nutrition Facts per serving: 173 cal., 4 g total fat
(1 g sat. fat), 0 mg chol., 330 mg sodium, 33 g carbo.,
4 g fiber, 6 g pro. Daily Values: 26% vit. A, 74% vit. C,
2% calcium, 16% iron

Grilled Stuffed Peppers

Prep: 15 min. • Grill: 5 min.

2   medium sweet peppers, halved lengthwise
1   ounce soft goat (chèvre) cheese
¼   cup shredded Monterey Jack cheese
        (1 ounce)
1   tablespoon snipped fresh chives
1   tablespoon snipped fresh basil or
        1 teaspoon dried basil, crushed

1. In a medium saucepan cook peppers, covered, in a small amount of boiling water for 2 minutes. Drain, cut sides down, on paper towels. Meanwhile, for cheese mixture, in a small bowl combine remaining ingredients. Spoon into pepper shells.

2. Fold a 24×18-inch piece of heavy foil in half to make a 12×18-inch rectangle. Place peppers in center of foil. Bring up two opposite edges of foil; seal with a double fold. Fold remaining ends to completely enclose peppers, leaving space for steam to build. Grill peppers on the rack of an uncovered grill directly over medium to medium-hot heat for 5 to 6 minutes or until peppers are crisp-tender and cheese is melted. **Makes 4 servings.**

Nutrition Facts per serving: 60 cal., 4 g total fat
(2 g sat. fat), 13 mg chol., 80 mg sodium, 3 g carbo.,
0 g fiber, 3 g pro. Daily Values: 30% vit. A, 104% vit. C,
4% calcium

Sweet-and-Sour Onions

Start to Finish: 35 min.

3   cups pearl white and/or red onions or
        one 16-ounce package frozen small
        whole onions
2   teaspoons butter or margarine
¼   cup white wine vinegar or balsamic vinegar
2   tablespoons brown sugar
1   ounce prosciutto or thinly sliced cooked
        ham, cut into short thin strips

1. In a medium saucepan cook unpeeled pearl onions (if using), covered, in a small amount of boiling water about 10 minutes or until onions are just tender. Drain. Cool onions slightly; trim ends and remove skins. (Or cook frozen onions in a medium saucepan according to package directions; drain.)

2. In the same saucepan melt butter over medium heat. Stir in the vinegar and brown sugar. Cook and stir about 30 seconds or until combined. Stir in onions and prosciutto. Cook, uncovered, for 7 to 8 minutes more or until the onions are golden brown and slightly glazed, stirring occasionally. **Makes 4 servings.**

Nutrition Facts per serving: 114 cal., 4 g total fat
(0 g sat. fat), 0 mg chol., 155 mg sodium, 16 g carbo.,
2 g fiber, 3 g pro. Daily Values: 2% vit. A, 12% vit. C,
3% calcium, 3% iron

Apple-Raisin Baked Beans

Start to Finish: 25 min.

2 16-ounce cans vegetarian baked beans
1 Granny Smith or other cooking apple,
    peeled, cored, and chopped
¼ cup raisins
1 tablespoon dried minced onion (optional)

1. In a medium saucepan stir together all ingredients. Bring to boiling; reduce heat. Simmer, uncovered, about 15 minutes or until mixture is of desired consistency and heated through, stirring occasionally.
Makes 6 to 8 servings.

Nutrition Facts per serving: 172 cal., 1 g total fat (0 g sat. fat), 0 mg chol., 601 mg sodium, 39 g carbo., 8 g fiber, 7 g pro. Daily Values: 5% vit. A, 10% vit. C, 8% calcium, 3% iron

Savory Black Beans

Start to Finish: 15 min.

2 15-ounce cans black beans
1 clove garlic, minced
1 teaspoon ground cumin
1 medium avocado, halved, seeded, peeled,
    and cubed
½ cup shredded Monterey Jack cheese
    (2 ounces)

1. Drain and rinse 1 of the cans of beans. In a medium saucepan combine both drained and undrained black beans, garlic, and cumin. Heat through, stirring occasionally. Transfer beans to a serving bowl; sprinkle with avocado and cheese.
Makes 6 to 8 servings.

Nutrition Facts per serving: 184 cal., 8 g total fat (3 g sat. fat), 8 mg chol., 403 mg sodium, 24 g carbo., 9 g fiber, 12 g pro. Daily Values: 8% vit. A, 7% vit. C, 13% calcium, 10% iron

Citrus-Splashed Squash

Prep: 10 min. • Bake: 35 min.

1　1½-pound kabocha, buttercup, and/or golden nugget squash, halved
4　small parsnips, peeled (about 12 ounces)
¼　cup butter or margarine, melted
¼　cup orange juice
2　tablespoons snipped fresh thyme or 1 teaspoon dried thyme, crushed

1. In a greased 13×9×2-inch baking pan place squash halves, cut sides down, in half of the pan. Add parsnips to other half of pan. Combine remaining ingredients. Drizzle ¼ cup of the orange juice mixture over parsnips; toss to coat.

2. Bake, uncovered, in a 350°F oven for 35 to 50 minutes or until vegetables are tender, stirring parsnips once. Remove squash carefully and cut each half into 4 wedges. Remove seeds, if desired. (Seeds are edible, but fibrous.) To serve, place squash and parsnips in a shallow bowl. Drizzle with remaining orange juice mixture.
Makes 4 servings.

Nutrition Facts per serving: 228 cal., 12 g total fat (7 g sat. fat), 31 mg chol., 148 mg sodium, 30 g carbo., 7 g fiber, 4 g pro. Daily Values: 68% vit. A, 68% vit. C, 9% calcium, 11% iron

Baked Sweet Potato Fries

Prep: 15 min. • Bake: 20 min.

　　Nonstick cooking spray
1　pound medium sweet potatoes
1　tablespoon butter or margarine, melted
¼　teaspoon seasoned salt
　　Dash ground nutmeg

1. Lightly coat a 15×10×1-inch baking pan with cooking spray. Scrub potatoes and cut lengthwise into quarters. Cut each quarter into 2 wedges. Arrange potatoes in a single layer in pan. Combine remaining ingredients. Brush onto potatoes. Bake in a 425°F oven for 20 to 30 minutes or until brown and tender.
Makes 4 servings.

Nutrition Facts per serving: 117 cal., 3 g total fat (2 g sat. fat), 7 mg chol., 122 mg sodium, 22 g carbo., 3 g fiber, 2 g pro. Daily Values: 196% vit. A, 36% vit. C

Steak Fries

Prep: 10 min. • Bake: 20 min.

2	teaspoons olive oil
4	large baking potatoes
1	teaspoon salt
¼	teaspoon freshly ground black pepper

1. Line a baking sheet with foil and brush with 1 teaspoon of the oil. Scrub potatoes and cut lengthwise into ½-inch wedges. Transfer to a bowl. Add remaining oil, the salt, and pepper; toss gently to coat. Spread potatoes on prepared baking sheet. Bake for 20 to 25 minutes or until golden and tender.
Makes 4 servings.

Nutrition Facts per serving: 166 cal., 2 g total fat (0 g sat. fat), 0 mg chol., 592 mg sodium, 33 g carbo., 3 g fiber, 4 g pro. Daily Values: 45% vit. C, 1% calcium, 8% iron

Potatoes 101

All potatoes are not created equally—or at least with the same uses in mind. For the lightest, crispiest french fries and the fluffiest mashed or baked potatoes, use russets. For roasting or making scalloped potatoes, try a medium-starch potato such as yellow Finn or Yukon gold. When making potato salad that won't turn to mush, try a low-starch potato or waxy potato such as round red, round white, or new potatoes.

Ranch Fries

Prep: 25 min. • Bake: 40 min.

	Nonstick cooking spray
3	pounds baking potatoes
1	2-ounce package ranch salad dressing mix

1. Lightly coat 2 baking sheets with cooking spray. Scrub potatoes and cut into 2×¼-inch pieces. Combine potatoes and dressing mix in large bowl. Spread half of the potatoes in a single layer on each prepared baking sheet. Lightly coat with cooking spray; bake in a 400°F oven for 20 minutes. Toss potatoes with metal spatula; spray again with cooking spray. Switch positions of pans; bake for 20 minutes more or until golden and crisp.
Makes 6 servings.

Nutrition Facts per serving: 191 cal., 0 g total fat (0 g sat. fat), 0 mg chol., 678 mg sodium, 42 g carbo., 4 g fiber, 5 g pro. Daily Values: 51% vit. C, 3% calcium, 17% iron

Garlic-Roasted Red Potatoes

Prep: 15 min. • Bake: 40 min.

2   pounds small red potatoes
1   tablespoon snipped fresh rosemary
1   teaspoon steak seasoning blend or
        seasoning salt
2   tablespoons olive oil
12   cloves garlic, peeled

1. Scrub potatoes; cut into quarters. Place in a 15×10×1-inch baking pan. Sprinkle potatoes with rosemary and seasoning blend. Drizzle with the oil, stirring gently to coat. Bake, uncovered, in a 400°F oven for 20 minutes. Stir in garlic cloves. Bake for 20 minutes more or until potatoes are tender and golden, stirring occasionally.
Makes 8 servings.

Nutrition Facts per serving: 120 cal., 4 g total fat
(0 g sat. fat), 0 mg chol., 9 mg sodium, 21 g carbo., 8 g fiber,
3 g pro. Daily Values: 28% vit. C, 2% calcium, 9% iron

Rosemary Buttered Potatoes

Prep: 10 min. • Cook: 17 min.

12   small red potatoes (about 3 pounds)
¼   cup butter or margarine
1   tablespoon snipped fresh rosemary or
        1 teaspoon dried rosemary, crushed
½   teaspoon salt
¼   teaspoon black pepper

1. Scrub potatoes; cut into quarters. In a 4-quart Dutch oven cook potatoes in a small amount of lightly salted boiling water for 15 to 20 minutes or until tender; drain.

2. Meanwhile, in a small skillet melt butter over low heat. Stir in remaining ingredients. Cook and stir over low heat for 2 minutes. In a bowl gently toss cooked potatoes with the butter mixture until potatoes are coated.
Makes 12 servings.

Nutrition Facts per serving: 143 cal., 4 g total fat
(2 g sat. fat), 10 mg chol., 36 mg sodium, 25 g carbo.,
1 g fiber, 3 g pro. Daily Values: 3% vit. A, 24% vit. C,
1% calcium, 12% iron

Caramelized Potatoes

Start to Finish: 35 min.

2 pounds tiny new potatoes

½ cup packed brown sugar

⅓ cup butter or margarine

½ teaspoon salt

1. Scrub potatoes. In a large saucepan cook potatoes, covered, in salted boiling water for 20 to 25 minutes or until tender. Drain; let cool. Peel potatoes, halving any large potatoes. In a large skillet combine remaining ingredients. Cook over medium heat, stirring constantly, until butter is melted and mixture is thickened and bubbly. Reduce heat. Carefully add potatoes. Stir gently until potatoes are coated and heated through.
Makes 8 servings.

Nutrition Facts per serving: 190 cal., 8 g total fat (5 g sat. fat), 22 mg chol., 237 mg sodium, 29 g carbo., 1 g fiber, 2 g pro. Daily Values: 6% vit. A, 20% vit. C, 2% calcium, 5% iron

Potatoes and Sugar Snap Peas

Prep: 10 min. • Cook: 15 min.

8 small red potatoes (1½ pounds), quartered

¾ pound fresh sugar snap peas

1 tablespoon olive oil

½ teaspoon dried thyme, crushed, or
　　dried dill

¼ teaspoon salt

1. Scrub potatoes. In a medium saucepan cook potatoes, covered, in a small amount of lightly salted boiling water for 12 minutes. Add peas. Cook, covered, about 3 minutes more or until peas are crisp-tender and potatoes are tender; drain. Add remaining ingredients. Toss to coat.
Makes 6 servings.

Nutrition Facts per serving: 128 cal., 3 g total fat (0 g sat. fat), 0 mg chol., 102 mg sodium, 22 g carbo., 4 g fiber, 4 g pro. Daily Values: 2% vit. A, 74% vit. C, 4% calcium, 12% iron

Caramel-Topped Sweet Potatoes

Prep: 15 min. • Bake: 40 min.

8   medium sweet potatoes (6 to 8 ounces each)
¼   cup butter or margarine
1   cup packed brown sugar
¼   cup whipping cream
     Chopped pecans, toasted (optional)

1. Scrub potatoes; pat dry. Prick potatoes with a fork. Bake in a 425°F oven for 40 to 60 minutes or until potatoes are tender.

2. For sauce, melt butter in a small saucepan. Stir in brown sugar and whipping cream. Cook, uncovered, over medium heat for 5 minutes, stirring constantly. Cut each potato open. Serve warm sauce over potatoes. If desired, sprinkle with pecans.
Makes 8 servings.

Nutrition Facts per serving: 312 cal., 9 g total fat (6 g sat. fat), 27 mg chol., 91 mg sodium, 57 g carbo., 4 g fiber, 2 g pro. Daily Values: 474% vit. A, 35% vit. C, 6% calcium, 7% iron

Honeyed Sweet Potatoes

Prep: 25 min. • Bake: 15 min.

3   pounds sweet potatoes, peeled and sliced ½ inch thick
¼   cup packed brown sugar
¼   cup honey
¼   cup butter or margarine, cut up
¼   teaspoon ground ginger

1. In a Dutch oven or large saucepan add enough water to cover potatoes. Bring to boiling; reduce heat. Simmer, covered, about 15 minutes or until potatoes are nearly tender when pierced with a fork. Drain; transfer to a greased 2-quart square baking dish.

2. In a small heavy saucepan combine remaining ingredients. Bring to boiling, stirring constantly until sugar is dissolved. Boil gently for 3 minutes. Pour over potatoes. Bake, uncovered, in a 350°F oven about 15 minutes or until potatoes are tender, basting occasionally with sauce.
Makes 8 to 10 servings.

Nutrition Facts per serving: 240 cal., 6 g total fat (6 g sat. fat), 30 mg chol., 73 mg sodium, 46 g carbo., 5 g fiber, 2 g pro. Daily Values: 294% vit. A, 54% vit. C

Mashed Potatoes

Start to Finish: 35 min.

3   medium baking potatoes or sweet potatoes
        (1 pound)
2   tablespoons butter or margarine
        Salt and black pepper
2   to 4 tablespoons milk

1. Scrub, peel, and quarter potatoes. If using sweet potatoes, remove any woody ends. In a large saucepan cook potatoes, covered, in a small amount of lightly salted boiling water for 20 to 25 minutes (25 to 35 minutes for sweet potatoes) or until tender; drain. Mash with a potato masher or beat with an electric mixer on low speed. Add butter. Season to taste with salt and pepper. Gradually beat in enough milk to make light and fluffy.
Makes 4 servings.

Nutrition Facts per serving: 139 cal., 6 g total fat (1 g sat. fat), 1 mg chol., 209 mg sodium, 20 g carbo., 1 g fiber, 2 g pro. Daily Values: 7% vit. A, 12% vit. C, 1% calcium, 2% iron

Boursin Mashed Potatoes

Prep: 30 min. • Bake: 25 min.

3½ pounds potatoes, peeled and cut into
        2-inch pieces (about 10 medium
        potatoes)
2   5.2-ounce packages boursin cheese with
        garlic and herbs
½   cup whole milk, half-and-half, or light
        cream
    Salt and black pepper

1. In a large saucepan cook potatoes, covered, in small amount of lightly salted boiling water for 20 to 25 minutes or until tender. Drain; return potatoes to pan. Mash with potato masher or beat with mixer on low speed until smooth. Add cheese; beat until combined. Beat in milk until combined. Season with salt and pepper. Transfer to a 2-quart casserole; cover. Bake in a 350°F oven for 25 minutes or until heated through.
Makes 8 to 10 servings.

Nutrition Facts per serving: 326 cal., 17 g total fat (11 g sat. fat), 3 mg chol., 239 mg sodium, 41 g carbo., 3 g fiber, 6 g pro. Daily Values: 24% vit. C

Veggie Mash

Prep: 15 min. • Cook: 15 min.

6   medium carrots, sliced (3 cups)
4   medium red potatoes (1¼ pounds),
      scrubbed and cut into cubes
1   cup coarsely chopped broccoli
½   of an 8-ounce container dairy sour cream
      French onion dip
½   teaspoon seasoned pepper

1. In a Dutch oven or large saucepan cook carrots and potatoes, covered, in boiling water for 15 minutes or until tender, adding broccoli the last 3 minutes of cooking time. Drain vegetables; return to pan. Mash with a potato masher or beat with an electric mixer on low speed. Add dip and seasoned pepper. Beat until fluffy.
Makes 6 servings.

Nutrition Facts per serving: 146 cal., 3 g total fat (2 g sat. fat), 0 mg chol., 173 mg sodium, 27 g carbo., 5 g fiber, 4 g pro. Daily Values: 387% vit. A, 51% vit. C, 4% calcium, 7% iron

Vegetable Rice Pilaf

Prep: 15 min. • Cook: 45 min.

1   cup finely chopped celery
⅓   cup chopped onion
¼   cup butter or margarine
1½   cups brown rice
3¾   cups chicken broth or reduced-sodium
      chicken broth

1. In a large saucepan, cook celery and onion in butter until tender. Add rice; cook until lightly brown. Carefully stir in chicken broth. Bring mixture to boiling; reduce heat. Simmer, covered, about 45 minutes or until rice is tender and all liquid is absorbed.
Makes 6 servings.

Nutrition Facts per serving: 268 cal., 11 g total fat (6 g sat. fat), 22 mg chol., 729 mg sodium, 38 g carbo., 2 g fiber, 5 g pro. Daily Values: 7% vit. A, 3% vit. C, 2% calcium, 4% iron

Easy Spanish Rice

Start to Finish: 25 min.

1   cup uncooked long grain rice
2   tablespoons cooking oil
1   14-ounce can chicken broth
¼   cup tomato sauce
¼   cup water

1. In a medium saucepan cook rice in oil about 3 to 5 minutes or until lightly brown. Stir in remaining ingredients. Bring to boiling; reduce heat. Simmer, covered, for 18 to 20 minutes or until rice is done.
Makes 4 servings.

Nutrition Facts per serving: 247 cal., 8 g total fat (1 g sat. fat), 0 mg chol., 533 mg sodium, 39 g carbo., 1 g fiber, 4 g pro. Daily Values: 3% vit. A, 4% vit. C, 2% calcium, 12% iron

Easy Oven Risotto

Prep: 10 min. • Bake: 55 min.

3¼   cups water
1   10¾-ounce can condensed cream of
     chicken with herbs soup or condensed
     cream of chicken soup
1¼   cups uncooked arborio or medium grain
     white rice
⅓   cup shredded carrot
½   cup frozen snow pea pods, bias-cut in half
½   cup grated Parmesan cheese

1. In a 2-quart casserole stir together water, soup, uncooked rice, and carrot. Bake, covered, in a 375°F oven for 55 to 60 minutes or until rice is tender, stirring twice during baking. Stir in peas the last 5 minutes of baking. Remove casserole from oven; gently stir in cheese. Let risotto stand for 10 minutes before serving.
Makes 6 servings.

Nutrition Facts per serving: 233 cal., 6 g total fat (3 g sat. fat), 11 mg chol., 563 mg sodium, 38 g carbo., 1 g fiber, 8 g pro. Daily Values: 4% vit. C, 12% calcium, 14% iron

Arborio Rice
Although other types of rice will give good results for Easy Oven Risotto, arborio rice is favored. The short, fat, high-starch kernels give this classic Italian dish a delicious creamy texture. Arborio rice is readily available at your local supermarket.

Light and Lemony Fettuccine

Start to Finish: 15 min.

1   9-ounce package fresh refrigerated regular or spinach fettuccine
2   tablespoons butter
½   teaspoon finely shredded lemon peel
¼   teaspoon each salt and black pepper

1. Cook pasta according to package directions. Drain well. Return pasta to hot saucepan. Add butter, lemon peel, salt, and pepper. Toss gently to coat.
Makes 3 servings.

Nutrition Facts per serving: 164 cal., 6 g total fat
(3 g sat. fat), 54 mg chol., 154 mg sodium, 23 g carbo.,
1 g fiber, 5 g pro. Daily Values: 3% vit. A, 1% calcium, 8% iron

Mixing Pastas

When you find yourself with several open boxes of dried pasta in your cupboard—and each contains just a few noodles—mix things up. Combine pastas with the same cooking time together in one box. You'll save a few pennies on pasta and cupboard space too.

Mixed Pastas with Fresh Herbs

Start to Finish: 20 min.

8   ounces assorted packaged dried pastas (with similar cooking times)
2   tablespoons olive oil
2   tablespoons snipped mixed fresh herbs, such as sage, rosemary, and basil
¼   teaspoon salt
¼   teaspoon coarsely ground black pepper

1. In a large saucepan cook pasta according to package directions. Drain. Toss hot pasta with remaining ingredients.
Makes 8 servings.

Nutrition Facts per serving: 136 cal., 4 g total fat
(0 g sat. fat), 0 mg chol., 74 mg sodium, 21 g carbo.,
11 g fiber, 4 g pro. Daily Values: 1% calcium, 5% iron

DESSERTS

Chapter seven

Almond-Butter Crunch

Prep: 15 min. • Cool: 1 hour

½ **cup butter, cut up**

1 **cup slivered almonds**

½ **cup sugar**

1 **tablespoon light-colored corn syrup**

1. Line a 9×1½-inch round baking pan with foil; butter foil. Set aside.

2. In a large skillet, combine the ½ cup butter, almonds, sugar, and corn syrup. Cook and stir over medium heat until mixture comes to a boil. Cook, stirring constantly, for 5 to 6 minutes more or until mixture is a medium-brown color and almonds are toasted. Quickly pour into the prepared pan. Cool on a wire rack. Remove from pan; peel off foil. Break into pieces. **Makes 12 servings.**

Nutrition Facts per serving: 172 cal., 14 g total fat (5 g sat. fat), 22 mg chol., 85 mg sodium, 11 g carbo., 1 g fiber, 2 g pro. Daily Values: 6% vit. A, 3% calcium, 3% iron

Double-Dipped Caramels

Prep: 30 min. • Stand: 30 min.

12 **ounces chocolate-flavored candy coating, cut up**

1 **10-ounce package almond brickle pieces, crushed, or 2 cups finely chopped pistachio nuts**

1 **14-ounce package vanilla caramels (about 48), unwrapped**

1. In a medium heavy saucepan heat the candy coating over low heat until just melted, stirring constantly. Remove from heat.

2. Place brickle pieces in a bowl. Dip 1 caramel into melted coating; turn to coat. With a fork, lift caramel out, drawing the fork across the rim of the pan to remove excess coating. Place dipped caramels in brickle pieces, turning to coat. Transfer caramel to a baking sheet lined with waxed paper. Repeat with remaining caramels. Let stand for 30 minutes or until firm. Store tightly covered for up to 1 week. **Makes 48 pieces.**

Nutrition Facts per piece: 103 cal., 6 g total fat (3 g sat. fat), 0 mg chol., 22 mg sodium, 12 g carbo., 0 g fiber, 2 g pro. Daily Values: 1% vit. A, 2% calcium, 2% iron

White Chocolate Candy

Prep: 35 min. • Stand: 30 min.

1¼ pounds vanilla-flavored candy coating,
      cut up
1½ cups tiny marshmallows
1½ cups peanut butter cereal
½ cup crisp rice cereal
1½ cups mixed nuts

1. In a large saucepan melt candy coating over low heat, stirring constantly. Meanwhile, in a large bowl combine remaining ingredients. Pour melted candy coating over mixture, stirring to coat. Drop mixture by rounded teaspoons onto baking sheets lined with waxed paper. Let stand until candy is set.
Makes about 40 pieces.

Nutrition Facts per piece: 129 cal., 8 g total fat
(4 g sat. fat), 0 mg chol., 22 mg sodium, 14 g carbo.,
1 g fiber, 1 g pro. Daily Values: 1% vit. A, 1% vit. C,
1% calcium, 3% iron

White Citrus Fudge

Prep: 15 min. • Chill: 2 hours

3 cups white baking pieces
1 14-ounce can sweetened condensed milk
      (1¼ cups)
2 teaspoons finely shredded lime peel
2 tablespoons bottled Key lime juice or
      regular lime juice
1 cup chopped macadamia nuts, toasted

1. Line an 8×8×2- or 9×9×2-inch baking pan with foil, extending foil over edges of pan. Butter foil; set aside.

2. In a large heavy saucepan stir baking pieces and sweetened condensed milk over low heat until pieces are melted and mixture is smooth. Remove from heat. Stir in lime peel and lime juice. Stir in nuts. Spread mixture evenly into the prepared pan. If desired, sprinkle a few additional coarsely chopped nuts over top. Cover and chill for 2 hours or until firm.

3. Lift fudge from pan using edges of foil. Peel off foil. Use a knife to cut into pieces. Store in an airtight container at room temperature for up to 1 week or in the freezer for up to 2 months.
Makes 2½ pounds (64 pieces).

Nutrition Facts per piece: 80 cal., 4 g total fat (2 g sat. fat),
5 mg chol., 16 mg sodium, 8 g carbo., 0 g fiber, 1 g pro.
Daily Values: 1% vit. C, 3% calcium

Chocolate-Toffee Candy Cookies

Prep: 15 min. • Bake: 5 min.

35 saltine crackers
1 cup butter
1 cup packed brown sugar
1 11½-ounce package milk chocolate pieces
1 cup chopped nuts

1. Line a 15×10×1-inch baking pan with foil. Place crackers in a single layer to completely cover bottom of baking pan (cut crackers to fit, if necessary). Set aside.

2. In a medium saucepan combine butter and brown sugar. Heat and stir over medium heat until mixture boils; boil gently for 3 minutes. Pour butter mixture evenly over crackers. Bake in a 375°F oven for 5 minutes.

3. Remove from oven. Immediately sprinkle chocolate pieces over top. Let stand a few minutes to melt; spread chocolate evenly over all. Sprinkle with nuts, pressing lightly. Chill until set. Cut into squares or diamonds to serve.
Makes about 48 cookies.

Nutrition Facts per cookie: 117 cal., 8 g total fat
(4 g sat. fat), 12 mg chol., 78 mg sodium, 10 g carbo.,
0 g fiber, 1 g pro. Daily Values: 3% vit. A, 2% calcium, 2% iron

Peanut Butter Balls

Start to Finish: 1 hour

½ cup peanut butter
3 tablespoons butter, softened
1 cup sifted powdered sugar
8 ounces chocolate-flavored candy coating, chopped

1. In a bowl stir together peanut butter and butter. Gradually add powdered sugar, stirring until combined. Shape into 1-inch balls; place on waxed paper. Let stand about 20 minutes or until dry.

2. In a heavy saucepan cook and stir candy coating over low heat until melted and smooth. Cool slightly. Dip balls, one at a time, into coating. Let excess coating drip off. Place balls on waxed paper; let stand until coating is firm. Store tightly covered in refrigerator.
Makes about 30 pieces.

Nutrition Facts per piece: 88 cal., 6 g total fat (2 g sat. fat),
3 mg chol., 39 mg sodium, 9 g carbo., 0 g fiber, 2 g pro.
Daily Values: 1% vit. A, 1% calcium

Macadamia Nut Shortbread

Prep: 25 min. • Bake: 10 min.

1¼ cups all-purpose flour

3 tablespoons brown sugar

½ cup butter

2 tablespoons finely chopped macadamia
   nuts
   Powdered sugar

1. In a medium bowl stir together flour and brown sugar. Using a pastry blender, cut in butter until mixture resembles fine crumbs and starts to cling. Stir in nuts. Form mixture into a ball and knead until smooth.

2. Put or roll dough on a lightly floured surface into an 11×6-inch rectangle. Using a crinkle cutter, if desired, cut into 3×¾-inch strips. Place strips about 1 inch apart on an ungreased baking sheet.

3. Bake in a 325°F oven about 10 minutes or until bottoms just start to brown. Transfer to wire racks to cool. Store in a tightly covered container at room temperature for up to 3 days or in the freezer for up to 3 months. To serve, sift powdered sugar lightly over cookies.
Makes 30 to 40 cookies.

Nutrition Facts per cookie: 55 cal., 4 g total fat
(2 g sat. fat), 9 mg chol., 34 mg sodium, 5 g carbo., 0 g fiber,
1 g pro. Daily Values: 2% vit. A, 1% iron

Pine Nut Cookies

Prep: 20 min. • Bake: 15 min.

1½ 8-ounce cans almond paste

½ cup granulated sugar

1 cup sifted powdered sugar

4 large egg whites

1½ cups pine nuts (8 ounces)

1. Line 2 baking sheets with foil; lightly grease foil. In a food processor bowl combine almond paste and granulated sugar; process until smooth. Add powdered sugar and 2 of the egg whites; process until smooth.

2. Whisk the remaining egg whites in a small bowl until lightly beaten. Place pine nuts on shallow plate. With lightly floured hands roll almond paste mixture into 1-inch balls. Roll balls in egg whites, letting excess drip off. Roll in pine nuts, pressing lightly to stick. Arrange balls on prepared baking sheets; flatten balls slightly to form 1½-inch rounds. Bake in a 325°F oven for 15 to 18 minutes or until lightly brown. Let stand on cookie sheet for 1 minute. Transfer to wire rack; cool.
Makes about 42 cookies.

Nutrition Facts per cookie: 86 cal., 5 g total fat
(1 g sat. fat), 0 mg chol., 6 mg sodium, 9 g carbo., 0 g fiber,
2 g pro. Daily Values: 2% calcium, 4% iron

Fudgy Peanut Butter Bites

Prep: 20 min. • Bake: 11 min.

Nonstick cooking spray
- ½ of an 18-ounce roll refrigerated peanut butter cookie dough
- ½ cup semisweet chocolate pieces
- ¼ cup sweetened condensed milk
- 2 tablespoons finely chopped peanuts (optional)

1. Coat twenty-four 1¾-inch muffin cups with cooking spray; set aside. Cut dough into 6 equal pieces. Cut each piece into 4 equal slices. Place each slice in a prepared cup.

2. Bake in a 350°F oven for 9 minutes or until edges are lightly brown and dough is slightly firm. Remove from oven. Indent each cookie shell with the back of a ½-teaspoon measuring spoon. Bake for 2 minutes or until edges are firm. Cool for 15 minutes. Remove shells from cups. Cool.

3. Place chocolate pieces and condensed milk in a heavy small saucepan; stir over medium heat until chocolate melts. Spoon filling into each shell. If desired, sprinkle with peanuts. Cool. **Makes 24 servings.**

Nutrition Facts per serving: 76 cal., 4 g total fat (1 g sat. fat), 4 mg chol., 46 mg sodium, 8 g carbo., 1 g fiber, 1 g pro. Daily Values: 2% calcium, 1% iron

Peanut Butter and Chocolate Pinwheels

Prep: 25 min. • Chill: 1 hour • Bake: 8 min.

- 1 18-ounce roll refrigerated peanut butter cookie dough
- ¼ cup all-purpose flour
- 1 18-ounce roll refrigerated sugar cookie dough
- ¼ cup unsweetened cocoa powder
- ½ cup finely chopped peanuts (optional)

1. In a large bowl stir together peanut butter cookie dough and flour. Divide dough in half. In another large bowl stir together sugar cookie dough and cocoa powder. Divide dough in half.

2. Between pieces of waxed paper, roll out half of the peanut butter dough and half of the sugar cookie dough into 12×6-inch rectangles. Remove the top pieces of waxed paper. Invert 1 rectangle on top of the other; press down to seal. Remove top piece of waxed paper. Starting from a long side, roll up. Repeat with remaining dough.

3. If desired, sprinkle half of the peanuts onto waxed paper. Roll 1 log of dough in peanuts. Wrap in waxed paper. Repeat with remaining dough and peanuts, if desired. Wrap and chill dough logs for 1 hour or until firm enough to slice.

4. Cut dough logs into ¼-inch slices. Place slices 2 inches apart on an ungreased baking sheet. Bake in a 375°F oven for 8 to 10 minutes or until edges are firm. Cool cookies on a wire rack. **Makes about 60 cookies.**

Nutrition Facts per cookie: 79 cal., 4 g total fat (1 g sat. fat), 5 mg chol., 70 mg sodium, 10 g carbo., 0 g fiber, 1 g pro. Daily Values: 2% calcium, 2% iron

Cherry-Coconut Drops

Prep: 15 min. • Bake: 12 min.

1 **7-ounce package flaked coconut (2²/₃ cups)**
²/₃ **cup chopped red or green candied cherries**
2 **tablespoons cornstarch**
¹/₂ **cup sweetened condensed milk**
1 **teaspoon vanilla**

1. In a medium bowl combine coconut, candied cherries, and cornstarch. Stir in sweetened condensed milk and vanilla until mixture is combined. Drop by small rounded teaspoonfuls about 1 inch apart onto a greased, floured baking sheet.

2. Bake in a 350°F oven for 12 to 15 minutes or until lightly brown on bottoms. Cool on baking sheet for 1 minute. Transfer cookies to a wire rack; cool.
Makes 24 to 30 drops.

Nutrition Facts per drop: 75 cal., 3 g total fat (3 g sat. fat), 2 mg chol., 10 mg sodium, 11 g carbo., 0 g fiber, 1 g pro. Daily Values: 2% calcium, 1% iron

Quick Strawberry Shortcakes

Start to Finish: 30 min.

4 **frozen unbaked buttermilk biscuits**
¹/₃ **cup strawberry jelly**
1 **pint fresh strawberries, sliced**
¹/₃ **cup lemon or strawberry curd**
   Sweetened whipped cream

1. Bake biscuits according to package directions. Cool completely.

2. In a small saucepan heat the jelly just until melted. Place strawberries in a bowl; add jelly. Toss gently to coat. Set aside.

3. Split biscuits horizontally. Spread biscuit bottoms with lemon curd; replace tops. Place biscuits on dessert plates. Spoon strawberries over biscuits and top with whipped cream.
Makes 4 servings.

Nutrition Facts per serving: 472 cal., 22 g total fat (10 g sat. fat), 61 mg chol., 619 mg sodium, 48 g carbo., 5 g fiber, 5 g pro. Daily Values: 9% vit. A, 69% vit. C, 5% calcium, 8% iron

Crunchy Pound Cake Slices

Prep: 15 min. • Broil: 2 min.

4   ½-inch slices purchased pound cake
¼   cup chocolate hazelnut spread
½   cup roasted mixed nuts, coarsely chopped
1   pint caramel or cinnamon ice cream

1. Place pound cake slices on a baking sheet. Broil 3 to 4 inches from heat for 1 minute on each side or until lightly brown. Cool slightly. Spread one side of each slice with chocolate hazelnut spread. Sprinkle with nuts; pat gently to form an even layer. Transfer each slice to a dessert plate and top with a scoop of ice cream. Serve immediately.
Makes 4 servings.

Nutrition Facts per serving: 763 cal., 45 g total fat (22 g sat. fat), 206 mg chol., 421 mg sodium, 82 g carbo., 2 g fiber, 12 g pro. Daily Values: 19% vit. A, 19% calcium, 11% iron

Cherry Trifle Cake

Prep: 20 min. • Chill: 2 hours

1   9½-inch tart-shaped sponge cake or
        8 individual sponge cakes or shortcakes
½   cup cherry juice blend or orange juice
¼   of an 8-ounce container frozen whipped
        dessert topping, thawed
1   6-ounce carton cherry-vanilla or desired
        flavor yogurt (⅔ cup)
2   cups fresh light or dark sweet cherries,
        such as Rainier or Bing, pitted and
        halved

1. Place cake on a serving platter; drizzle with juice. Set aside. In a small bowl stir together the whipped topping and yogurt; spoon onto cake. Cover and chill for up to 2 hours. Just before serving, arrange cherries, cut side down, on top of the yogurt mixture.
Makes 8 servings.

Nutrition Facts per serving: 263 cal., 5 g total fat (2 g sat. fat), 109 mg chol., 158 mg sodium, 50 g carbo., 1 g fiber, 6 g pro. Daily Values: 5% vit. A, 5% vit. C, 7% calcium, 6% iron

Coffee Angel Dessert

Prep: 20 min. • Chill: 4 to 24 hours

1   **cup whipping cream**
¼   **cup sifted powdered sugar**
⅓   **cup coffee liqueur or coffee**
½   **of an 8- or 10-inch angel food cake**
¼   **cup shaved semisweet chocolate (1 ounce)**

1. In a medium mixing bowl beat together whipping cream, powdered sugar, and 1 tablespoon of the liqueur with an electric mixer until stiff peaks form. Set aside.

2. Cut cake into bite-size cubes. Place half of the cake cubes in 4 parfait glasses. Drizzle each with some of the remaining liqueur. Spoon half of the whipping cream mixture over cake in glasses. Sprinkle some of the chocolate shavings over each. Repeat layers. Cover and chill for 4 to 24 hours.
Makes 4 servings.

Nutrition Facts per serving: 466 cal., 25 g total fat (15 g sat. fat), 82 mg chol., 396 mg sodium, 48 g carbo., 1 g fiber, 5 g pro. Daily Values: 18% vit. A, 1% vit. C, 11% calcium, 4% iron

Tropical Angel Cake

Start to Finish: 25 min.

1   **8- to 9-inch or one 15-ounce purchased angel food cake**
3   **cups fruit-flavored sherbet**
¼   **cup frozen juice concentrate**
1   **cup whipping cream, whipped Coconut (optional)**

1. Slice cake in half horizontally. Hollow out insides, leaving two 1-inch shells. Spoon sherbet into bottom shell. Set top half, hollow side down, over bottom. Poke holes in top. Drizzle with juice concentrate. Frost with whipped cream. If desired, sprinkle with coconut. Serve immediately or cover loosely with foil and freeze for up to 1 week. Let stand for 10 minutes before serving, if frozen.
Makes 10 servings.

Nutrition Facts per serving: 315 cal., 10 g total fat (6 g sat. fat), 36 mg chol., 123 mg sodium, 52 g carbo., 0 g fiber, 5 g pro. Daily Values: 11% vit. A, 22% vit. C, 4% calcium, 3% iron

Whipping Cream Success
To make your whipping cream firm up faster and hold its shape better once it's whipped, chill the beaters of your electric mixer and the bowl you're using in the freezer for at least 30 minutes before whipping the cream. To sweeten the cream, add 1 to 2 tablespoons of sugar and 1 teaspoon of vanilla per cup of cream before beating.

Praline Baked Apples

Prep: 20 min. • Bake: 30 min.

½ cup apple juice

¼ teaspoon ground cinnamon

4   small red baking apples

¼ cup pecans or walnuts, coarsely chopped

¼ cup packed brown sugar

1. In a small bowl combine apple juice and ⅛ teaspoon of the cinnamon. Divide mixture among four 6-ounce custard cups. Core apples; remove peel from the top of each. Place apples in prepared custard cups.

2. Place custard cups in a shallow baking pan. Combine nuts, brown sugar, and remaining cinnamon. Sprinkle over apples. Bake, covered, in a 350°F oven for 30 to 40 minutes or until apples are tender.
Makes 4 servings.

Nutrition Facts per serving: 195 cal., 5 g total fat
(1 g sat. fat), 0 mg chol., 6 mg sodium, 39 g carbo., 4 g fiber,
1 g pro. Daily Values: 1% vit. A, 11% vit. C, 3% calcium,
5% iron

Easy Fruit Crisp

Prep: 20 min. • Bake: 30 min.

5   cups peeled and sliced apples, pears, or peaches or frozen unsweetened peach slices, thawed

¼ cup dried cherries, cranberries, or mixed dried fruit bits

2   tablespoons sugar

1½ cups granola

3   tablespoons butter, melted

1. Place sliced fruit and dried fruit in a 2-quart square baking dish; sprinkle with sugar. Combine granola and melted butter; sprinkle over fruit. Bake, uncovered, in 350°F oven for 30 to 35 minutes or until fruit is tender. Serve warm.
Makes 6 servings.

Nutrition Facts per serving: 306 cal., 13 g total fat
(5 g sat. fat), 16 mg chol., 66 mg sodium, 46 g carbo.,
5 g fiber, 3 g pro. Daily Values: 8% vit. A, 7% vit. C,
3% calcium, 6% iron

Mocha Pears

**Prep: 10 min. • Cook: 15 min.
Chill: 4 hours**

- **2 16-ounce cans or one 29-ounce can pear halves in heavy syrup (12 pear halves)**
- **2 teaspoons instant coffee crystals**
- **1 teaspoon vanilla**
- **¾ cup vanilla low-fat yogurt
  Miniature semisweet chocolate pieces**

1. Drain pears, reserving syrup. Place pears in a bowl; set aside. In a saucepan combine reserved syrup and coffee crystals. Bring to boiling; reduce heat. Simmer, uncovered, about 15 minutes or until mixture is slightly thickened and reduced to ½ cup. Stir in vanilla. Pour coffee mixture over pears. Cover; refrigerate for at least 4 hours, turning pears once.

2. Use a slotted spoon to remove pear halves from coffee mixture. Place 2 pear halves into each of 6 dessert dishes; drizzle with coffee mixture. Top with yogurt and chocolate pieces.
Makes 6 servings.

Nutrition Facts per serving: 168 cal., 2 g total fat
(1 g sat. fat), 2 mg chol., 30 mg sodium, 37 g carbo.,
3 g fiber, 2 g pro. Daily Values: 1% vit. A, 3% vit. C,
6% calcium, 3% iron

Raspberries on a Citrus Cloud

Start to Finish: 15 min.

- **2 cups fresh red raspberries**
- **4 teaspoons raspberry liqueur (optional)**
- **1 8-ounce carton lemon-flavored yogurt**
- **¼ of an 8-ounce container frozen fat-free whipped dessert topping, thawed**
- **¼ cup chocolate syrup**

1. Reserve ¼ cup raspberries. In a medium bowl gently toss remaining raspberries with the liqueur, if desired.

2. In a small bowl stir together yogurt and dessert topping. Spoon raspberry-liqueur mixture into 4 dessert dishes. Spoon yogurt mixture onto raspberries. Drizzle chocolate syrup over each. Top with reserved raspberries. Serve immediately.
Makes 4 servings.

Nutrition Facts per serving: 128 cal., 3 g total fat
(2 g sat. fat), 4 mg chol., 46 mg sodium, 23 g carbo.,
4 g fiber, 3 g pro. Daily Values: 3% vit. A, 27% vit. C,
11% calcium, 3% iron

Raspberry Whip

Prep: 10 min. • Chill: 1¼ hours

1 cup fresh or frozen raspberries
1 3-ounce package raspberry-flavored
   gelatin
1 cup boiling water
²/₃ cup cold water
1 8-ounce carton vanilla low-fat yogurt

1. Thaw raspberries, if frozen; drain. In a medium mixing bowl dissolve gelatin in the boiling water. Add the cold water. Cover and chill about 45 minutes or until partially set (the consistency of unbeaten egg whites).

2. Add yogurt. Beat with an electric mixer on medium speed for 1 to 2 minutes or until light and foamy. If necessary, chill mixture until it mounds when spooned.

3. Meanwhile, divide half of the raspberries among 6 dessert dishes. Spoon gelatin mixture on top. Top with remaining raspberries. Chill for 30 minutes or until firm or cover and chill for up to 24 hours.
Makes 6 servings.

Nutrition Facts per serving: 99 cal., 1 g total fat (0 g sat. fat), 2 mg chol., 65 mg sodium, 21 g carbo., 1 g fiber, 3 g pro. Daily Values: 1% vit. A, 9% vit. C, 8% calcium, 1% iron

Dessert Waffles with Raspberry Sauce

Start to Finish: 10 min.

1 10-ounce package frozen raspberries in
   syrup, thawed
¼ cup sifted powdered sugar
2 tablespoons créme de cassis (optional)
6 frozen waffles, toasted
3 cups vanilla ice cream

1. For raspberry sauce, press raspberries and syrup through a fine-mesh sieve; discard seeds. In a small bowl combine sieved raspberries, powdered sugar, and créme de cassis, if desired.

2. To serve, cut each waffle diagonally in half. Place 2 waffle halves on each of 6 dessert plates; top with ice cream. Drizzle with sauce.
Makes 6 servings.

Nutrition Facts per serving: 300 cal., 11 g total fat (4 g sat. fat), 29 mg chol., 310 mg sodium, 48 g carbo., 3 g fiber, 5 g pro. Daily Values: 17% vit. A, 13% vit. C, 10% calcium, 14% iron

Fruit-Filled Napoleons

Prep: 20 min. • Bake: 20 min.

½ of a 17¼-ounce package puff pastry
     (1 sheet), thawed
2 cups pudding, fruit-flavored yogurt,
     sweetened whipped cream, or softened
     ice cream
1 cup peeled, sliced kiwifruit, halved
     seedless red grapes, berries, and/or
     halved orange slices
     Sifted powdered sugar (optional)

1. On a lightly floured surface, unfold thawed pastry. Using a sharp knife, cut pastry into 8 rectangles. Place pastry rectangles on an ungreased baking sheet. Bake in a 375°F oven about 20 minutes or until puffed and golden. Cool on wire racks.

2. Just before serving, split each pastry rectangle in half horizontally. Spoon pudding into pastry bottoms. Top with fruit and pastry tops. If desired, sprinkle tops with powdered sugar. Serve immediately.
Makes 8 servings.

Nutrition Facts per serving: 266 cal., 13 g total fat (0 g sat. fat), 1 mg chol., 184 mg sodium, 35 g carbo., 1 g fiber, 3 g pro. Daily Values: 4% vit. A, 67% vit. C, 8% calcium, 2% iron

Quick and Creamy Rice Pudding

Start to Finish: 25 min.

1 4-serving-size package instant vanilla
     pudding mix
3¼ cups milk
1 cup quick-cooking rice
¼ cup dried tart cherries or blueberries or
     snipped dried apricots
¼ teaspoon ground cardamom or cinnamon

1. Prepare pudding mix according to package directions using 2 cups of the milk; set aside. Meanwhile, heat remaining milk over medium heat just to boiling. Stir in rice and dried fruit. Remove from heat; cover and let stand for 5 minutes. Stir in prepared pudding and cardamom. Serve warm or cover surface with plastic wrap and chill.
Makes 4 servings.

Nutrition Facts per serving: 234 cal., 2 g total fat (1 g sat. fat), 6 mg chol., 178 mg sodium, 51 g carbo., 0 g fiber, 5 g pro. Daily Values: 9% vit. A, 1% vit. C, 8% calcium, 7% iron

Stirred Custard

Prep: 15 min. • Chill: 2 hours

5	beaten egg yolks
1½	cups milk
¼	cup sugar
1½	teaspoons vanilla
	Fresh fruit, such as blueberries, blackberries, or strawberries (optional)

1. In a medium heavy saucepan use a wooden spoon to stir together egg yolks, milk, and sugar. Cook over medium heat, stirring constantly with a wooden spoon, until mixture just coats the back of a clean metal spoon. Remove pan from heat. Stir in vanilla.

2. Quickly cool custard by placing saucepan in a large bowl of ice water for 1 to 2 minutes, stirring constantly. Pour custard mixture into a bowl. Cover surface with plastic wrap. Chill for at least 2 hours or until serving time. Do not stir. If desired, serve custard over fresh fruit. **Makes 8 servings.**

Nutrition Facts per serving: 85 cal., 4 g total fat (2 g sat. fat), 136 mg chol., 27 mg sodium, 8 g carbo., 0 g fiber, 3 g pro. Daily Values: 9% vit. A, 1% vit. C, 7% calcium, 2% iron

Flan

Prep: 20 min. • Bake: 35 min.
Chill: 4 to 24 hours

⅔	cup sugar
3	beaten eggs
1	12-ounce can evaporated milk (1½ cups)
1	teaspoon vanilla

1. Cook half of the sugar in a heavy skillet over medium heat until it begins to melt, shaking skillet occasionally. Do not stir. Once sugar begins to melt, reduce heat to low. Cook for 5 minutes or until all of the sugar turns golden brown, stirring occasionally with a wooden spoon.

2. Remove skillet from heat; immediately pour caramelized sugar into six 6-ounce custard cups. Working quickly, turn cups so sugar evenly coats the bottoms. Place custard cups in a 13×9×2-inch baking pan. Set aside.

3. In a mixing bowl combine remaining ingredients. Beat gently with a wire whisk or mixer. Pour egg mixture into custard cups. Pour hot water into baking pan around the cups to a depth of about 1 inch. Bake in a 325°F oven for 35 to 40 minutes or until a knife inserted near the center of custard comes out clean. Carefully remove cups from baking pan. Cool on a wire rack. Cover; chill for 4 to 24 hours.

4. To serve, slip a knife down sides of cups to loosen edges. Invert a dessert plate over each custard cup; turn over dish and cup together to release custard. **Makes 6 servings.**

Nutrition Facts per serving: 198 cal., 7 g total fat (3 g sat. fat), 123 mg chol., 92 mg sodium, 28 g carbo., 0 g fiber, 7 g pro. Daily Values: 6% vit. A, 2% vit. C, 16% calcium, 3% iron

Chocolate Pots de Crème

Prep: 15 min. • Chill: 2 to 24 hours

 1   cup half-and-half or light cream
 1   4-ounce package sweet baking chocolate,
     coarsely chopped
 2   teaspoons sugar
 3   slightly beaten egg yolks
 ¹/₂ teaspoon vanilla

1. In a small heavy saucepan combine half-and-half, chocolate, and sugar. Cook and stir over medium heat about 10 minutes or until mixture reaches a full boil and thickens.

2. Gradually stir about half of the hot mixture into beaten egg yolks. Return all of the egg yolk mixture to saucepan. Cook and stir over low heat for 2 minutes. Remove from heat; stir in vanilla. Pour chocolate mixture into 4 or 6 small cups or dessert dishes. Cover; chill for 2 to 24 hours.
Makes 4 to 6 servings.

Nutrition Facts per serving: 276 cal., 21 g total fat
(11 g sat. fat), 182 mg chol., 31 mg sodium, 22 g carbo.,
2 g fiber, 5 g pro. Daily Values: 32% vit. A, 7% calcium,
7% iron

Chocolate Cookie Cheesecakes

Prep: 20 min. • Bake: 20 min.
Chill: 1 to 24 hours

12   chocolate sandwich cookies with
     white filling
 2   8-ounce packages cream cheese, softened
 ¹/₂ cup sugar
 1   teaspoon vanilla
 2   eggs

1. Split each cookie, keeping filling intact on 1 cookie half. Line twelve 2¹/₂-inch muffin cups with foil bake cups. Place a cookie half with filling in each cup, filling side up. In a medium mixing bowl beat cream cheese, sugar, and vanilla until smooth. Add eggs. Beat on low speed just until combined. Spoon mixture into cups. Crush remaining cookies; sprinkle over filling.

2. Bake in a 325°F oven for 20 to 25 minutes or until set (top may indent slightly). Cool. Cover and chill for at least 1 hour or up to 24 hours. To serve, remove bake cups.
Makes 12 servings.

Nutrition Facts per serving: 223 cal., 16 g total fat
(9 g sat. fat), 77 mg chol., 183 mg sodium, 16 g carbo.,
0 g fiber, 4 g pro. Daily Values: 12% vit. A, 4% calcium,
5% iron

Peanut Butter S'more Tarts

**Prep: 15 min. · Chill: 2 to 24 hours
Stand: 30 min.**

1   cup semisweet chocolate pieces (6 ounces)
½   cup peanut butter
1½   cups miniature marshmallows
½   cup chopped peanuts
1   4-ounce package graham cracker tart
      shells (6)

1. In a small saucepan melt chocolate pieces over low heat, stirring constantly. Remove from heat. Stir in peanut butter until smooth. Stir in marshmallows and peanuts. Spoon into tart shells. Cover and chill for 2 hours or overnight. Let stand at room temperature for 30 minutes before serving.
Makes 6 servings.

Nutrition Facts per serving: 505 cal., 31 g total fat (8 g sat. fat), 0 mg chol., 257 mg sodium, 42 g carbo., 7 g fiber, 10 g pro. Daily Values: 2% calcium, 7% iron

Fruit-Topped Phyllo Cups

Prep: 15 min.

3   tablespoons apple jelly
½   of an 8-ounce package cream cheese,
      softened
1   2.1-ounce package miniature phyllo
      tart shells (15)
15   red and/or green seedless grape halves or
      strawberry halves

1. In a small saucepan heat and stir apple jelly over medium-low heat until melted. Stir 2 tablespoons of the jelly into cream cheese until smooth. Divide cream cheese mixture among tart shells.

2. In a small bowl combine fruit and remaining jelly; stir gently to coat. Spoon a piece of fruit on top of each tart. Serve immediately or chill for up to 4 hours.
Makes 15 servings.

Nutrition Facts per serving: 62 cal., 4 g total fat (2 g sat. fat), 8 mg chol., 33 mg sodium, 6 g carbo., 0 g fiber, 1 g pro. Daily Values: 2% vit. A, 1% vit. C, 1% calcium, 1% iron

Raspberry and Chocolate Tulips

Start to Finish: 15 min.

½ cup frozen raspberries

2 tablespoons sugar

1 2.1-ounce package miniature phyllo tart shells (15)

4 teaspoons chocolate-flavored syrup
Pressurized whipped dessert topping

1. In a small saucepan combine raspberries and sugar. Cook over medium heat, stirring frequently, for 3 to 5 minutes or just until sugar is melted and raspberries are completely thawed. Remove from heat; cool until slightly warm or room temperature.

2. To serve, place tart shells on a platter. Spoon about ½ teaspoon raspberry mixture into the bottom of each shell; top with ¼ teaspoon chocolate-flavored syrup and a small amount of whipped dessert topping.
Makes 15 servings.

Nutrition Facts per serving: 46 cal., 2 g total fat
(0 g sat. fat), 0 mg chol., 11 mg sodium, 6 g carbo., 0 g fiber,
0 g pro. Daily Values: 1% vit. C, 1% iron

Raspberry Pie

Prep: 25 min. • Bake: 45 min.

4 cups fresh or frozen raspberries

1 cup sugar

3 tablespoons quick-cooking tapioca

2 tablespoons butter, melted

1 15-ounce package refrigerated unbaked piecrust (2 crusts)

1. For filling, combine berries, sugar, tapioca, and butter; toss until combined. (If using frozen berries, let stand for 15 to 30 minutes or until fruit is partially thawed but still icy; stir well.)

2. For bottom crust, unwrap pastry according to package directions. Place 1 unbaked crust in a 9-inch pie plate. Trim pastry to ½ inch beyond edge of pie plate. For lattice top, roll remaining unbaked crust to a 12-inch diameter. Cut into ½-inch-wide strips.

3. Spoon raspberry mixture into pastry-lined pie plate. Weave strips over the filling to make a lattice. Press ends of the strips into the rim of the crust. Fold bottom pastry over strips; seal and flute edge. Cover edge with foil.

4. Place pie on a baking sheet. Bake in a 375°F oven for 25 minutes. Remove foil. Bake for 20 to 25 minutes more or until the top is golden. (Or for frozen raspberries, bake for 50 minutes. Remove foil; bake for 20 to 30 minutes more or until top is golden.) Cool pie on a wire rack.
Makes 8 servings.

Nutrition Facts per serving: 405 cal., 17 g total fat
(8 g sat. fat), 18 mg chol., 231 mg sodium, 61 g carbo.,
4 g fiber, 2 g pro. Daily Values: 4% vit. A, 26% vit. C,
1% calcium, 2% iron

Parfait Pie with Coconut Shell

Prep: 20 min. • Bake: 20 min.
Chill: 4 hours

- 2 cups flaked coconut
- 3 tablespoons butter or margarine, melted
- 1 10-ounce package frozen red raspberries, thawed
- 1 3-ounce package raspberry-flavored gelatin
- 1 pint vanilla ice cream

1. In a medium bowl combine coconut and melted butter. Press evenly into the bottom and sides of a 9-inch pie plate. Bake in a 325°F oven for 20 minutes. Cool on a wire rack.

2. Drain raspberries, reserving syrup. Set aside. Add enough water to the syrup to measure 1¼ cups. In a medium saucepan combine the gelatin and the syrup mixture. Heat and stir until gelatin is dissolved. Remove from heat.

3. Add the ice cream by spoonfuls to syrup mixture; stir until melted. Cover and chill until mixture mounds when spooned. Fold in raspberries. Pour into coconut shell. Refrigerate for at least 4 hours or until set.
Makes 8 servings.

Nutrition Facts per serving: 291 cal., 14 g total fat
(10 g sat. fat), 27 mg chol., 114 mg sodium, 40 g carbo.,
2 g fiber, 3 g pro. Daily Values: 6% vit. A, 5% vit. C,
5% calcium, 5% iron

Strawberry-Chocolate Pie

Prep: 20 min. • Chill: 1 hour

- 1 6-ounce package (1 cup) semisweet chocolate pieces
- 1 8-ounce package cream cheese, softened
- 3 tablespoons honey
- 1 baked 9-inch piecrust, cooled
- 4 cups fresh whole strawberries, stems and caps removed

1. In a small heavy saucepan heat chocolate pieces over low heat, stirring constantly, until melted and smooth. Remove from heat; let stand at room temperature to cool.

2. In a medium mixing bowl beat cream cheese with an electric mixer on low speed until softened. Gradually beat in cooled chocolate and honey. Spread mixture in piecrust. Cover pie; chill for 1 to 2 hours. Arrange strawberries on pie. Serve immediately.
Makes 8 servings.

Nutrition Facts per serving: 387 cal., 25 g total fat
(12 g sat. fat), 31 mg chol., 160 mg sodium, 40 g carbo.,
3 g fiber, 5 g pro. Daily Values: 9% vit. A, 68% vit. C,
4% calcium, 12% iron

Frozen Cranberry Pie

Prep: 20 min. • Freeze: 4 hours

> Nonstick cooking spray
> 6 chocolate wafer cookies, finely crushed
>   (about ⅓ cup)
> 1 quart vanilla low-fat or light ice cream
> 1 cup whole-berry cranberry sauce
> 1 teaspoon finely shredded orange peel

1. Coat a 9-inch pie plate with cooking spray. Cover with the crushed cookies. Set aside.

2. In a chilled medium bowl stir ice cream with a wooden spoon just until softened. Fold in remaining ingredients until combined. Spoon mixture into prepared pie plate. Cover and freeze for at least 4 hours or until firm.
Makes 8 servings.

Nutrition Facts per serving: 176 cal., 3 g total fat
(1 g sat. fat), 10 mg chol., 92 mg sodium, 36 g carbo.,
1 g fiber, 2 g pro. Daily Values: 1% vit. C, 3% calcium, 1% iron

Easy Peppermint Stick Pie

Prep: 10 min. • Freeze: 4 hours

> 1 half-gallon peppermint ice cream
> 1 chocolate-flavored crumb pie shell
> 1 12-ounce jar fudge ice cream topping

1. In a chilled bowl stir the ice cream until softened. Spoon ice cream into pie shell, spreading evenly. Return to freezer for at least 4 hours or until serving time.

2. To serve, warm the fudge topping in the microwave oven according to directions. Let pie stand at room temperature for 5 minutes before slicing. Serve with warmed topping.
Makes 8 servings.

Nutrition Facts per serving: 554 cal., 24 g total fat
(13 g sat. fat), 63 mg chol., 474 mg sodium, 72 g carbo.,
1 g fiber, 8 g pro. Daily Values: 14% calcium, 50% iron

Double Berry Soup

Start to Finish: 20 min.

2 cups frozen unsweetened blueberries

1 10-ounce package frozen sliced
  strawberries in syrup

½ teaspoon finely shredded orange peel
  (optional)

¾ cup orange juice

2 cups orange or other fruit sorbet or sherbet

1. In a medium saucepan combine frozen blueberries with their syrup, half of the frozen strawberries with their syrup, the orange peel (if using), and orange juice. Cook over medium heat, stirring occasionally, for 4 to 5 minutes or just until the berries are thawed. Remove from heat. Stir in remaining frozen strawberries; let stand for 5 minutes. Ladle soup into 4 shallow dessert bowls. Top each with a scoop of sorbet.
Makes 4 servings.

Nutrition Facts per serving: 262 cal., 2 g total fat
(1 g sat. fat), 5 mg chol., 37 mg sodium, 63 g carbo.,
8 g fiber, 2 g pro. Daily Values: 3% vit. A, 110% vit. C,
5% calcium, 4% iron

Easy Berry Sorbet

Prep: 15 min. • Freeze: 1 hour

2 cups fresh blueberries

2 cups fresh raspberries

½ cup cold water

¼ cup frozen pineapple-orange-banana juice
  concentrate or citrus beverage
  concentrate

1. Place berries in a single layer on a baking pan; freeze for 1 hour. In a large bowl combine frozen berries, water, and frozen concentrate. Place half of the mixture in a food processor bowl. Cover and process until nearly smooth. Repeat with remaining mixture. Serve immediately. (Or transfer mixture to a baking dish. Cover and freeze about 4 hours or until firm. Serve within 2 days.)
Makes 6 to 8 servings.

Nutrition Facts per serving: 66 cal., 0 g total fat
(0 g sat. fat), 0 mg chol., 4 mg sodium, 16 g carbo., 3 g fiber,
1 g pro. Daily Values: 1% vit. A, 46% vit. C, 1% calcium,
5% iron

Daiquiri Sorbet

Prep: 10 min. • Freeze: 4 to 24 hours

1   16-ounce package frozen unsweetened
      peach slices or unsweetened whole
      strawberries
½   cup water
¼   cup bottled daiquiri drink mix (no alcohol)
⅓   cup powdered sugar
3   tablespoons rum or orange juice

1. In a food processor bowl combine all
ingredients. Cover; process until smooth and
fluffy. Transfer to a freezer container. Cover and
freeze for 4 to 24 hours.
Makes 6 servings.

Nutrition Facts per serving: 76 cal., 0 g total fat
(0 g sat. fat), 0 mg chol., 11 mg sodium, 15 g carbo.,
1 g fiber, 1 g pro. Daily Values: 27% vit. A, 151% vit. C,
1% iron

Quick Ice Cream Shake

Start to Finish: 5 min.

1   pint vanilla ice cream
¼   cup amaretto, Irish cream, or hazelnut liquid
      creamer, or strawberry-flavored syrup
      Milk

1. In a blender container combine ice cream and
amaretto creamer. Cover and blend until smooth. If
necessary, add milk to reach desired consistency.
Makes 3 servings.

Nutrition Facts per serving: 250 cal., 10 g total fat
(6 g sat. fat), 39 mg chol., 74 mg sodium, 30 g carbo.,
0 g fiber, 3 g pro. Daily Values: 7% vit. A, 1% vit. C,
12% calcium, 1% iron

Cherry-Bananas Foster

Start to Finish: 15 min.

¼   cup butter
⅓   cup packed brown sugar
3   ripe bananas, peeled and sliced
      (about 2 cups)
⅓   cup dried tart cherries
⅓   cup spiced rum or rum (optional)

1. In a large skillet melt butter over medium
heat; stir in brown sugar until combined. Add
bananas and cherries; cook and gently stir over
medium heat for 1 to 2 minutes or until heated
through. If using rum, in a small saucepan heat
the rum until it almost simmers. Ignite rum with
a long match. Pour over bananas and cherries.
Serve immediately over ice cream, pound cake,
or angel food cake.
Makes 4 servings.

Nutrition Facts per serving: 290 cal., 13 g total fat
(8 g sat. fat), 33 mg chol., 132 mg sodium, 46 g carbo.,
3 g fiber, 1 g pro. Daily Values: 11% vit. A, 13% vit. C,
2% calcium, 4% iron

Butterscotch-Caramel Sauce

Start to Finish: 10 min.

- 1½ cups light-colored corn syrup
- 1 cup packed brown sugar
- 2 tablespoons butter
- ¼ cup half-and-half or light cream

1. In a medium heavy skillet combine corn syrup, brown sugar, and butter. Cook and stir over medium heat until sugar dissolves and mixture begins to boil. Remove from heat; cool slightly. Stir in half-and-half. Serve warm over ice cream or toasted pound cake slices.
Makes 2¼ cups.

Nutrition Facts per 2 tablespoons: 68 cal., 1 g total fat
(0 g sat. fat), 2 mg chol., 26 mg sodium, 16 g carbo.,
0 g fiber, 0 g pro. Daily Values: 1% vit. A, 1% calcium, 1% iron

Glazed Nut Topping

Start to Finish: 5 min.

- ½ cup chopped walnuts
- 2 tablespoons butter or margarine
- 3 tablespoons brown sugar
- 1 tablespoon milk

1. In a small saucepan combine walnuts and butter. Cook and stir over medium heat until nuts are lightly brown; stir in brown sugar. Stir in milk. Heat and stir until sugar is dissolved. Serve over ice cream.
Makes about ½ cup.

Nutrition Facts per 2 tablespoons: 179 cal., 16 g total fat
(5 g sat. fat), 17 mg chol., 67 mg sodium, 9 g carbo.,
1 g fiber, 2 g pro. Daily Values: 5% vit. A, 3% calcium, 3% iron

Hot Fudge Sauce

Prep: 10 min. • Cook: 4 min.

- ½ cup unsweetened cocoa powder
- ⅓ cup granulated sugar
- ⅓ cup packed dark brown sugar
- 3 tablespoons butter or margarine
- ½ cup whipping cream

1. In a small bowl stir together cocoa powder, granulated sugar, and brown sugar; set aside. In a small heavy saucepan melt butter with cream over low heat, stirring constantly. Cook and stir over medium heat about 3 minutes or until mixture bubbles around edges. Add sugar mixture. Cook, stirring constantly, for 1 to 2 minutes more until sugar is dissolved and mixture is smooth and thickened. Serve immediately over ice cream, cake, or other desserts. Or cover and store in the refrigerator for up to 1 week.

2. To reheat fudge sauce, in a small heavy saucepan cook over low heat, stirring frequently until heated through.
Makes 1 cup.

Nutrition Facts per tablespoon: 89 cal., 5 g total fat
(4 g sat. fat), 73 mg chol., 34 mg sodium, 10 g carbo.,
0 g fiber, 1 g pro. Daily Values: 5% vit. A, 3% calcium, 2% iron

JUST FOR KIDS

Chapter eight

Green and Orange Drink

Prep: 10 min. • Chill: 1½ hours

3   cups apple juice
1   3-ounce package lime-flavored gelatin
3   cups orange drink, chilled

1. In a saucepan stir together 1½ cups of the apple juice and the gelatin. Cook over low heat until gelatin dissolves, stirring constantly. Remove from heat; stir in remaining apple juice. Pour into a pitcher. Chill mixture for 1½ to 2 hours or until slightly thickened.

2. Divide gelatin mixture evenly among 6 glasses. Slowly pour about ½ cup of the orange drink down the side of each glass so it floats on top of the green mixture.
Makes 6 servings.

Nutrition Facts per serving: 169 cal., 0 g total fat (0 g sat. fat), 0 mg chol., 46 mg sodium, 42 g carbo., 1 g fiber, 1 g pro. Daily Values: 18% vit. A, 103% vit. C, 4% calcium, 3% iron

Sangria for Kids

Start to Finish: 5 min.

4   cups orange juice, chilled
1½ cups purple or white unsweetened grape juice, chilled
1   1-liter bottle ginger ale, chilled
2   cups ice cubes
2   cups assorted fresh fruit, such as orange wedges, thinly sliced lemons and/or limes, pineapple wedges, peach slices, and halved strawberries

1. In a large bowl or pitcher stir together orange juice and grape juice. Add ginger ale; stir gently. Add ice and fruit.
Makes 20 servings.

Nutrition Facts per serving: 57 cal., 0 g total fat (0 g sat. fat), 0 mg chol., 5 mg sodium, 14 g carbo., 0 g fiber, 0 g pro. Daily Values: 1% vit. A, 35% vit. C, 2% iron

Chocolate-Marshmallow Malt

Start to Finish: 10 min.

1   pint vanilla ice cream
¼   cup milk
¼   cup chocolate syrup
¼   cup purchased marshmallow topping or marshmallow creme
1   tablespoon malted milk powder

1. In a blender container combine all ingredients. Cover and blend until smooth.
Makes 2 servings.

Nutrition Facts per serving: 526 cal., 16 g total fat (10 g sat. fat), 62 mg chol., 209 mg sodium, 92 g carbo., 1 g fiber, 8 g pro. Daily Values: 13% vit. A, 2% vit. C, 24% calcium, 6% iron

Veggie Dip

Start to Finish: 5 min.

1   8-ounce carton fat-free dairy sour cream
  or one 8-ounce tub cream cheese
1   8-ounce carton plain fat-free yogurt
1   0.4-ounce envelope dry ranch salad
  dressing mix
  Cut-up vegetables

1. In a medium bowl stir together sour cream, yogurt, and dressing mix. (If using cream cheese, beat with an electric mixer on medium speed until smooth.) Serve with cut-up vegetables.
Makes about 2 cups.

Nutrition Facts per tablespoon: 10 cal., 0 g total fat
(0 g sat. fat), 1 mg chol., 40 mg sodium, 2 g carbo., 0 g fiber,
1 g pro. Daily Values: 1% vit. A, 2% calcium

Creamy Peanut Butter Spread

Start to Finish: 5 minutes

1   cup light-colored corn syrup
½   cup creamy peanut butter
¼   cup marshmallow creme

1. In a small bowl stir together all ingredients until combined. Store in a covered container in the refrigerator. Bring to room temperature to spread on bread, crackers, or apple slices.
Makes about 1½ cups.

Nutrition Facts per tablespoon: 73 cal., 3 g total fat
(1 g sat. fat), 0 mg chol., 42 mg sodium, 12 g carbo.,
0 g fiber, 1 g pro. Daily Values: 1% iron

Peanutty Dip

Start to Finish: 10 min.

½   cup peanut butter
½   cup plain yogurt
2   to 3 tablespoons honey
  Dippers, such as apple wedges, celery
   sticks, cucumber sticks, sliced carrots,
   and/or crackers

1. In a small bowl stir together peanut butter and yogurt until combined. Add honey to taste. Serve with dippers. Transfer any leftover dip to a storage container. Store tightly covered in the refrigerator for up to 2 days.
Makes about 1 cup.

Nutrition Facts per tablespoon: 60 cal., 4 g total fat
(1 g sat. fat), 1 mg chol., 41 mg sodium, 4 g carbo., 0 g fiber,
2 g pro. Daily Values: 1% calcium, 1% iron

Crunchy Banana Boats

Start to Finish: 15 min.

1 medium banana
   Fruit-flavored tub cream cheese or
      peanut butter
   Granola

1. Halve banana lengthwise. Spread one cut side of banana with some cream cheese. Press some granola into the cheese. Top with the other banana half. Cut filled banana in half crosswise.
Makes 1 or 2 servings.

Nutrition Facts per serving: 95 cal., 3 g total fat (2 g sat. fat), 6 mg chol., 27 mg sodium, 17 g carbo., 2 g fiber, 1 g pro. Daily Values: 2% vit. A, 9% vit. C, 2% calcium, 1% iron

Carrot, Raisin, and Peanut Butter Sandwich

Start to Finish: 15 min.

8 slices white, whole wheat, or cinnamon-
      raisin bread
$\frac{1}{2}$ to $\frac{2}{3}$ cup peanut butter
$\frac{1}{4}$ cup raisins
$\frac{1}{4}$ cup shredded carrot

1. Spread half of the bread slices with peanut butter; top with raisins, carrot, and remaining bread slices. Broil 4 inches from the heat for 2 to 4 minutes or until toasted, turning once.
Makes 4 servings.

Nutrition Facts per serving: 354 cal., 18 g total fat (4 g sat. fat), 1 mg chol., 422 mg sodium, 39 g carbo., 4 g fiber, 13 g pro. Daily Values: 43% vit. A, 2% vit. C, 7% calcium, 13% iron

Cinnamon Snails

Start to Finish: 25 min.

   Nonstick cooking spray
3 tablespoons sugar
$\frac{1}{2}$ teaspoon ground cinnamon
$\frac{1}{4}$ cup finely chopped nuts
1 8-ounce package refrigerated
      breadsticks (8)

1. Coat a baking sheet with nonstick spray. Combine sugar, cinnamon, and nuts. Sprinkle sugar mixture on a rolling surface. Unroll 1 breadstick. Coil tightly. Wrap another breadstick around coil, forming a larger coil. Place on the sugared surface. Roll to $\frac{1}{8}$-inch thickness. Place sugared side up on baking sheet. Repeat with remaining 6 breadsticks. Bake in a 375°F oven about 15 minutes or until golden. Serve warm.
Makes 4 servings.

Nutrition Facts per serving: 305 cal., 10 g total fat (1 g sat. fat), 0 mg chol., 580 mg sodium, 46 g carbo., 2 g fiber, 7 g pro. Daily Values: 1% calcium, 14% iron

Banana-Raisin Trail Mix

Start to Finish: 10 min.

2   cups raisins

2   cups dried banana chips

2   cups unsalted dry roasted peanuts

1   6-ounce package mixed dried fruit bits
      (1⅓ cups)

1. In a storage container combine all ingredients. Cover and shake to mix. Store in a cool, dry place for up to 1 week.
Makes about 7 cups.

Nutrition Facts per ½ cup: 172 cal., 9 g total fat
(4 g sat. fat), 0 mg chol., 6 mg sodium, 22 g carbo., 1 g fiber,
3 g pro. Daily Values: 1% vit. A, 2% vit. C, 3% iron

Blaze-a-Trail Mix

Start to Finish: 10 min.

2   cups honey graham cereal

1   cup tiny marshmallows

1   cup peanuts

½   cup semisweet chocolate pieces

½   cup raisins

1. In a storage container combine all the ingredients. Cover and shake to mix. Store in a cool, dry place for up to 2 weeks.
Makes 5 cups.

Nutrition Facts per ½ cup: 199 cal., 10 g total fat
(3 g sat. fat), 0 mg chol., 81 mg sodium, 26 g carbo.,
2 g fiber, 5 g pro. Daily Values: 2% calcium, 10% iron

Dive-in Caramel Corn

Start to Finish: 25 min.

3   tablespoons butter or margarine

¼   cup corn syrup

1   tablespoon molasses

6   cups popped popcorn

1   cup dry roasted peanuts

1. In a small saucepan melt butter. Remove from heat; stir in corn syrup and molasses. In a 13×9×2-inch baking pan drizzle molasses mixture over popcorn, tossing to coat.

2. Bake in a 325°F oven about 15 minutes, stirring twice. Transfer mixture to a serving bowl. Stir in peanuts. Store in a tightly covered container at room temperature.
Makes 8 servings.

Nutrition Facts per serving: 205 cal., 14 g total fat
(4 g sat. fat), 12 mg chol., 61 mg sodium, 18 g carbo.,
2 g fiber, 5 g pro. Daily Values: 4% vit. A, 17% calcium,
4% iron

Fancy Stack Pancakes

Start to Finish: 15 min.

8   frozen microwave pancakes

1/2 cup tub cream cheese

3   tablespoons apricot, raspberry, blackberry, or blueberry spreadable fruit

1. Carefully spread each frozen pancake with 1 tablespoon cream cheese. Spoon 1 teaspoon of spreadable fruit on top of the cream cheese. Make 4 stacks of 2 pancakes each. Place on a large microwave-safe platter. Microwave on 50 percent power (medium) for 3 1/2 to 4 1/2 minutes or until the stacks are heated through. Serve warm.
Makes 4 servings.

Nutrition Facts per serving: 296 cal., 12 g total fat (8 g sat. fat), 36 mg chol., 466 mg sodium, 41 g carbo., 1 g fiber, 6 g pro. Daily Values: 7% vit. A, 6% calcium, 14% iron

The Magic Pancake

Prep: 10 min. • Bake: 20 min.

4   beaten eggs

2/3 cup all-purpose flour

2/3 cup milk

1   cup finely shredded Swiss, cheddar, or Monterey Jack cheese (4 ounces)

2   tablespoons cooked bacon pieces

1. Grease a 10-inch ovenproof skillet with shortening. Place in a 400°F oven. Meanwhile, in a medium mixing bowl beat together the eggs, flour, and milk until smooth. Pour into hot skillet. Bake about 20 minutes or until pancake is puffed and golden. Sprinkle with cheese and bacon pieces. Cut into wedges.
Makes 4 servings.

Nutrition Facts per serving: 289 cal., 15 g total fat (8 g sat. fat), 244 mg chol., 207 mg sodium, 18 g carbo., 1 g fiber, 19 g pro. Daily Values: 13% vit. A, 1% vit. C, 35% calcium, 9% iron

Baked Parmesan Chicken

Prep: 10 min. • Bake: 30 min.

- ½ **cup crushed cornflakes**
- 2 **tablespoons grated Parmesan cheese**
- ¼ **teaspoon dried Italian seasoning, crushed**
- 4 **skinless, boneless chicken breast halves (1¼ pounds)**
- 3 **tablespoons butter or margarine, melted**

1. In a bowl combine cornflakes, cheese, and seasoning. Dip chicken pieces in melted butter; roll in cornflake mixture. Place on a baking rack in a shallow baking pan. Bake in a 375°F oven about 30 minutes or until chicken is tender and no longer pink (170°F).
Makes 4 main-dish servings.

Nutrition Facts per serving: 287 cal., 12 g total fat (7 g sat. fat), 109 mg chol., 318 mg sodium, 9 g carbo., 0 g fiber, 35 g pro. Daily Values: 8% vit. A, 2% vit. C, 5% calcium, 16% iron

Little Chicken Dippers

Start to Finish: 15 min.

- 1 **10-ounce package frozen breaded chicken chunks**
- ¼ **cup bottled barbecue sauce**
- 2 **tablespoons grape jelly**

1. Bake chicken chunks according to package directions. For dipping sauce, in a small saucepan heat together barbecue sauce and grape jelly just until the jelly melts. Serve dipping sauce with chicken.
Makes 3 main-dish servings.

Nutrition Facts per serving: 366 cal., 23 g total fat (6 g sat. fat), 56 mg chol., 725 mg sodium, 27 g carbo., 0 g fiber, 13 g pro. Daily Values: 4% vit. A, 3% vit. C, 5% iron

Chicken Salad Stacks

Start to Finish: 15 min.

4 7- to 8-inch flour tortillas

½ cup tub cream cheese

1 cup deli chicken or tuna salad

3 lettuce leaves

3 to 4 pimiento-stuffed olives, pitted ripe
   olives, or cherry tomatoes (optional)

1. Spread 3 tortillas with cream cheese. Top
each with some chicken salad and a lettuce
leaf. Stack tortillas; top with remaining tortilla.
Cut stack into wedges to serve. Pierce each
wedge with a decorative pick or a toothpick
topped with olives or tomatoes, if desired.
Makes 3 servings.

Nutrition Facts per serving: 392 cal., 27 g total fat
(12 g sat. fat), 75 mg chol., 391 mg sodium, 22 g carbo.,
1 g fiber, 15 g pro. Daily Values: 10% vit. A, 2% vit. C,
8% calcium, 10% iron

Tasty Wheels

Prep: 20 min. • Chill: 2 hours

6 6- or 7-inch flour tortillas

1 8-ounce tub cream cheese

6 lettuce leaves

6 slices thinly sliced cooked ham

1. Wrap tortillas in paper towels. Microwave on
100 percent power (high) for 30 seconds. Keep
covered. Spread 1 tablespoon cream cheese
over one side of a tortilla. Top with a lettuce
leaf. Place a thin slice of ham on top of lettuce.
Spread with another tablespoon of cream
cheese. Roll up tightly to form a log. Using a
serrated knife cut into 1-inch portions. Cover;
chill for 2 hours.
Makes 24 servings.

Nutrition Facts per serving: 66 cal., 4 g total fat
(2 g sat. fat), 12 mg chol., 137 mg sodium, 5 g carbo.,
0 g fiber, 2 g pro. Daily Values: 3% vit. A, 1% vit. C, 2% iron

Ham and Cheese Pizza Tortillas

Prep: 15 min. • Bake: 12 min.

- ¼ cup purchased pesto
- 12 7- to 8-inch flour tortillas
- ½ pound finely chopped cooked ham (1½ cups)
- 2 cups shredded mozzarella cheese (8 ounces)
- 1 8-ounce can pizza sauce or ½ cup Alfredo pasta sauce

1. Spread pesto on one side of 4 tortillas. Top each with a second tortilla to make 4 stacks. Stir together the ham and half of the cheese. Sprinkle ham mixture over second layer of each tortilla stack. Top with the remaining tortillas. Spread top layer with pizza sauce, sprinkle with remaining cheese.

2. Place tortilla stacks on an ungreased baking sheet. Bake in a 425°F oven for 12 to 15 minutes or until cheese is melted. To serve, cut each stack into wedges.
Makes 8 main-dish servings.

Nutrition Facts per serving: 315 cal., 16 g total fat (6 g sat. fat), 32 mg chol., 772 mg sodium, 26 g carbo., 1 g fiber, 16 g pro. Daily Values: 13% vit. A, 5% vit. C, 28% calcium, 12% iron

Snowflake Sandwiches

Prep: 65 min. • Bake: 10 min.

- 8 frozen white or wheat Texas-style rolls, thawed
- 1 pound thinly sliced cooked ham or turkey
- 8 slices American cheese (6 to 8 ounces) Bottled ranch or creamy Italian salad dressing

1. Flatten a thawed roll into a 4-inch round. With kitchen shears, make five or six 1-inch, V-shaped cuts toward center of round (about 1½ inches apart), and discard triangular dough pieces. Make 2 small diagonal cuts in dough on each side of each V, creating a snowflake design. Repeat with remaining rolls.

2. Place shaped rolls 2 inches apart on a large greased baking sheet. Let rise in a warm place until nearly double in size (30 to 40 minutes). Bake in a 350°F oven for 10 to 12 minutes or until golden. Cool on rack.

3. Split cooled rolls in half. Layer ham and cheese on bottom halves of rolls. Add dressing and top halves of rolls.
Makes 8 sandwiches.

Nutrition Facts per sandwich: 396 cal., 22 g total fat (8 g sat. fat), 59 mg chol., 1,462 mg sodium, 30 g carbo., 1 g fiber, 21 g pro. Daily Values: 7% vit. A, 18% calcium, 14% iron

Cheese Calzone

Prep: 15 min. • Bake: 18 min.

Nonstick cooking spray
1   10-ounce package refrigerated pizza dough
2   cups shredded cheddar cheese (8 ounces)
½   cup ricotta cheese
¼   grated Parmesan cheese
1   cup thick-style spaghetti sauce or one
        8-ounce can pizza sauce

1. Line a 12-inch pizza pan with foil and coat with cooking spray. Press dough onto foil in pan, forming a 12-inch circle. In a large bowl stir together the cheeses. Spoon cheese mixture on half of the pizza dough. Fold dough over filling to form a half-circle. Pinch to seal edges. Cut slits in dough so steam can escape.

2. Bake in a 400°F oven for 18 to 20 minutes or until cheese is melted. Cover with foil after 10 minutes of baking to prevent overbrowning. Cool in pan on a wire rack for 5 minutes before serving. Meanwhile, in a small saucepan heat spaghetti sauce. Serve warm sauce with calzone.
Makes 4 main-dish servings.

Nutrition Facts per serving: 520 cal., 28 g total fat (16 g sat. fat), 80 mg chol., 1,194 mg sodium, 40 g carbo., 3 g fiber, 27 g pro. Daily Values: 16% vit. A, 10% vit. C, 57% calcium, 15% iron

Cheese and Bean Quesadillas

Start to Finish: 20 min.

¼   cup refried beans
4   6- to 8-inch flour tortillas
⅔   cup shredded co-jack cheese
        Salsa (optional)

1. Spread beans on 2 of the tortillas. Sprinkle with cheese; top with remaining 2 tortillas. In a medium skillet or griddle cook tortillas, one at a time, over medium heat about 5 minutes or until cheese melts, turning once. Cut each quesadilla into 4 triangles. If desired, serve with salsa.
Makes 4 side-dish servings.

Nutrition Facts per serving: 191 cal., 8 g total fat (5 g sat. fat), 18 mg chol., 326 mg sodium, 21 g carbo., 2 g fiber, 8 g pro. Daily Values: 3% vit. A, 2% vit. C, 18% calcium, 7% iron

Cheeseburger Pizza

Prep: 20 min. • Bake: 15 min.

1   10-ounce package refrigerated pizza crust
1   pound ground beef
2   cups shredded cheddar cheese (8 ounces)
1   8-ounce can pizza sauce
½   cup chopped dill pickle or pickle relish

1. Press dough into a greased 13×9×2-inch baking pan. Build up edges of crust slightly. In a skillet brown the ground meat. Drain off fat. Sprinkle about three-fourths of the cheese over the crust. Pour sauce over cheese. Top with cooked meat and the remaining cheese. Bake in a 425°F oven for 15 to 20 minutes or until crust is golden. Sprinkle with dill pickle.
Makes 4 to 6 main-dish servings.

Nutrition Facts per serving: 670 cal., 35 g total fat (17 g sat. fat), 131 mg chol., 1,222 mg sodium, 44 g carbo., 0 g fiber, 42 g pro. Daily Values: 12% vit. A, 41% calcium, 25% iron

Two Pizzas in One

Prep: 10 min. • Bake: 45 min.

½   pound bulk Italian sausage or ground beef
2   15- to 15½-ounce frozen cheese pizzas
½   cup chopped sweet pepper
1   2-ounce can mushroom stems and pieces, drained
1   cup shredded colby or Monterey Jack cheese (4 ounces)

1. In a skillet cook sausage until brown. Drain off fat. Place 1 cheese pizza on a greased baking sheet. Top with cooked sausage, pepper, and mushrooms. Top with remaining pizza, crust side up. Cover pizza with foil.

2. Bake in a 375°F oven for 30 minutes. Remove foil and bake for 10 minutes more. Sprinkle cheese over pizza. Bake about 5 minutes more or until cheese melts.
Makes 6 main-dish servings.

Nutrition Facts per serving: 505 cal., 22 g total fat (11 g sat. fat), 64 mg chol., 1,131 mg sodium, 50 g carbo., 0 g fiber, 27 g pro. Daily Values: 21% vit. A, 24% vit. C, 41% calcium, 10% iron

Cheeseburger and Fries Casserole

Prep: 15 min. • Bake: 45 min.

2 pounds lean ground beef
1 10¾-ounce can condensed golden
    mushroom soup
1 10¾-ounce can condensed cheddar cheese
    soup
1 20-ounce package frozen, fried crinkle-
    cut potatoes
    Toppings, such as catsup, pickles, mustard,
    and chopped tomato (optional)

1. In a large skillet cook ground beef, half at a time, until brown. Drain off fat. Place cooked meat in the bottom of a 3-quart rectangular baking dish. In a medium bowl combine soups. Spread over meat in baking dish. Sprinkle potatoes over soup. Bake, uncovered, in a 350°F oven for 45 to 55 minutes or until potatoes are golden. If desired, serve with toppings.
Makes 8 to 10 main-dish servings.

Nutrition Facts per serving: 348 cal., 18 g total fat (6 g sat. fat), 78 mg chol., 654 mg sodium, 24 g carbo., 2 g fiber, 24 g pro. Daily Values: 11% vit. A, 9% vit. C, 4% calcium, 15% iron

Ready-Right-Now Sloppy Joes

Start to Finish: 15 min.

1 pound ground beef, ground pork, or ground
    raw turkey
1 8-ounce can tomato sauce
⅓ cup bottled barbecue sauce
1 teaspoon dried minced onion
6 hamburger buns, split

1. In a large skillet cook meat until brown. Drain off fat. Stir in tomato sauce, barbecue sauce, and onion. Bring to boiling. Remove from heat. Spoon into buns.
Makes 6 servings.

Nutrition Facts per serving: 433 cal., 18 g total fat (6 g sat. fat), 71 mg chol., 849 mg sodium, 38 g carbo., 2 g fiber, 28 g pro. Daily Values: 4% vit. A, 3% vit. C, 10% calcium, 25% iron

Chili Dogs

Start to Finish: 10 min.

1 7½-ounce can chili with beans, undrained
2 tablespoons bottled barbecue sauce
1 teaspoon prepared mustard
4 frankfurters
4 hot dog buns, split

1. In a microwave-safe 1-quart casserole combine the undrained chili, barbecue sauce, and mustard. Place frankfurters on top of chili mixture. Cover and microwave on 100 percent power (high) for 4 to 5 minutes or until mixture is heated through, stirring once. Place frankfurters on buns. Top with chili mixture.
Makes 4 main-dish servings.

Nutrition Facts per serving: 376 cal., 22 g total fat (8 g sat. fat), 38 mg chol., 1,276 mg sodium, 32 g carbo., 4 g fiber, 13 g pro. Daily Values: 4% vit. A, 2% vit. C, 9% calcium, 21% iron

Sausage-Corn Chowder

Start to Finish: 20 min.

12 ounces cooked link smoked turkey sausage or frankfurters
1 10¾-ounce can condensed cream of potato soup
1⅓ cups milk
1 8½-ounce can cream-style corn
2 or 3 slices American cheese, torn into pieces (2 or 3 ounces)

1. Halve sausage lengthwise; cut into ½-inch slices. Set aside. In a 2-quart saucepan combine the soup, milk, and corn. Stir in sausage and cheese. Cook and stir over medium heat until heated through.
Makes 4 main-dish servings.

Nutrition Facts per serving: 312 cal., 15 g total fat (6 g sat. fat), 80 mg chol., 1,774 mg sodium, 24 g carbo., 1 g fiber, 21 g pro. Daily Values: 11% vit. A, 6% vit. C, 21% calcium, 9% iron

Lip-Smackin' Mac 'n' Cheese

Prep: 15 min. • Cook: 12 min.

2 cups rotini or elbow macaroni
¼ cup chopped onion
6 ounces American cheese slices, torn
     into pieces
½ cup fat-free milk
    Dash black pepper

1. In a saucepan cook pasta and onion according to pasta package directions. Drain. Return mixture to saucepan. Stir in cheese, milk, and pepper. Cook for 4 to 5 minutes or until cheese is melted, stirring constantly.
Makes 3 main-dish servings.

Nutrition Facts per serving: 392 cal., 14 g total fat (10 g sat. fat), 42 mg chol., 791 mg sodium, 46 g carbo., 2 g fiber, 18 g pro. Daily Values: 15% vit. A, 3% vit. C, 40% calcium, 8% iron

Cheesy Broccoli and Rice

Start to Finish: 15 min.

1 10-ounce package frozen cut broccoli
1 cup uncooked instant rice
1 cup water
1 cup shredded cheddar or Swiss cheese
    (4 ounces)

1. In a medium saucepan combine frozen broccoli, uncooked rice, and water. Bring to boiling, stirring occasionally to break up broccoli. Remove from heat. Cover and let stand for 5 minutes. Over low heat, stir in cheese just until it melts.
Makes 4 main-dish servings.

Nutrition Facts per serving: 224 cal., 10 g total fat (6 g sat. fat), 30 mg chol., 196 mg sodium, 24 g carbo., 2 g fiber, 11 g pro. Daily Values: 33% vit. A, 47% vit. C, 25% calcium, 9% iron

Spud with Broccoli Topper

Start to Finish: 20 min.

4   medium potatoes (6 to 8 ounces each)
1   cup frozen cut broccoli
1   tablespoon water
½   of an 8-ounce tub cream cheese
½   teaspoon Worcestershire sauce

1. Scrub potatoes and pierce with a fork. Arrange about 1 inch apart on a microwave-safe plate. Microwave on 100 percent power (high) for 12 to 18 minutes or until tender, turning potatoes after 6 minutes. Remove from oven. Cover with foil; let stand for 6 minutes.

2. Meanwhile, in a microwave-safe 1-quart casserole microwave broccoli and water for 3 to 4 minutes or until tender. Cut up any large pieces. Stir in remaining ingredients. Microwave on 100 percent power (high), covered, for 1 to 2 minutes or until heated through. Cut each potato open. Spoon topping over each potato. **Makes 4 side-dish servings.**

Nutrition Facts per serving: 231 cal., 10 g total fat (7 g sat. fat), 28 mg chol., 118 mg sodium, 30 g carbo., 4 g fiber, 7 g pro. Daily Values: 23% vit. A, 72% vit. C, 6% calcium, 10% iron

Pepperoni-Pizza Potatoes

Start to Finish: 25 min.

4   medium potatoes (6 to 8 ounces each)
1   8-ounce jar pizza sauce
3½   ounces sliced pepperoni
¾   cup shredded mozzarella cheese (3 ounces)

1. Scrub potatoes and pierce with a fork. Arrange about 1 inch apart on a microwave-safe plate. Microwave on 100 percent power (high) for 12 to 18 minutes or until tender, turning potatoes after 6 minutes. Remove from oven. Cover potatoes with foil; let stand for 6 minutes.

2. Meanwhile, in a microwave-safe 2-cup measuring cup, combine pizza sauce and pepperoni. Cover with vented microwave-safe plastic wrap. Microwave on 100 percent power (high) for 3 to 4 minutes or until heated through, stirring after 2 minutes.

3. Cut each potato open. Spoon pepperoni mixture over each potato. Sprinkle with cheese. Return to microwave oven. Microwave for 2 to 3 minutes more or until the cheese melts. **Makes 4 main-dish servings.**

Nutrition Facts per serving: 366 cal., 16 g total fat (7 g sat. fat), 32 mg chol., 611 mg sodium, 42 g carbo., 5 g fiber, 16 g pro. Daily Values: 16% vit. A, 61% vit. C, 20% calcium, 25% iron

Chocolate-Mint Sandwich Cookies

Start to Finish: 20 min.

1/2 **cup canned vanilla frosting**
3 **tablespoons finely crushed striped round peppermint candies**
44 **chocolate wafers**

1. In a small bowl stir together frosting and crushed candies. Spread 1 teaspoon frosting mixture on the flat side of 22 chocolate wafers. Top with the remaining chocolate wafers, flat side toward frosting mixture.
Makes 22 cookies.

Nutrition Facts per cookie: 88 cal., 3 g total fat (1 g sat. fat), 1 mg chol., 104 mg sodium, 15 g carbo., 0 g fiber, 1 g pro. Daily Values: 1% vit. A, 1% calcium, 3% iron

Crispy Chocolate Heart Cookies

Prep: 15 min. • Chill: 20 min.

  Butter or margarine
1 **cup semisweet chocolate pieces**
1/4 **cup light-colored corn syrup**
2 **tablespoons butter or margarine**
3 **cups crisp rice cereal**

1. Line a baking sheet with waxed paper. Grease the waxed paper with butter. Set aside.

2. In a heavy medium saucepan combine chocolate pieces, corn syrup, and the 2 tablespoons butter. Cook over low heat until chocolate and butter are melted, stirring constantly. Stir the cereal into the melted chocolate mixture until evenly coated.

3. Transfer cereal mixture to prepared baking sheet. Pat it into a 12×6-inch rectangle. Chill about 20 minutes or until slightly firm. Cut into heart shapes with a 3-inch heart-shaped cookie cutter. Chill until serving time.
Makes 8 or 9 hearts.

Nutrition Facts per heart: 197 cal., 10 g total fat (6 g sat. fat), 9 mg chol., 153 mg sodium, 30 g carbo., 1 g fiber, 2 g pro. Daily Values: 7% vit. A, 8% vit. C, 1% calcium, 7% iron

Puzzle Cookies

Prep: 25 min. • Bake: 7 min.

¼ **cup all-purpose flour**
1 **18-ounce roll refrigerated sugar**
    cookie dough
2 **egg yolks**
2 **teaspoons water**
   Liquid or paste food coloring

1. In a medium bowl knead flour into sugar cookie dough. Divide dough into 6 portions. On an ungreased baking sheet, pat each portion into a 5-inch square. Press a well-floured 3- to 4-inch cookie cutter into the square (use smaller cutters, if desired). Carefully remove cookie cutter without removing dough. Using a table knife, cut outside portion of square into large puzzle pieces.

2. In a small mixing bowl beat egg yolks and water. Divide mixture among 3 or 4 small bowls. To each bowl add 2 to 3 drops of liquid food coloring or desired amount of paste food coloring in desired color; mix well. Use a small, clean paintbrush to brush dough puzzle pieces with different colors of egg yolk mixture. If mixture thickens while standing, stir in water, 1 drop at a time.

3. Bake in a 350°F oven for 7 to 8 minutes or until bottoms of cookies just start to brown and centers are set. While still warm, carefully recut pieces with cookie cutter and knife. Trim edges as needed. Transfer cookies to a wire rack to cool.
Makes 6 cookies (24 servings).

Nutrition Facts per serving: 102 cal., 5 g total fat
(1 g sat. fat), 24 mg chol., 90 mg sodium, 13 g carbo.,
0 g fiber, 1 g pro. Daily Values: 1% vit. A, 2% calcium, 3% iron

Chewy Granola Goodies

Start to Finish: 20 min.

1 **10-ounce bag marshmallows**
¼ **cup butter or margarine**
4 **cups granola with raisins**
1½ **cups crisp rice cereal**
½ **cup sunflower nuts**

1. Line a 13×9×2-inch pan with foil. Butter foil; set aside. In a large saucepan combine marshmallows and the ¼ cup butter. Cook and stir until the marshmallows are melted. Stir in granola, cereal, and sunflower nuts. Press mixture into prepared pan. Cool. Lift by foil to remove from pan. Peel off foil and cut into bars.
Makes 24 bars.

Nutrition Facts per bar: 154 cal., 7 g total fat (3 g sat. fat),
6 mg chol., 50 mg sodium, 23 g carbo., 1 g fiber, 3 g pro.
Daily Values: 1% vit. A, 2% vit. C, 2% calcium, 4% iron

Chocolate-Dipped Waffles

Prep: 20 min. • Chill: 30 min.

1   cup semisweet chocolate pieces (6 ounces)
1   cup milk chocolate pieces (6 ounces)
2   teaspoons shortening
5   frozen buttermilk waffles or Belgian
     waffles
     Almond brickle pieces, colorful sprinkles,
     toasted coconut, or other crunchy
     toppings

1. In a small saucepan melt chocolate and shortening over low heat, stirring constantly. Meanwhile, place waffles in a single layer on an ungreased baking sheet; toast in the oven according to package directions. Halve each waffle crosswise.

2. Dip waffles in chocolate or spoon chocolate over waffles to coat. Remove from chocolate with a fork, allowing excess chocolate to drip back into pan. Insert a wooden skewer or ice cream stick into each waffle half. Place on a baking sheet lined with waxed paper. Sprinkle with desired topping. Chill for 30 minutes or until chocolate is set.
Makes 10 servings.

Nutrition Facts per serving: 289 cal., 16 g total fat (8 g sat. fat), 11 mg chol., 169 mg sodium, 35 g carbo., 1 g fiber, 3 g pro. Daily Values: 5% vit. A, 8% calcium, 7% iron

Chocolate Brownie Pudding

Start to Finish: 15 min.

1/3   cup whipping cream
2   purchased chocolate brownies (about
     2×2-inch squares)
2   3 1/2- to 4-ounce containers chocolate
     pudding, chilled
1/4   cup English toffee pieces
1/4   cup chopped pecans, toasted

1. In a chilled medium mixing bowl beat whipping cream until soft peaks form. Crumble one of the brownies; divide evenly between 2 dessert dishes. Divide 1 container of pudding between dishes. Top with half of the whipped cream, toffee pieces, and pecans. Repeat layers. Serve at once or cover and chill for up to 1 hour.
Makes 2 to 3 servings.

Nutrition Facts per serving: 661 cal., 45 g total fat (18 g sat. fat), 82 mg chol., 407 mg sodium, 61 g carbo., 2 g fiber, 7 g pro. Daily Values: 18% vit. A, 1% vit. C, 15% calcium, 10% iron

Berry Parfaits

Start to Finish: 12 min.

- 1   **4-ounce container vanilla pudding**
- ¼   **cup whipped cream or frozen whipped dessert topping, thawed**
- 1   **drop red food coloring (optional)**
- 2   **1-inch slices angel food cake, cut into 1-inch cubes**
- ¾   **cup fresh strawberries, sliced, and/or raspberries**

1. In a small bowl gently fold together the vanilla pudding and whipped cream. If desired, stir in red food coloring.

2. Place one-fourth of the cake cubes in the bottom of 2 parfait or sundae glasses. Add one-fourth of the berries and one-fourth of the pudding mixture. Repeat layers. Serve parfaits immediately.
Makes 2 servings.

Nutrition Facts per serving: 270 cal., 8 g total fat (4 g sat. fat), 25 mg chol., 337 mg sodium, 46 g carbo., 1 g fiber, 5 g pro. Daily Values: 56% vit. A, 51% vit. C, 11% calcium, 2% iron

Lollipop Pudding Pops

Prep: 15 min. • Freeze: 4 hours

-   **Small multicolored decorative candies**
- 1   **4-serving-size package instant chocolate pudding mix**
- 2½   **cups chocolate-flavored milk**

1. Put 10 paper bake cups in an 8×8×2- or 9×9×2-inch baking pan. Sprinkle decorative candies in the bottom of each paper cup. In a medium mixing bowl combine the pudding mix and milk. Beat with a wire whisk or rotary beater until combined. Spoon pudding into paper cups.

2. Cover each cup with a square of foil. Use a knife to make a small slit in center of each square. Slide a wooden crafts stick through the slit and into the pudding in the cup. Freeze for 4 to 6 hours or until firm. Remove from freezer. To serve, remove foil and tear paper cups away from the pops.
Makes 10 pops.

Nutrition Facts per pop: 89 cal., 1 g total fat (1 g sat. fat), 4 mg chol., 203 mg sodium, 17 g carbo., 2 g fiber, 2 g pro. Daily Values: 3% vit. A, 1% vit. C, 7% calcium, 2% iron

Metric Information

The charts on this page provide a guide for converting measurements from the U.S. customary system, which is used throughout this book, to the metric system.

Product Differences

Most of the ingredients called for in the recipes in this book are available in most countries. However, some are known by different names. Here are some common American ingredients and their possible counterparts:

- Sugar (white) is granulated, fine granulated, or castor sugar.
- Powdered sugar is icing sugar.
- All-purpose flour is enriched, bleached or unbleached white household flour. When self-rising flour is used in place of all-purpose flour in a recipe that calls for leavening, omit the leavening agent (baking soda or baking powder) and salt.
- Light-colored corn syrup is golden syrup.
- Cornstarch is cornflour.
- Baking soda is bicarbonate of soda.
- Vanilla or vanilla extract is vanilla essence.
- Green, red, or yellow sweet peppers are capsicums or bell peppers.
- Golden raisins are sultanas.

Volume and Weight

The United States traditionally uses cup measures for liquid and solid ingredients. The chart below shows the approximate imperial and metric equivalents. If you are accustomed to weighing solid ingredients, the following approximate equivalents will be helpful.

- 1 cup butter, castor sugar, or rice = 8 ounces = ½ pound = 250 grams
- 1 cup flour = 4 ounces = ¼ pound = 125 grams
- 1 cup icing sugar = 5 ounces = 150 grams

Canadian and U.S. volume for a cup measure is 8 fluid ounces (237 ml), but the standard metric equivalent is 250 ml.

1 British imperial cup is 10 fluid ounces.

In Australia, 1 tablespoon equals 20 ml, and there are 4 teaspoons in the Australian tablespoon.

Spoon measures are used for smaller amounts of ingredients. Although the size of the tablespoon varies slightly in different countries, for practical purposes and for recipes in this book, a straight substitution is all that's necessary. Measurements made using cups or spoons always should be level unless stated otherwise.

Common Weight Range Replacements

Imperial / U.S.	Metric
½ ounce	15 g
1 ounce	25 g or 30 g
4 ounces (¼ pound)	115 g or 125 g
8 ounces (½ pound)	225 g or 250 g
16 ounces (1 pound)	450 g or 500 g
1¼ pounds	625 g
1½ pounds	750 g
2 pounds or 2¼ pounds	1,000 g or 1 Kg

Oven Temperature Equivalents

Fahrenheit Setting	Celsius Setting*	Gas Setting
300°F	150°C	Gas Mark 2 (very low)
325°F	160°C	Gas Mark 3 (low)
350°F	180°C	Gas Mark 4 (moderate)
375°F	190°C	Gas Mark 5 (moderate)
400°F	200°C	Gas Mark 6 (hot)
425°F	220°C	Gas Mark 7 (hot)
450°F	230°C	Gas Mark 8 (very hot)
475°F	240°C	Gas Mark 9 (very hot)
500°F	260°C	Gas Mark 10 (extremely hot)
Broil	Broil	Grill

*Electric and gas ovens may be calibrated using celsius. However, for an electric oven, increase celsius setting 10 to 20 degrees when cooking above 160°C. For convection or forced air ovens (gas or electric) lower the temperature setting 25°F/10°C when cooking at all heat levels.

Baking Pan Sizes

Imperial / U.S.	Metric
9×1½-inch round cake pan	22- or 23×4-cm (1.5 L)
9×1½-inch pie plate	22- or 23×4-cm (1 L)
8×8×2-inch square cake pan	20×5-cm (2 L)
9×9×2-inch square cake pan	22- or 23×4.5-cm (2.5 L)
11×7×1½-inch baking pan	28×17×4-cm (2 L)
2-quart rectangular baking pan	30×19×4.5-cm (3 L)
13×9×2-inch baking pan	34×22×4.5-cm (3.5 L)
15×10×1-inch jelly roll pan	40×25×2-cm
9×5×3-inch loaf pan	23×13×8-cm (2 L)
2-quart casserole	2 L

U.S. / Standard Metric Equivalents

⅛ teaspoon = 0.5 ml	
¼ teaspoon = 1 ml	
½ teaspoon = 2 ml	
1 teaspoon = 5 ml	
1 tablespoon = 15 ml	
2 tablespoons = 25 ml	
¼ cup = 2 fluid ounces = 50 ml	
⅓ cup = 3 fluid ounces = 75 ml	
½ cup = 4 fluid ounces = 125 ml	
⅔ cup = 5 fluid ounces = 150 ml	
¾ cup = 6 fluid ounces = 175 ml	
1 cup = 8 fluid ounces = 250 ml	
2 cups = 1 pint = 500 ml	
1 quart = 1 litre	